Cambridge IGCSE®

Mathematics

Revision Guide

Martin Law

CAMBRIDGE
UNIVERSITY PRESS

CAMBRIDGE
UNIVERSITY PRESS

University Printing House, Cambridge CB2 8BS, United Kingdom

Cambridge University Press is part of the University of Cambridge.

It furthers the University's mission by disseminating knowledge in the pursuit of education, learning and research at the highest international levels of excellence.

www.cambridge.org
Information on this title: education.cambridge.org

First published 2016

Printed in India by Multivista Global Ltd

A catalogue record for this publication is available from the British Library

ISBN 978-1-107-61195-5 Paperback

Cover image: Seamus Ditmeyer/Alamy

....

....

Table of Contents

Revision checklist

The following list is a very concise summary of the syllabus. Core students only study the core syllabus while Extended students will need to study both the core and the extended topics (red text).

UNIT	CORE TOPICS	EXTENDED TOPICS
1. Number, set notation and language	Know natural numbers, integers, primes, factors, multiples, rational and irrational numbers. Describe sequences and patterns using words and the *n*th term.	Set symbols for elements, union, intersection, universal set, complement, subset, empty sets, greater/less than. Venn diagrams.
2. Squares, roots and cubes, directed numbers, fractions, decimals and percentages	Perform calculations with squares, roots and cubes with and without calculator. Directed numbers in practical situations, arithmetic with directed numbers. Fraction and percentage calculations and conversions, equivalence.	
3. Ordering, standard form, four rules and estimation	Order numbers by magnitude using $\neq$, $\geqslant$, $\leqslant$, $=$, $>$, $<$. Write numbers in standard form and vice versa. Calculations with whole numbers, decimals, fractions, BODMAS. Estimate numbers using rounding, decimal places, significant figures.	
4. Limits of accuracy	Limits of accuracy, upper and lower bounds of numbers.	Upper and lower bounds to solutions of simple problems, e.g. areas and perimeters, given data to a specified accuracy.
5. Ratio, proportion and rate	Ratio, direct and inverse proportion, scales, average speed.	Direct and inverse variation ($\propto$) in algebraic terms, increase and decrease by a given ratio.
6. Percentages	Percentages of quantities, % increase and decrease. One quantity as a percentage of another.	Reverse percentages, e.g. find the cost price given the selling price and the percentage profit.
7. Use of calculator, measures and time	Efficient use of a calculator, appropriate checks of accuracy. Use current units of mass, length, capacity, area and volume in practical situations and express quantities in terms of larger or smaller units. Conversions between 12 and 24 hour clocks, time calculations, read dials and timetables.	
8. Money, personal, household and small business finance	Currency conversions, calculations involving money. Use data to solve problems on personal and household finance, e.g. earnings, discount, profit/loss, reading associated tables and charts.	
9. Graphs in practical situations	Co-ordinate, travel and conversion graphs, construction and interpretation.	Distance–time, speed–time graphs, e.g. acceleration/deceleration, distance travelled from area under a speed–time graph.

UNIT	CORE TOPICS	EXTENDED TOPICS
10. Graphs of functions	Calculate table values, draw linear and quadratic graphs, find gradients, solve functions using graphical methods.	Harder functions involving powers (ax^n), estimate gradients of curves using tangents. Solve associated equations using graphical methods.
11. Straight line graphs	Interpret straight line graphs, obtain their equation in the form $y = mx + c$. Equation of a straight line parallel to a given line.	Calculate gradient/length of line from co-ordinates of two points on it. Find mid-point from co-ordinates of end points.
12. Algebraic representation and formulae	Algebraic representation, substitution, simplification, rearranging. Construct simple expressions and set up simple equations.	Construct and transform more complicated equations and formulae.
13. Algebraic manipulation	Manipulate directed numbers, use brackets and extract common factors.	Harder algebraic expressions, algebraic fractions, factorisation using difference of two squares, quadratic, grouping methods.
14. Functions		Find inputs (x), outputs, inverse and composite functions.
15. Indices	Rules for positive, negative, zero powers.	Fractional indices.
16. Solution of equations and inequalities	Solving linear and simultaneous equations.	Solve quadratic equations by factorisation and formula or completing the square. Solve simple linear inequalities.
17. Linear programming		Graphical inequalities, shade regions, solve for x and y.
18. Geometric terms and relationships	Angle calculation, point, line, parallel, right, acute, obtuse, reflex, perpendiculars, similarity, congruence. Types of triangles, quadrilaterals, circles and polygons and solid figures. Nets.	Areas and volumes of similar triangles, figures and solids.
19. Geometrical constructions	Construct lines, angles, bisectors and simple shapes using ruler, protractor and compass. Scale drawings.	
20. Symmetry	Line and rotational symmetry, symmetrical properties of simple shapes.	Solid shape symmetries, equal chords, perpendicular/tangent symmetry.
21. Angle properties	Angles in parallel lines, shapes, circle theorems.	Irregular polygons, more difficult circle theorems.
22. Locus	Constructions using compass and ruler from fixed point, straight line, two points, two straight lines (angle bisector).	
23. Mensuration	Perimeter, area of rectangle, triangle, parallelogram, trapezium, circumference, area of circles, volume of cuboids, prism, cylinder, surface areas of cuboid and cylinder.	Arc length, sector areas, surface area, volume of sphere, pyramid and cone.
24. Trigonometry	Find missing sides, angles in right-angled triangles. Pythagoras' theorem, using bearings.	Elevation and depression, sine and cosine rules, sine and cosine function between 90° and 180°, area of triangles, three-dimensional trigonometry.

UNIT	CORE TOPICS	EXTENDED TOPICS
25. Statistics	Interpret, tabulate and draw bar charts, pictograms, pie charts, histograms (equal intervals) from data. Scatter diagrams, line of best fit. Mean, mode and median and range calculations and uses. Discrete and continuous data.	Histograms (unequal intervals), cumulative frequency diagrams, median, upper/lower quartiles, interquartile range, estimate of mean, modal class.
26. Probability	Probability calculations of single events as fractions or decimals. Probability scales, probability complement.	Combined probabilities using trees, possibility diagrams.
27. Vectors	Description, addition, multiplication by scalar quantities, using vectors.	Magnitude of vector, resultant vectors, position vectors. Algebraic representation.
28. Matrices		Notation, addition, subtraction, multiplication of matrices, equations involving matrices. Determinants and inverses. Identity and zero matrices.
29. Transformations	Describe and perform reflections, rotations (multiples of 90°), enlargements, translations.	Combinations of transformations and matrix transformations.

Formulae

CORE CURRICULUM

Rectangle: area = length × width   perimeter = 2 × length + 2 × width (distance around shape)

Triangle: area = $\frac{1}{2}$ × base × height   perimeter = add up all the sides

Parallelogram: area = base × height   **Trapezium:** area = $\frac{1}{2}$ × sum of parallel sides × height

Circle: area = πr^2 circumference = $2\pi r$ (where r is the radius)

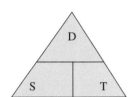

Distance = speed × time

Speed = distance ÷ time

Time = distance ÷ speed

$$c = \sqrt{a^2 + b^2}$$
$$a = \sqrt{c^2 - b^2}$$
$$b = \sqrt{c^2 - a^2}$$

Gradient of a graph = $\dfrac{\text{change in } y \text{ co-ordinates}}{\text{change in } x \text{ co-ordinates}}$ **Mean** = total of values ÷ sum of values

Mode = most frequent number

Median = middle value when numbers in order of size   **% increase/decrease** = $\dfrac{\text{actual change} \times 100}{\text{original}}$

Total degrees in polygon = $(n - 2) \times 180°$ **Regular polygon** = total degrees ÷ n (n = number of sides)

sin $\theta = \dfrac{\text{opposite}}{\text{hypotenuse}}$ **cos** $\theta = \dfrac{\text{adjacent}}{\text{hypotenuse}}$ **tan** $\theta = \dfrac{\text{opposite}}{\text{adjacent}}$

Exterior angle of regular polygon = $\dfrac{360°}{\text{exterior angle}}$

Equation of linear graph: $y = mx + c$ m = gradient, c = y-intercept

Simple interest: $I = \dfrac{PTR}{100}$, where P is the principal amount, T is the time and R is the rate.

Compound interest: Value of investment = $P\left(1 + \frac{r}{100}\right)^n$, where P = amount invested, r = percentage interest rate, and n = number of years of compound interest.

EXTENDED CURRICULUM

Volume of any shape = cross-sectional area × length (or height)

Sine rule: $\dfrac{a}{\sin A} = \dfrac{b}{\sin B} = \dfrac{c}{\sin C}$ **Cosine rule:** $a^2 = b^2 + c^2 - 2bc \cos A$ $\cos A = \dfrac{b^2 + c^2 - a^2}{2bc}$

Area of triangle = $\dfrac{1}{2} ab \sin C$ **Arc length** = $\dfrac{\theta}{360} \times 2\pi r$ **Sector area** = $\dfrac{\theta}{360} \times \pi r^2$

Venn diagram formula: $n(A \cup B) = n(A) + n(B) - n(A \cap B)$

Quadratic formula: $x = \dfrac{-b \pm \sqrt{b^2 - 4ac}}{2a}$

Matrices: $X = \begin{pmatrix} a & b \\ c & d \end{pmatrix}$ **Determinant:** $|X| = ad - bc$ **Inverse:** $X^{-1} = \dfrac{1}{|X|}\begin{pmatrix} d & -b \\ -c & a \end{pmatrix}$

Acceleration/deceleration = $\dfrac{\text{change in speed}}{\text{time taken}}$ **Distance travelled** = area under speed–time graph

Introduction

TIP

Ensure you are familiar with your calculator and its many functions (see Unit 7).

Revise the metric units of measurement.

Make a list of the symbols used in the revision guide.

This revision guide has been written to help students studying for Cambridge International Examinations IGCSE Mathematics. The structure of the guide broadly follows the syllabus headings, and is designed to accompany the IGCSE course book.

Each unit includes:

- definitions and explanations of key concepts for each of the syllabus areas;
- appropriate charts or diagrams to highlight important ideas;
- tips and notes to provide helpful guidance on key points;
- links to show where concepts in different units overlap;
- progress check questions to allow you to test your understanding;
- worked examples to highlight common mistakes or misunderstandings;
- exam-style questions for you to practise.

There are sections on examination technique and guidance notes to help you revise.

Key skills

The Cambridge IGCSE examination is designed to assess two main sets of skills: your knowledge of mathematical techniques and your ability to apply those techniques to solve problems. The specific assessment objectives of the Cambridge IGCSE are listed below (taken from the syllabus).

Mathematical techniques

TIP

There can often be more than one way to arrive at the final answer.

It is important that you show all your steps in a logical, easy to follow, order.

- Organise, interpret and present information accurately in written, tabular, graphical and diagrammatic forms.
- Perform calculations by suitable methods, using an electronic calculator where appropriate.
- Understand systems of measurement in everyday use and utilise in problem-solving.
- Estimate, approximate and work to appropriate degrees of accuracy; convert between numerical forms.
- Use mathematical and other instruments for measuring and construction to a suitable degree of accuracy.
- Interpret and transform mathematical statements expressed in words or symbols.
- Recognise and use spatial relationships in two and three dimensions, particularly in solving problems.
- Recall, apply and interpret mathematical knowledge in the context of everyday situations.

Applying mathematical techniques to solve problems

- Make logical deductions from given mathematical data, recognise patterns and structures in a variety of situations, and form generalisations.
- Respond to a problem relating to a relatively unstructured situation by translating it into an appropriately structured form.
- Analyse a problem, select a suitable strategy and apply an appropriate technique to obtain its solution.
- Apply combinations of mathematical skills and techniques in problem solving.
- Set out mathematical work, including the solution of problems, in a logical and clear form using appropriate symbols and terminology.

Exam-style questions

Referring to the Key skills section, ensure you are confident with each of the 'knowledge' and 'application' aspects mentioned.

Mathematical techniques

These are 'knowledge' questions, examples may include:

- Write down the number of planes of symmetry of a cuboid.
- Calculate the area of the triangle shown.
- Label each region of the Venn diagram shown.
- Give your answer to 4 significant figures.
- Construct the perpendicular bisector of the line AB.

Applying mathematical techniques to solve problems

These questions test whether you can apply your mathematical knowledge to a range of questions and contexts. Examples may include:

TIP

You may decide to roughly sketch the two points first, apply the gradient formula and use $y = mx + c$ to find the y intercept.

We need to be able to apply our knowledge of calculations with time units, and remember to multiply out to find total buying and selling costs, then use subtraction to find the profit before applying percentage techniques.

- The points $(2, 5)$, $(3, 3)$ lie on a straight line. Find the equation of the line.
- At 0508 Mr Jin bought 820 fish at a fish market for \$2.45 each. He sold them all 93 minutes later to a supermarket for \$2.88 each.

   a) What was the time when he sold the fish?
   b) Calculate his total percentage profit.

Revision guidance

There are many ways to revise, but here are some simple points to bear in mind.

1. **Ensure you know what you need to learn.** Look at the syllabus carefully and concentrate on the key aspects. Mathematics is a vast subject that some students find easier to grasp than others. Ask your teacher for more guidance on what your strengths or weaknesses are and plan accordingly. If you are sitting the core examination then only concentrate on the core syllabus; if you are an extended student, ensure the core material is well understood before tackling the extended syllabus.
2. **Make a revision timetable.** Set aside a regular time for revising a specific subject, either on a daily or weekly basis. Allow several weeks before the actual exam to avoid a last-minute panic, and to give yourself time to either revisit a more difficult topic or ask your teacher for clarification. Allow time for relaxation between study periods.

TIP

Learn the key facts. Many of these questions will involve simple recall of formulae and technique. Remember to understand and learn formulae before an exam as formulae sheets are NOT provided.

TIP

Check the wording of the question carefully. Is there a formula that can be applied? Would a sketch make the question easier to understand?

3. **Revise effectively.** Try not to spend more than 30 to 40 minutes revising at a time. Allow at least 10 to 15 minutes to sit back and reflect on what you have learnt.

4. **Make your revision active.** When studying a particular topic, refer to the appropriate syllabus section. Make notes in the margins as you revise and try to link together topics with common themes. This revision guide identifies connected topics to assist you.

5. **Test yourself regularly to check that you have understood.** With each topic locate relevant exercises from your textbook to test what you have learnt. At the start of each revision session spend a few minutes going over your previous study notes. This will give you confidence to tackle the next set of notes.

6. **Practise past examination or sample questions.** This will help to familiarise you with the style of questions that you will come across and will also help you to time your answers accordingly.

7. **Get into the habit of showing your working.** It can be very tempting to just jot down an answer quickly while rushing a question. When answering questions always set out your method neatly and logically in the space provided, then copy your answer to the correct place.

Some important things to remember during an examination

1. Make yourself familiar with the instructions on the front page of the examination paper. Key things to remember include:
   - Answer all the questions.
   - Degree of accuracy: If the answer is not exact round it to 3 significant figures unless specified; answers in degrees to 1 decimal place.
   - Use an electronic calculator for more difficult calculations.
   - For π, use 3.142 or your calculator.
   - Use a blue or black pen for writing your answers; only use a pencil for diagrams or graphs.

2. Ensure you have the required equipment: pen, pencil, ruler, protractor, compasses, calculator, eraser. Make sure that you know how to use them.

3. Identify the command words in the question such as 'calculate', 'find the value', 'solve', 'simplify', 'shade', then answer accordingly.

4. Although all questions have to be attempted, you can do the questions in any order. Some students will naturally find some topics easier than others. You may want to complete these first, to give yourself confidence as time moves on.

5. Underline key words in the question, such as 'smallest' when dealing with an ordering question, or 'standard form' when asked to give your final answer.

6. Jot down relevant formulae for questions. This revision guide contains a formulae sheet which you should make yourself very familiar with.

7. Look at the marks allocated to a question, as this will give you a guide to how much time and effort you should allocate to a question.

8. Try not to get too bogged down with a particular question, as you may be able to come back to it later.

9. Always show your method. An incorrect answer can be carried through to the next part of the question without further penalty.

Remember: show all your working!

Number, set notation and language

CORE CURRICULUM

1.01 Numbers

Natural numbers

These are the counting numbers: 1, 2, 3, 4, …

Integers

These are positive or negative whole numbers, e.g. $-5, 3, 25$. If the number contains a fraction part or a decimal point, then it cannot be an integer. For example, the numbers 4.2 and $\frac{1}{2}$ are not integers.

Prime numbers

Numbers that can only be divided by themselves, e.g. 2, 3, 5, 7, 11, 13, are prime numbers. Note that 1 is not considered prime and 2 is the only even prime number.

Progress check

1.01 Explain the difference between natural numbers and integers.

1.02 Give two examples of prime numbers between 20 and 30.

1.02 Factors

A number is a factor of another number if it divides exactly into that number without leaving a remainder. For example, the factors of 6 are 1, 2, 3, 6; the factors of 15 are 1, 3, 5, 15.

To find the factors of a number quickly, find which numbers were multiplied together to give that number. For example, the products which give 8 are 1×8 or 2×4, so the factors of 8 are 1, 2, 4, 8.

Prime factors

A prime factor is a prime number that is also a factor of another number. For example, the prime factors of 24 are 2 and 3, since $2 \times 2 \times 2 \times 2 \times 3 = 24$.

Highest Common Factor (HCF)

This is the highest factor which is common to a group of numbers.

1.01 Worked example

Find the HCF of the numbers 6, 8 and 12.

Factors of 6	=	1, **2**, 3, 6
Factors of 8	=	1, **2**, 4, 8
Factors of 12	=	1, **2**, 3, 4, 6, 12

As the number 2 is a the highest factor of the three numbers, HCF = 2.

1.03 Multiples

These are the 'times table' of a number. For example, multiples of 4 are 4, 8, 12, 16, …; multiples of 9 are 9, 18, 27, 36, …

Lowest Common Multiple (LCM)

This is the lowest multiple which is common to a group of numbers. It is found by listing all the multiples of a group of numbers and finding the lowest number which is common to each set of multiples.

1.02 Worked example

Find the Lowest Common Multiple of the numbers 2, 3 and 9.

Multiples of 2 are	2, 4, 6, 8, 10, 12, 14, 16, **18**, 20, …
Multiples of 3 are	3, 6, 9, 12, 15, **18**, 21, 24, …
Multiples of 9 are	9, **18**, 27, 36, …

The number 18 is the lowest number that occurs as a multiple of each of the numbers, so the LCM is 18.

Progress check

1.03 Find the HCF and LCM of the numbers 24 and 36.

1.04 Rational and irrational numbers

Rational numbers

Rational numbers are numbers that can be shown as fractions, they either terminate or have repeating digits, for example $\frac{3}{4}$, 4.333, 5.343434…, etc.

Note that recurring decimals are rational.

TIP

Recurring decimals can be displayed in a variety of ways. One way of representing a repeating decimal is by placing a dot over the recurring figure:

5.3$\dot{4}$

Another common way of indicating that a decimal is recurring is by placing a horizontal line over the figure which repeats:

5.3$\overline{4}$

Irrational numbers

An irrational number cannot be expressed as a fraction, e.g. $\sqrt{2}, \sqrt{3}, \sqrt{5}, \pi$. Since these numbers never terminate, we cannot possibly show them as fractions. The square root of any odd number apart from the square numbers is irrational. (Try them on your calculator, you will find that they do not terminate.) Also, any decimal number which neither repeats nor terminates is irrational.

For more information on square numbers look up special number sequences at the end of this unit.

Progress check

1.04 In general, square roots of which type of numbers are always rational?

1.05 Number sequences

A number sequence is a set of numbers that follow a certain pattern, for example:

1, 3, 5, 7, ...   Here the pattern is either 'consecutive odd numbers' or 'add 2'.
1, 3, 9, 27, ...   The pattern is '3 × previous number'.

The pattern could be add, subtract, multiply or divide. To make it easier to find the pattern, remember that for a number to get bigger, you generally have to use the add or multiply operation. If the number gets smaller, then it will usually be the subtract or divide operation.

Sometimes the pattern uses more than one operation, for example:

1, 3, 7, 15, 31, ... Here the pattern is 'multiply the previous number by 2 and then add 1'.

The nth term

For certain number sequences it is necessary, and indeed very useful, to find a general formula for the number sequence.

Consider the number sequence 4, 7, 10, 13, 16, 19, ...

We can see that the sequence is 'add 3 to the previous number', but what if we wanted the 50th number in the sequence?

This would mean us continuing the sequence up to the 50th value, which would be very time consuming.

A quicker method is to find a general formula for any value of n and then substitute 50 to find its corresponding value. The following examples show the steps involved.

1.03 Worked example

Find the nth term and hence the 50th term of the number sequence
4, 7, 10, 13, 16, 19, …

We can see that you add 3 to the previous number. To find a formula for the nth term, follow the steps below:

Step 1 Construct a table and include a difference row.

n	1	2	3	4	5	6
Sequence	4	7	10	13	16	19

1st difference   3   3   3   3   3

Step 2 Look at the table to see where the differences remain constant.

We can see that the differences are always 3 in the (n) row; this means that the formula involves $3n$. If we then add 1 we get the sequence number, as shown below.

When $n = 1$:   When $n = 2$:
$3 \times (1) + 1 = 4$ $3 \times (2) + 1 = 7$

Step 3 Form a general nth term formula and check:

Knowing that we have to multiply n by 3 and then add 1:

$$n\text{th term} = 3n + 1$$

This formula is extremely powerful as we can now find the corresponding term in the sequence for any value of n. To find the 50th term in the sequence:

Using nth term $= 3n + 1$ when $n = 50$:

$$3(50) + 1 = 151$$

Therefore the 50th term in the sequence will be 151.
This is a much quicker method than extending the sequence up to $n = 50$.

Sometimes, however, we have sequences where the first difference row is not constant, so we have to continue the difference rows, as shown in the following example.

TIP

Some more complicated sequences will require a third difference row (n^3) for the differences to be constant, so we have to manipulate n^3 to get the final formula.

Some special sequences

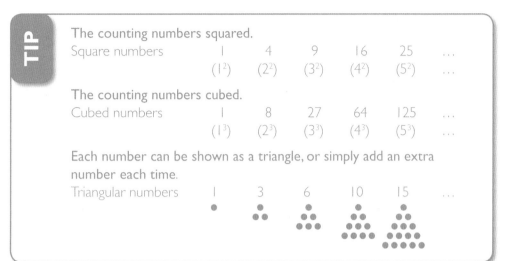

TIP

The counting numbers squared.

Square numbers	1	4	9	16	25	...
	(1^2)	(2^2)	(3^2)	(4^2)	(5^2)	...

The counting numbers cubed.

Cubed numbers	1	8	27	64	125	...
	(1^3)	(2^3)	(3^3)	(4^3)	(5^3)	...

Each number can be shown as a triangle, or simply add an extra number each time.

Triangular numbers	1	3	6	10	15	...

Progress check

1.05 Find the *n*th term and 20th term of 5, 8, 11, 14, 17, ...

TERMS

- **Natural numbers**
  The positive counting numbers, 1, 2, 3, etc.

- **Integers**
  Whole numbers, including zero.

- **Prime numbers**
  Only divide by themselves and 1.

- **Factors**
  Numbers that divide into other numbers exactly.

- **Multiples**
  Times table of numbers.

- **LCM**
  Lowest Common Multiple of two or more numbers.

- **HCF**
  Highest Common Factor of two or more numbers.

- **Rational numbers**
  Numbers that terminate or have same recurring digit(s).

- **Irrational numbers**
  Numbers that exhibit continuous random digits.

- **Sequence**
  A set of numbers that exhibit a definite pattern.

- ***n*th term**
  A general formula for a number sequence.

Exam-style questions

1.01 Write down the next two prime numbers after 53. (2)

1.02 For the set of numbers $2, -2.3, \sqrt{5}, \pi, 5, 0.3333\ldots$, write down which are:
a integers
b rational numbers
c prime numbers (3)

1.03 What is the sum of the 2nd square number and the 3rd triangular number? (2)

EXTENDED CURRICULUM

Learning outcomes

By the end of this unit you should be able to understand and use:

■ set notation such as $n(A), \in, \notin, \xi, A', \cap, \cup, \subseteq$

■ Venn diagrams and appropriate shading of well-defined regions

■ calculations involving missing regions in sets

■ exponential sequences and combinations.

1.06 Sets

Definition of a set

A set is a collection of objects, numbers, ideas, etc. The different objects, numbers, ideas and so on in the set are called the **elements** or **members** of the set.

1.04 Worked example

Set A contains the even numbers from 1 to 10 inclusive. Write this as a set.

The elements of this set will be 2, 4, 6, 8, 10, so we write:
$A = \{2, 4, 6, 8, 10\}$

1.05 Worked example

Set B contains the prime numbers between 10 and 20 inclusive. Write this as a set.

The elements of this set will be 11, 13, 17 and 19, so:
$B = \{11, 13, 17, 19\}$

Progress check

1.06 Set C contains the triangular numbers between 1 and 20 inclusive. Write as a set.

The number of elements in a set

The number of elements in set A is denoted $n(A)$, and is found by counting the number of elements in the set.

1.06 Worked example

Set C contains the odd numbers from 1 to 10 inclusive. Find $n(C)$.

$C = \{1, 3, 5, 7, 9\}$. There are 5 elements in the set, so:

$n(C) = 5$

Inclusion in a set

The symbols $\in$ and $\notin$ indicate whether or not an item is an element of a set.

1.07 Worked example

Set $A = \{2, 5, 6, 9\}$. Describe which of the numbers 2, 3 or 4 are elements and which are not elements of set A.

Set A contains the element 2, therefore $\qquad$ $2 \in A$.

Set A does not contain the elements 3 or 4, therefore $\qquad$ $3, 4 \notin A$.

The universal set and the complement of a set

The universal set, ξ, for any problem is the set which contains all the available elements for that problem.

The complement of a set A, A', is the set of elements of ξ which do not belong to A.

1.08 Worked example

The universal set is all of the odd numbers up to and including 11.

$\xi = \{1, 3, 5, 7, 9, 11\}$

1.09 Worked example

If $A = \{3, 5\}$ and the universal set is the same as the previous example, write down the complement of A.

$A' = \{1, 7, 9, 11\}$

The empty set

This is a set that contains no elements, and is denoted $\varnothing$ or { }. For example, for some readers, the set of people who wear glasses in their family will have no members. The empty set is sometimes referred to as the null set.

Subsets

If all the elements of a set A are also elements of a set B then A is said to be a **subset** of B, $A \subseteq B$.

Every set has at least two subsets, itself and the null set.

1.10 Worked example

List all the subsets of $\{a, b, c\}$.

The subsets are $\varnothing$, $\{a\}$, $\{b\}$, $\{c\}$, $\{a, b\}$, $\{a, c\}$, $\{b, c\}$ and $\{a, b, c\}$, because all of these elements can occur in their own right inside the main set.

Subsets A ⊆ B and proper subsets

If all the elements of a set A are also elements of a set B then A is said to be a **subset** of B.

Every set has at least two subsets, itself and the null set.

Proper subsets will contain all elements except the whole set and the null set.

1.11 Worked example

Set A = $\{2, 3, 5\}$, find:

a the subsets   **b** the proper subsets

a $\{\ \}$ $\{2\}$, $\{3\}$, $\{5\}$, $\{2, 3\}$, $\{2, 5\}$, $\{3, 5\}$, $\{2, 3, 5\}$, note $\{\ \}$ is the empty set and can also be written as

b $\{2\}$, $\{3\}$, $\{5\}$, $\{2, 3\}$, $\{2, 5\}$, $\{3, 5\}$

Intersection and union

The **intersection** of two sets A and B is the set of elements which are common to both A and B, and is denoted by $A \cap B$.

The **union** the sets A and B is the set of all the elements contained in A and B, and is denoted by $A \cup B$.

1.12 Worked example

If A = $\{2, 3, 5, 8, 9\}$ and B = $\{1, 3, 4, 8\}$, find:

a $A \cap B$ **b** $A \cup B$

a $A \cap B = \{3, 8\}$, because these elements are common to both sets.

b $A \cup B = \{1, 2, 3, 4, 5, 8, 9\}$, because these are all the elements contained in both A and B.

Progress check

1.07 Describe the difference between the union and intersection of two or more sets.

1.08 What does the complement of a set mean?

1.09 If set A is $\{1, 2, 3, 5\}$ and set B is $\{3, 4, 6, 9\}$, write down:
  a $n(A)$ **b** $A \cap B$ **c** $A \cup B$

Venn diagrams

Set problems may be solved by using Venn diagrams. The universal set is represented by a rectangle and subsets of this set are represented by circles or loops. Some of the definitions explained earlier can be shown using these diagrams.

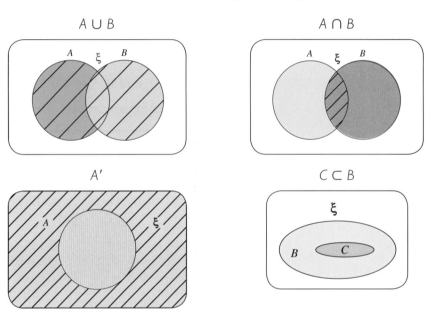

Some more complex Venn diagrams:

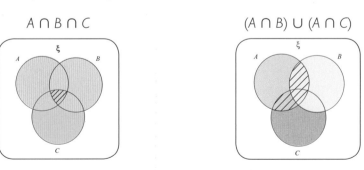

Obviously there are many different arrangements possible with these diagrams but now let us try some more difficult problems.

Unit 1 Number, set notation and language — Extended

9

1.13 Worked example

If $A = \{3, 4, 5, 6\}$, $B = \{2, 3, 5, 7, 9\}$ and $\xi = \{1, 2, 3, 4, 5, 6, 7, 8, 9, 10, 11\}$, draw a Venn diagram to represent this information. Hence write down the elements of:

a A' **b** $A \cap B$ **c** $A \cup B$

We only have 2 sets (A, B), so there are two circles inside the universal set.

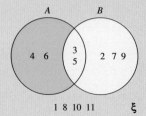

From the Venn diagram it can be seen that:

a $A' = \{1, 2, 7, 8, 9, 10, 11\}$
b $A \cap B = \{3, 5\}$
c $A \cup B = \{2, 3, 4, 5, 6, 7, 9\}$

Problems with the number of elements of a set

For two intersecting sets A and B we can use the rule:

$$n(A \cup B) = n(A) + n(B) - n(A \cap B)$$

This formula can be used for any problem involving two sets; here is an example.

1.14 Worked example

In a class of 25 members, 15 take history, 17 take geography and 3 take neither subject. How many class members take both subjects?

Let H = set of history students, so $n(H) = 15$.
Let G = set of geography students, so $n(G) = 17$.
Also, $n(H \cup G) = 22$ (since 3 students take neither subject).
Let x represent the number taking both subjects.

Now we can draw the Venn diagram.
Using the formula:

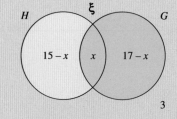

$$n(H \cup G) = n(H) + n(G) - n(H \cap G)$$
$$22 = 15 + 17 - x$$

So $x = 10$.

Hence the number taking both subjects is 10.
The history-only region is labelled $15 - x$.
This is because a number of these students also take geography.

Progress check

1.10 In a class of 35 students, 19 take French, 18 take German and 3 take neither. Calculate how many take:
   a both French and German
   b just French
   c just German.

1.07 Exponential sequences

These take the form a^n, where a is a positive integer. For example, 2^n, 2^{n+1}, 3^n.

Here is a table showing some typical exponential sequences:

n	1	2	3	4	5	6
2^n	$2^1 = 2$	$2^2 = 4$	8	16	32	64
3^n	$3^1 = 3$	$3^2 = 9$	27	81	243	729

Notice that the differences between successive terms are steadily increasing, but they represent powers of 2, 3, etc.

1.15 Worked example

Write down the first five terms of the sequence $2^{n+1} + n^2$.

$n = 1, 2^{(1)+1} + (1)^2 = 5$
$n = 2, 2^{(2)+1} + (2)^2 = 13$
$n = 3, 2^{(3)+1} + (3)^2 = 25$
$n = 4, 2^{(4)+1} + (4)^2 = 48$
$n = 5, 2^{(5)+1} + (5)^2 = 89$

So the first five terms are 5, 13, 25, 48, 89.

1.16 Worked example

Find the nth term and hence the 50th term for the sequence 0, 3, 8, 15, 24, 35, ...

Construct a table:

n	1	2	3	4	5	6
Sequence	0	3	8	15	24	35

1st difference   3   5   7   9   11

2nd difference   2   2   2   2

Now we notice that the differences are equal in the *second* row, so the formula involves n^2. If we square the first few terms of n we get 1, 4, 9, 16, etc. We can see that we have to subtract 1 from these numbers to get the terms in the sequence. So:

nth term $= n^2 - 1$

Now we have the nth term, to find the 50th term we use simple substitution:

50th term $= (50)^2 - 1 = 2499$

- n(A)
  The number of elements in set A.

- $\in, \notin$
  An element is or is not an element of a set.

- ξ
  The universal set, which contains all possible elements for the problem.

- A'
  The complement of a set: the elements in the universal set but not in set A.

- $\cap$
  The intersection of two sets: the common elements of both sets.

- $\cup$
  The union of two sets: those elements in either set A or set B.

- $\subseteq$
  The subset of a set: another set made from some or all of the elements in the main set.

Exam-style questions

1.04 All the students in a class of 20 took tests in mathematics and chemistry. The following table shows the results of these two tests.

	Pass	Fail
Mathematics	12	8
Chemistry	11	9

M is the set of students who passed the mathematics test.
C is the set of students who passed the chemistry test.
x is the number of students who passed both tests.

a   Write 3 expressions **in terms of x** to complete the Venn diagram.

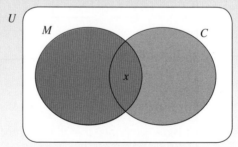

b   Two pupils failed both mathematics and chemistry. Find the value of x, the number of students who passed both tests.

Source: Cambridge IGCSE Mathematics 0580 Paper 21 Q10a, b June 2011.

Squares, roots and cubes, directed numbers, fractions, decimals and percentages

CORE CURRICULUM

Learning outcomes

By the end of this unit you should be able to understand and use:

- squares, roots and cubes of numbers
- positive and negative numbers in practical situations, e.g. temperature changes
- fractions, decimals and percentages, conversions and equivalence

2.01 Squares

The square of a number (x^2) is that number multiplied by itself.

$$4^2 = 4 \times 4 = 16$$
$$8^2 = 8 \times 8 = 64$$

2.02 Square roots ($\sqrt{\ }$)

A square root is the inverse of a square. It can be quickly obtained from the calculator using the ◻√ key.

For example, $\sqrt{16} = 4$ (see above), $\sqrt{49} = 7$ (since $7 \times 7 = 49$).

2.03 Cubes

The cube of a number (x^3) is that number multiplied by itself twice.

$$5^3 = 5 \times 5 \times 5 = 125$$
$$10^3 = 10 \times 10 \times 10 = 1000$$

TIP

Find the square, root and power keys on your scientific calculator and check these calculations.

2.04 Cube roots ($\sqrt[3]{\ }$)

A cube root is the inverse of a cube. It can be obtained from the calculator using the ◻$\sqrt[3]{\ }$ key.

For example, $\sqrt[3]{27} = 3$ (since $3 \times 3 \times 3 = 27$).

TIP

The roots of 63 and 7 give continuing numbers after the point so it's best to leave them in the calculator display when multiplying them.

Four cubed, and indeed two cubed, can be done on the calculator, using the x^y key or by simply multiplying the numbers together, i.e. $4 \times 4 \times 4 = 64$.

When using the x^y key on your calculator, press the following:

$4^3 \div 2^3 = $

2.01 Worked example

Find the value of

a $\sqrt{63} \times \sqrt{7}$ **b** $4^3 \div 2^3$

giving your answer in the same format.

a $\sqrt{63} \times \sqrt{7} = 7.9372... \times 2.6457... = 21$

b $4^3 \div 2^3 = 64 \div 8 = 8 = 2^3$

For easy reference, the first ten numbers and their corresponding squares and cubes are shown in Table 2.01.

Table 2.01 The squares and cubes of the first ten numbers

x	1	2	3	4	5	6	7	8	9	10
x^2	1	4	9	16	25	36	49	64	81	100
x^3	1	8	27	64	125	216	343	512	729	1000

Progress check

2.01 Find the value of $\sqrt{42} \times \sqrt{6}$, giving your answer to 2 decimal places.

2.02 Calculate $8^2 \div 2^4$, giving your answer in power (indices) form.

2.05 Directed numbers

These are numbers with direction; their sign, either positive or negative, indicates their direction.

Positive numbers are above zero on the temperature scale or to the right of zero on a number line, and negative numbers are below zero or to the left of zero on the number line, as illustrated in Figures 2.01 and 2.02.

TIP

A positive number displays either an upwards movement or a left-to-right movement.
A negative number displays either a downward movement or a right-to-left movement.

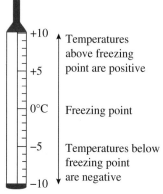

Fig. 2.01 A temperature scale

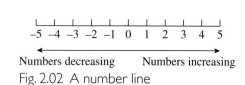

Fig. 2.02 A number line

2.02 Worked example

Figure 2.03 shows part of a water-level marker. The water level shown is −20 cm. What will be the reading on the marker if the water level:

a rises by 30 cm   **b** then falls by 17 cm?

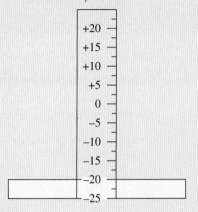

Fig. 2.03 Water-level marker

a If the water rises, then this is a positive movement, so we therefore add 30 to −20:

$$-20\,cm + 30\,cm = 10\,cm$$

b The water then falls. This is a negative movement, so we have to subtract:

$$10\,cm - 17\,cm = -7\,cm$$

2.03 Worked example

In July the average temperature in Saudi Arabia is 43 °C, while in Antarctica it averages −17 °C. Find the difference in temperature.

$$43 - (-17) = 60$$

We have to move 43 units down the scale to reach zero, then another 17 degrees below zero to reach the point of −17 °C.

Progress check

2.03 The average temperature for Siberia, Russia in January 2004 was −15 °C, while in Kuwait City, the average temperature for July 2004 was 47 °C. Find the difference between these temperatures.

2.06 Fractions

A fraction is a part of something. The top number is called the numerator and the bottom number the denominator.

For example:

numerator $\longrightarrow$ $\dfrac{1}{2}$ = 1 part out of 2

denominator $\longrightarrow$

There are two main types of fraction:

- Mixed fractions contain a whole number and a fraction part.
- Improper fractions are 'top-heavy' fractions in which the numerator is bigger than the denominator.

Mixed and improper fractions can have the same value but they are shown differently as shown in Table 2.02.

Table 2.02 The same values expressed as either mixed or improper fractions.

Mixed	Improper
$1\dfrac{2}{3}$ $\longleftrightarrow$	$\dfrac{5}{3}$
$2\dfrac{4}{7}$ $\longleftrightarrow$	$\dfrac{18}{7}$
$3\dfrac{3}{5}$ $\longleftrightarrow$	$\dfrac{18}{5}$
$4\dfrac{5}{6}$ $\longleftrightarrow$	$\dfrac{29}{6}$

Conversion between mixed and improper fractions

The mixed fraction $4\frac{2}{5}$ can be changed to improper by multiplying the whole number by the fraction denominator and then adding the numerator part. This number is then simply the numerator of the new top-heavy fraction. In other words:

$$4\frac{2}{5} = \frac{(4 \times 5) + 2}{5} = \frac{22}{5}$$

To change improper to mixed fractions, simply reverse the process. For example:

$\frac{15}{4} = 15 \div 4 = 3$ wholes with 3 remainder, therefore the fraction is $3\frac{3}{4}$.

Fraction operations

Fractions can be added, subtracted, multiplied or divided.

Adding and subtracting fractions

If the denominators are the same, then just add or subtract the numerators.

2.04 Worked example

a $\dfrac{3}{7} + \dfrac{2}{7} = \dfrac{5}{7}$ $\qquad$ b $\dfrac{5}{9} - \dfrac{2}{9} = \dfrac{3}{9}$

TIP

We can check our answers with a scientific calculator; press these keys:

 $3\dfrac{3}{4}$

If the denominators are different, then follow the steps shown in the next example.

2.05 Worked example

Find $\dfrac{2}{3} + \dfrac{3}{4}$.

$$\dfrac{2}{3} = \dfrac{8}{12} \text{ and } \dfrac{3}{4} = \dfrac{9}{12}.$$

$$\dfrac{8}{12} + \dfrac{9}{12} = \dfrac{17}{12} = 1\dfrac{5}{12}$$

The process is similar for subtracting. Once both fractions have the same denominator, we **subtract** the numerators.

Multiplying fractions

The easiest of the operations: we just multiply the numerators together and then the denominators together.

2.06 Worked example

Find $\dfrac{3}{8} \times \dfrac{4}{7}$.

$$\dfrac{3}{8} \times \dfrac{4}{7} = \dfrac{12}{56}$$

$$= \dfrac{3}{14} \text{ (whenever possible, simplify the final answer)}$$

Dividing fractions

First turn the second fraction around and then multiply as normal.

2.07 Worked example

Find $\dfrac{2}{3} \div \dfrac{1}{12}$.

Invert the second fraction and then multiply the numerators and denominators:

$$\dfrac{2}{3} \times \dfrac{12}{1} = \dfrac{24}{3}$$

$$= 8 \text{ (Finally, simplify the answer.)}$$

Alternatively, we could cancel the fractions:

$$\dfrac{2}{3} \times \dfrac{\cancel{12}^{\,4}}{1} = 2 \times 4 = 8$$

The calculator method

The methods shown are useful to learn, but a great deal of time can be saved, or you can quickly check your answers, by using a scientific calculator.

First: locate the fraction key, usually the $\boxed{a\frac{b}{c}}$ key, and follow the steps in the following example.

$$\frac{7}{9} \div \frac{2}{3} = \boxed{7}\ \boxed{a^{b/c}}\ \boxed{9}\ \boxed{\div}\ \boxed{2}\ \boxed{a^{b/c}}\ \boxed{3}\ \boxed{=}\ 1\frac{1}{6}$$

2.07 Decimals, fractions and percentages: conversions

When given decimals, for example 0.5, 0.75, they can be written as equivalent-value fractions.

$$0.5 = \frac{5}{10} = \frac{1}{2} \qquad\qquad 0.75 = \frac{75}{100} = \frac{3}{4}$$

Note how we have simplified the fractions by dividing through with the highest common factor.

Percentages are fractions with denominators of 100. In solving many problems it is useful to express a fraction or a decimal as a percentage. Let's look at how to interchange fractions, decimals and percentages.

Fraction → decimal

Divide numerator by denominator.

$$\text{i.e. } \frac{3}{8} = 3 \div 8 = 0.375$$

Fraction or decimal → percentage

Multiply the fraction or decimal by 100:

a $\dfrac{4}{5} = \dfrac{4}{5} \times 100 = 80\%$ b $0.375 = 0.375 \times 100 = 37.5\%$

To convert back from percentage to decimal, simply reverse the process ($\div$ 100).

Percentage → fraction

Place percentage value over 100, then simplify if possible:

a $30\% = \dfrac{30}{100} = \dfrac{3}{10}$ (divide by 10)   b $145\% = 1\dfrac{45}{100} = 1\dfrac{9}{20}$ (divide by 5)

Equivalence

Equivalent fractions have the same value.

$$\frac{2}{3} \xrightarrow[\times 2]{\times 2} \frac{4}{6} \xrightarrow[\times 2]{\times 2} \frac{8}{12} \xrightarrow[\times 3]{\times 3} \frac{24}{36} \quad \text{etc...}$$

The operations used to change the numerators and the denominators must be the same.

Progress check

2.04 Write the following in order of size, smallest first. $\dfrac{399}{401}\ \dfrac{698}{701}\ \dfrac{598}{601}$

Source: *Cambridge IGCSE Mathematics 0580 Paper 21 Q6 June 2008.*

2.05 Write the following in order of size, largest first: $\sqrt[3]{\dfrac{9}{13}}$, 84%, $\left(\dfrac{4}{3}\right)^{-1}$, 0.756.

TERMS

- $x^2, x^3, \sqrt{x}, \sqrt[3]{x}$
  The square, cube, square root and cube root of a number.

- $\dfrac{a}{b}$
  Fraction notation: a is the numerator, b is the denominator.

- %
  Percentage, out of a hundred.

- **Conversions**
  To change a fraction or a decimal to a percentage, multiply by a hundred.

- **Equivalence**
  When values are equal but in a different format, e.g. $25\% = 0.25 = \frac{1}{4}$.

Exam-style questions

2.01 Rani scored 9 marks in a test and Winston scored 12 marks. Calculate Rani's mark as a percentage of Winston's mark.

2.02 A tin of soup has the following information on the label.

200 grams of soup contains		
Protein	Carbohydrate	Fat
4 g	8.7 g	5.8 g

   a What fraction of the soup is Protein? Give your answer in its simplest form.
   b What percentage of the soup is Carbohydrate?
   Source: *Cambridge IGCSE Mathematics 0580 Paper 2 Q5a, b June 2007.*

2.03 The table below gives the average surface temperature (°C) on the following planets.

Planet	Earth	Mercury	Neptune	Pluto	Saturn	Uranus
Average temperature	15	350	−220	−240	−180	−200

   a Calculate the range of these temperatures.
   b Which planet has a temperature 20 °C lower than that of Uranus?
   Source: *Cambridge IGCSE Mathematics 0580 Paper 2 Q3a, b June 2006.*

2.04 Write the following in order of size, smallest first.

$$\dfrac{\pi}{4} \qquad \dfrac{1}{\sqrt{2}} \qquad \dfrac{3}{4} \qquad \sin 47°$$

   Source: *Cambridge IGCSE Mathematics 0580 Paper 2 Q8 June 2006.*

2.08 Conversion of recurring decimals to fractions

Recurring decimals such as 0.333..., 0.454545..., etc. can be converted to fractions in the form $\frac{a}{b}$, where a and b are integers.

For example, 0.333... can be written as $\frac{1}{3}$, and 0.4545... can be written as $\frac{45}{99}$.

2.08 Worked example

Convert the following recurring decimals into fractions:

a 0.555...   b 0.232323...   c 0.345345345...

a Let $x = 0.555...$	**b** Let $x = 0.232323...$	**c** Let $x = 0.345345345...$
$10x = 5.555...$	$100x = 23.2323...$	$1000x = 345.345345...$
$9x = 5$	$99x = 23$	$999x = 345$
Subtract the equations		
$x = \dfrac{5}{9}$	$x = \dfrac{23}{99}$	$x = \dfrac{345}{999}$

To convert a recurring decimal with one repeating digit, multiply by 10; with two repeating digits, multiply by 100; etc.

Exam-style questions

2.05   Convert the following recurring decimals to fractions:

a 0.444...   b 0.313131...   c 1.272272272

Ordering, standard form, four rules and estimation

CORE CURRICULUM

Learning outcomes

By the end of this unit you should be able to understand and use:

- ordering of numbers, including the mathematical symbols

- standard form, representing large and small numbers in terms of powers of 10

- ordering of operations (BODMAS); calculations with whole numbers and fractions

- estimation, including rounding, decimal places, significant figures, reasonable degree of accuracy

3.01 Ordering

We need to familiarise ourselves with the basic mathematical symbols that are used to compare sizes (magnitudes):

The symbols $=, \neq, >, <, \geq, \leq$

$a = b$	a is equal to b	$a \neq b$	a is not equal to b
$a > b$	a is greater than b	$a < b$	a is less than b
$a \geq b$	a is greater than or equal to b	$a \leq b$	a is less than or equal to b

Now that we know the symbols, we can put different terms in order, as shown in the following examples.

3.01 Worked example

Arrange the following terms in order of size, using the appropriate symbol:

$$0.55, \frac{1}{2}, 48\%.$$

We have three terms shown in three different ways, i.e. a decimal, a fraction and a percentage. First we'll make them all decimals so that we can compare them more easily:

$$0.55 = 0.55 \text{ (already a decimal)}$$
$$\frac{1}{2} = 1 \div 2 = 0.5$$
$$48\% = 48 \div 100 = 0.48$$

Now that we have the numbers as decimals, we can see that $\frac{1}{2}$ is greater than 0.48 but smaller than 0.55, so we can order them:

$$48\% < \frac{1}{2} < 0.55$$

Alternatively, we could have changed them to percentages.

3.02 Worked example

Give all the possible values of x for the following expression: $3 \leqslant x < 8$

If x is less than 8, it could be 7, 6, 5, 4, 3, 2, etc.
If x is greater than or equal to 3, it could be 3, 4, 5, 6, 7, 8, 9, etc.
x must satisfy both inequalities, so x must be greater than or equal to 3 **and** x must be less than 8.
The values of x which satisfy both inequalities are 3, 4, 5, 6 and 7.

Progress check

3.01 Using appropriate symbols, write the following numbers in order of size, smallest first.

$$\frac{23}{7} \qquad \sqrt{11} \qquad \pi \qquad 3.14$$

3.02 Standard form

We use standard form (also called scientific notation) to show large or very small numbers in terms of powers of 10. For example, we can write 10 000 000 as 1×10^7, or 0.000000000001 as 1×10^{-12}, which is a much more compact way to write them.

Rules for standard form

i Only one whole number between 1 and 9 inclusive is allowed before the decimal point.
ii The number must be written as a power of 10.

Changing large numbers into standard form

Take, for example, the number 210 000 000. We'll change it into standard form:

2 1 0 0 0 0 0 0   is the same as   2 1 0 0 0 0 0 0 . 0 0 0 0 0

As we are only allowed **one whole number between 1 and 9** before the decimal point, we have to move the figures so that the point appears immediately after the 2, as shown:

2 . 1 0 0 0 0 0 0 0 . 0 0 0

To do this, the figures have moved 8 positions to the right, so the new number must be written as:

$2.1 \times (10 \times 10 \times 10 \times 10 \times 10 \times 10 \times 10 \times 10)$
$= 2.1 \times 10^8$

Changing small numbers into standard form

Let's take, for example, 0.00000345:

0 . 0 0 0 0 0 3 . 4 5

The figures have moved 6 places to the left, so as a power of ten it becomes:

$3.45 \times (10^{-1} \times 10^{-1} \times 10^{-1} \times 10^{-1} \times 10^{-1} \times 10^{-1})$
$= 3.45 \times 10^{-6}$

TIP

Numbers less than 1 have a negative power of 10.

3.03 Worked example

Find the sum of 4×10^3 and 5×10^2, giving the answer in standard form.

First change the numbers to ordinary numbers: $\quad 4 \times 10^3 = 4000$
$5 \times 10^2 = 500$

Then we add them to get $4000 + 500 = 4500$.

Now change 4500 back into standard form:
$4500 = 4.5 \times 10^3$ (the decimal point had to be moved 3 times)

3.04 Worked example

Write the answers to the following calculations in standard form:

a $(2.5 \times 10^6) \times (3.0 \times 10^4)$ **b** $(4.5 \times 10^4) + (30.5 \times 10^3)$

  a $(2.5 \times 10^6) \times (3.0 \times 10^4) = (2.5 \times 3.0) \times 10^{6+4}$
       $= 7.5 \times 10^{10}$

The numbers are multiplied as normal to give 7.5. The powers are added when multiplying terms (see Unit 15).

  b $(4.5 \times 10^4) + (30.5 \times 10^3) = (4.5 \times 10^4) + (3.05 \times 10^4) = 7.55 \times 10^4$

Make the powers the same by changing the second number. Add the numbers as normal, taking the existing power.

The calculator method

Your scientific calculator can also be used to work out questions involving standard form. First find the key marked $\boxed{\times 10^x}$, then follow the example below.

3.05 Worked example

Find the product of 2.34×10^2 and 4.56×10^{-1}.

Press the following keys on your calculator:

[2] [.] [3] [4] [×] [10ˣ] [2] [×] [4] [.] [5] [6] [×]
[10ˣ] [-] [1] [=]

You should get the answer: 106.704

Standard form answers displayed on a calculator

When a result is either very large or very small (too many digits for the display), or if your calculator is just configured differently, it will give the answer in standard form. We need to be able to interpret the answer:

Result = 5^{-03} means that 5 has been divided by 10 three times (3rd number after point) = 0.005

Result = 14336^{13} means 1.4336×10^{13}, an extremely large number!

If you find that results with relatively few digits are still being displayed in standard form, ask your teacher how to change the calculator's configuration to amend this.

Calculator displays

There are several models of scientific calculators and the display format for Standard form can be shown in different ways:

The keys $\times 10^x$ Exp EE are used to calculate with standard form.

3.06 Worked example

a Find 2.32×10^{-2}

b $(3.46 \times 10^3) + (1.7 \times 10^5)$

a 2 . 3 2 Exp − 2 =

the answer displayed will be 0.0232

b 3 . 4 6 EE 3 + 1 . 7 EE 5 =

the answer displayed will be 173460

Progress check

3.02 Calculate the value of $5(6 \times 10^3 + 400)$, giving your answer in standard form.

3.03 The four rules

The mathematical operations are add, subtract, multiply and divide. We shall only revise multiplication and division.

Long multiplication

It is important that we remember **place value** when carrying out long multiplication. Take, for example, the number 234.68. Each of these digits has a certain value, as shown below.

	Hundreds	Tens	Units	Point	Tenths	Hundredths	...
	2	3	4	.	6	8	
Value =	200	30	4	.	0.6	0.08	

3.07 Worked example

Calculate 184×36.

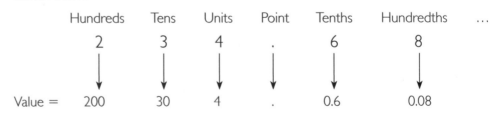

		1	8	4	
	×		3	6	
	1	1	0	4	(184×6)
+	5	5	2	0	(184×30)
	6	6	2	4	(184×36)

> Going through line by line:
> 6 is in the units column, so we calculate $6 \times 184 = 1104$.
> 3 is in the tens column, so we put a zero in the units column and multiply by 3: $30 \times 184 = 5520$.
> Then we add them together to get 6624.

Short division

With short division, if there is a remainder then it is carried over to the next number.

3.08 Worked example

Calculate $451 \div 4$.

$$
4 \overline{)\; 4 \quad {}^0 5 \quad {}^1 1 \;.\; {}^3 0 \quad {}^2 0 }
$$

$$
1 \quad 1 \quad 2 \;.\; 7 \quad 5 \qquad \text{Answer} = 112.75
$$

    (1) (2) (3)   (4) (5)

(1) $4 \div 4 = 1$, no remainder
(2) $5 \div 4 = 1$, with remainder 1
(3) $11 \div 4 = 2$, with remainder 3
(4) $30 \div 4 = 7$, with remainder 2
(5) $20 \div 4 = 5$: no remainder so calculation is complete.

Note that sometimes the answer is required in remainder form, i.e. 112 rem 3.

Long division

Long division is a more time-consuming method where each part of the calculation is shown under the previous part.

3.09 Worked example

Calculate $7165 \div 4$ to one decimal place.

$$
\begin{array}{r}
1\;7\;9\;1\,.\,2\;5 \\
4\,\overline{)\,7\;1\;6\;5\,.\,0\;0} \\
\underline{4} \\
3\;1 \\
\underline{2\;8} \\
3\;6 \\
\underline{3\;6} \\
0\;5 \\
\underline{4} \\
1\;0 \\
\underline{8} \\
2\;0 \\
\underline{2\;0}
\end{array}
$$

Answer = 1791.3 (1 decimal place)

This time the remainders are shown after subtracting the multiples of 4. We then bring down the next digit (see arrows) to join the remainder and continue dividing by 4. Once we have no remainder and all of the original number has been divided by 4 we can stop the process.

Note that some numbers will continue to give the same remainders (recurring decimals).

Operations with decimals

When adding or subtracting decimals, the most important rule is to make sure the numbers are in the right position relative to each other, i.e. the decimal points are in line under each other.

3.10 Worked example

Add 4.65 to 3.295.

```
  4.650
+ 3.295
  7.945
```

The decimal points are lined up and hence the other numbers are also. The zero in the thousandths column is not strictly necessary for adding operations, but it is good practice to include it.

3.11 Worked example

Subtract 2.675 from 4.86.

```
  4 . 8⁷ 6̷⁵ ¹0
 −2 . 6  7   5
  2 . 1  8   5
```

The higher number goes on top. Remember to add a zero. We have borrowed and carried where required to get the final answer.

Note that if we are subtracting a decimal such as 4.36 from a whole number such as 25, we can rewrite 25 as 25.00. Now the place values line up and the calculation is straightforward.

Multiplying and dividing decimals

First multiply or divide the whole numbers and then insert the decimal point as shown in the examples below. (It is also good practice to make an estimate of the expected answer to check that the calculation is correct.)

3.12 Worked example

Calculate 0.65 × 2.1.

Estimate = 1.3.

First change each number to a whole number:

0.65 → 65 (decimal point moves 2 places)
2.1 → 21 (decimal point moves 1 place)

Perform the calculation using the whole numbers (21 × 65).

```
        6   5
    ×   2   1
  _____
  1   3   6   5
```

In total the point has moved 2 + 1 = 3 places. When we get the answer, we simply move the point back 3 places to get the final answer (1.365).

```
  1 . 3   6   5.
```

3.13 Worked example

Calculate 4.26 ÷ 0.5.

Estimate = 8.

This time we have to move the decimal point 2 places in each number since the number with the greatest degree of accuracy is given to 2 decimal places:

4.26 → 426 (decimal point moves 2 places)
0.5 → 50 (decimal point moves 2 places)

Perform the calculation using the whole numbers.

```
         8 . 5   2
  50 | 4 2   6 . 0   0
```

Answer = 8.52
Note that there is no need to move the decimal point with divide operations.

Correct ordering of operations (mixed calculations)

This is one of the most important topics you will learn. Every mixed calculation must follow certain steps in order to get the correct final answer. We use a method called **BODMAS** to tell us the importance of each operation in mathematics – that is, which operation to do first:

B	O	D	M	A	S
r	u	i	u	d	u
a	t	v	l	d	b
c		i	t		t
k		d	i		r
e		e	p		a
t			l		c
s			y		t

← More important   Less important →

The diagram above tells us that the most important operation is brackets, so we do this first if applicable, then deal with powers, followed by divide or multiply and then either add or subtract, depending on the sign.

3.14 Worked example

Work out the value of:

a $19 \times 27 + 23 \times 8$ **b** $48 \div 6 - 54 \div 9$ **c** $11 - 12 \div 4 + 3(7 - 2)$

a As we have two multiply operations, these are performed at the same time, then the addition is carried out.

$$\underbrace{19 \quad \times \quad 27}_{\text{1st operation}} + \underbrace{23 \quad \times \quad 8}_{\text{1st operation}}$$

$$= \underbrace{513 + 184}_{\text{2nd operation}}$$

$$= 697$$

b We now have two divide operations. Perform these at the same time, then the subtract operation.

$$\underbrace{48 \quad \div \quad 6}_{\text{1st operation}} - \underbrace{54 \quad \div \quad 9}_{\text{1st operation}}$$

$$= \underbrace{8 \quad - \quad 6}_{\text{2nd operation}}$$

$$2$$

c There are brackets present so this must be the first operation, followed by the divide. Then, as the add and subtract have equal importance, we perform the first of these operations reading from left to right, in this case the subtract. Finally the addition is performed to get the final answer.

$$11 \quad - \quad 12 \quad \div \quad 4 \quad + \quad \underbrace{3(7-2)}_{\text{1st operation}}$$

$$= 11 \quad \underbrace{- \quad 12 \quad \div \quad 4}_{\text{2nd operation}} \quad + \quad 15$$

$$= 11 \quad - \quad 3 \quad + \quad 15$$

$$= 23$$

Any mixed calculation containing decimals or fractions can be performed using the same method. Follow the rules of BODMAS.

Progress check

3.03 Work out the value of:

a $21 \times 24 + 16 \div 8$ b $11 - 16 \div 4 + 5(9 - 2)$

3.04 Estimation

In many cases, exact numbers are not necessary or even desirable. In these circumstances approximations are given instead. The most common types of approximations are:

- rounding
- decimal places (d.p.)
- significant figures (s.f.)

Rounding

This type of approximation is usually done for large numbers; the number is rounded to the required multiple of ten, e.g. the nearest 10, nearest 100, nearest 1000, etc. Occasionally it can be used for small numbers, e.g. the nearest whole number, nearest $\frac{1}{10}$, nearest $\frac{1}{100}$, etc.

The following examples show the rounding of large and small numbers.

3.15 Worked example

In a recent football match there were 42 365 people attending. Approximate this number to:

a the nearest 10   **b** the nearest 100   **c** the nearest 1000

a The number in the tens column is the 6. As the number after it is 5 or greater, we round the 6 up to a 7.

42 365 to the nearest 10 = 42 370

b The number in the hundreds column is the 3. As the number directly after it is greater than 5 we round the 3 up to a 4.

42 365 to the nearest 100 = 42 400

c The number in the thousand column is the 2. The number directly after it is less than 5, so we leave the 2 unchanged and simply replace the numbers following it with zeros.

42 365 to the nearest 1000 = 42 000

3.16 Worked example

Round the number 24.923 to:

a the nearest whole number **b** the nearest tenth

a The whole number is the unit or ones column, which in this case is the 4. As the number after it is greater than or equal to 5 we round up the 4 to a 5.

24.923 to the nearest whole number = 25

b The number 9 is in the tenths column and there is no need to round up.

24.923 to the nearest tenth = 24.9

Decimal places

This refers to the numbers after the decimal point. Very often the calculator gives us an answer that has too many decimal places – we can correct the answer to a given number of decimal places.

3.17 Worked example

Round the number 24.47932 to:

a 3 decimal places **b** 2 d.p. **c** 1 d.p.

a We count to the third number after the decimal point, which in this case is the 9. Check if the number after it is 5 or greater. It is not, so the 9 stays unchanged. The rest of the digits are discarded.

2 4 . 4 7 9 3 2 = 24.479 correct to 3 d. p.
      1 2 3

b This time we count to the second number after the point. We have to round up the 7 to an 8.

2 4 . 4 7 9 3 2 = 24.48 correct to 2 d. p.
      1 2

c The first number after the point is the 4. This has to be rounded up to a 5.

2 4 . 4 7 9 3 2 = 24.5 correct to 1 d. p.
      1

Significant figures

Consider the number 24.67. The digit 2 is the most significant, as it has the highest value: 20. The 4 is the next most significant, then the 6 and finally the 7, which is the least significant.

We can therefore say that the number is given to **four significant figures**.

Some of the answers we obtain to problems contain too many figures for our purposes, so we need to approximate them to a given degree of accuracy just as we did for decimal places. This time the decimal point does not affect our final answer.

TIP

If you have an answer which is not exact, round it to 3 significant figures, e.g. 12.97563 would become 12.976.

3.18 Worked example

Write 23.456 to:

a 3 s.f.   **b** 2 s.f.   **c** 1 s.f.

a The third most significant figure is the 4. As the number after it is 5 or greater, we round it up to a 5.

2 3 . 4 5 6 = 23.5 to 3 s.f.
1 2   3 4 5 significant figures

b The second most significant figure is the 3. As the number after it is less than 5, there is no need to round this up.

2 3 . 4 5 6 = 23 to 2 s.f.
1 2   3 4 5 significant figures

c The 2 is the first significant figure. There is no need to round it up, but we must ensure the numbers are approximately the same size so we need to add the zero after the 2 to make it 20.

2 3 . 4 5 6 = 20 to 1 s.f.

As significant figures are more difficult, we will try another example.

3.19 Worked example

Write   **a** 0.0046 and   **b** 9.999 to 1 significant figure.

a The first significant figure is the first digit which is not a zero, i.e. 4 in this case. The 4 then rounds up to a 5 as the number after it is 5 or greater.

0 . 0 0 4 6 = 0.005 (to 1 s.f.)

b The first significant figure is the first 9, which has to be rounded to the next highest figure which is a 10.

9 . 9 9 9 = 10 (to 1 s.f.)

Progress check

3.04 Write the number 1046.2692 to:

    a 2 decimal places   b 2 significant figures

Giving answers to reasonable degrees of accuracy

On the front instruction page of all IGCSE papers, you are told by the examiner to give answers involving degrees to one decimal place and, if the answer is not exact, to three significant figures, **unless stated otherwise**. If you come across a problem which does not state the degree of accuracy required, then follow a simple rule:

Give your answer to the same degree of accuracy as the question.

3.20 Worked example

Calculate $23.4 \div 4.56$, giving your answer to an appropriate degree of accuracy.

The greatest degree of accuracy in the question is 2 decimal places, so the answer must also be to 2 decimal places.

$23.4 \div 4.56 = 5.13$ (to 2 d.p.)

3.21 Worked example

A cuboid's dimensions are given as 3.873 metres by 2.5 metres by 3.2 metres. Calculate its volume, giving your answer to an appropriate degree of accuracy.

Volume of cuboid $=$ length $\times$ width $\times$ height $= 3.873 \times 2.5 \times 3.2$
$= 30.984 \, m^3$ (Three d.p. is as accurate as the question allows.)

3.22 Worked example

Find the area of a right-angled triangle with base 4.3 cm and perpendicular height 7 cm.

Three d.p. is as accurate as the question allows:

Area $= \frac{1}{2} \times$ base $\times$ height $= \frac{1}{2} \times 4.3 \times 7 = 15.1 \, cm^2$ (to 1 d.p.)

Progress check

3.05 A cuboid's dimensions are given as 4.24 metres by 3.2 metres by 3.122 metres. Calculate its volume, giving your answer to an appropriate degree of accuracy.

Estimating answers to calculations

Many calculations can be done quickly using a calculator, but it is very easy to make mistakes when typing in the digits, so it is useful to be able to make a quick check.

For example, estimate the answer to 58×207 to check the answer obtained using your calculator.

58 can be rounded to 60 and 207 can be rounded to 200, so now we have:

$60 \times 200 = 12\,000$, which is very close to our calculator answer of $12\,006$, so it is unlikely that a mistake was made.

Summary

- When rounding answers to a given degree of accuracy, count up to the required number of places and then look at the number immediately after it. If that number is 5 or greater, round up.
- Unless stated otherwise, always give your answers to the same degree of accuracy as the question.
- Always make an approximate check on your calculator answer.

- When dealing with significant figures, remember that the approximated answer should be very similar in size to the original number. Add zeros if required to make the number of digits before the decimal point the same.
- With numbers less than 1, the first significant figure is the first digit which is not a zero.

TERMS

- =
  Equal values.

- ≠
  Unequal values.

- >
  Greater than.

- <
  Less than.

- ≥
  Greater than or equal to.

- ≤
  Less than or equal to.

- BODMAS
  Correct order of operations: Brackets/Powers/ Division or Multiplication/Add or Subtract.

- Standard form
  Numbers in standard form are represented as powers of 10.

- Decimal places
  When rounding to a certain number of decimal places, if the number after the cut-off is 5 or greater, always round up the last digit.

- Significant figures
  Start counting significant figures using digits 1 to 9 only. Ensure that the final and estimated answers are approximately the same size.

Exam-style questions

3.01   A block of cheese, of mass 8 kilograms, is cut by a machine into 500 equal slices.

    a   Calculate the mass of one slice of cheese in kilograms.
    b   Write your answer to part **(a)** in standard form.
Source: Cambridge IGCSE Mathematics 0580 Paper 2 Q3a, b June 2005.

3.02   The planet Neptune is 4 496 000 000 kilometres from the Sun. Write this distance in standard form.

3.03   The area of a small country is 783.265 square kilometres.

    a   Write this area correct to 1 significant figure.
    b   Write the answer from part (a) in standard form.

3.04   Write in order of size, smallest first,

$$\frac{5}{98}, \qquad 0.049, \qquad 5\%.$$

    Answer: ………….. < …………….. < …………
Source: Cambridge IGCSE Mathematics 0580 Paper 2 Q1 June 2003.

3.05   Calculate $(3 + 2\sqrt{3})^4$, giving your answer correct to 1 decimal place.

3.06   Write the number 3463.588 correct to

    a 3 significant figures   b 2 decimal places   c the nearest hundred

Limits of accuracy

CORE CURRICULUM

4.01 Accuracy limits

All numbers can be written to different degrees of accuracy. For example, the number 5 is the same as 5.0 or 5.00, except that it has been shown to a different degree of accuracy each time.

If, for example, the number 3.5 has been rounded to one decimal place, then, before rounding, the number could have been anywhere in the range from 3.45 up to but not including 3.55.

We could write this as an inequality,

$$3.45 \leqslant x < 3.55$$

where the lower bound is 3.45 and the upper bound is 3.55, or even show it on a number line as in Figure 4.01. Note that the lower bound of 3.45 could be an actual value of x so it is drawn as a black circle, but the upper bound cannot be an actual value (as it would have to be rounded up to 3.6) so it is drawn as a clear circle.

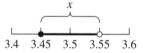

3.4   3.45   3.5   3.55   3.6

Fig. 4.01 $3.45 \leqslant x < 3.55$

Many students can find the upper and lower bounds quite easily in their head, but there is a method you can use if you find this difficult.

4.01 Worked example

A boy's height is given as 145 cm to the nearest centimetre. Find the upper and lower bounds within which his height could lie, giving your answer as an inequality.

The range is 1 cm, so if we first divide this by 2:   1 cm ÷ 2 = 0.5 cm

Upper bound = 145 cm + 0.5 cm = 145.5 cm
Lower bound = 145 cm − 0.5 cm = 144.5 cm

The inequality is therefore: 144.5 cm $\leqslant$ height < 145.5 cm

4.02 Worked example

The length of a field is measured as 90 metres to the nearest ten metres. Give the upper and lower bounds of the length.

10 m ÷ 2 = 5 m, so:
upper bound = 90 + 5 = 95 m
lower bound = 90 − 5 = 85 m

As an inequality:　　85 m ⩽ length < 95 m

Progress check

4.01　A girl's mass is given as 60 kg to the nearest ten kilograms. Calculate the upper and lower bounds of her mass.

4.02　The height of a three-year-old tree sapling is 21.4 cm to one decimal place. Give the upper limit.

4.03　The dimensions of a swimming pool are given as 3.5 m by 8.6 m, to the nearest 10 cm. Calculate the maximum possible surface area of the pool.

4.04　The mass of a sack of potatoes is given as 6.8 kg. Using m kg for the mass, express the range of values in which m must lie as an inequality.

4.05　Mark's motorcycle has a mass of 232 kg to the nearest whole number. Calculate the least possible mass of the motorcycle.

TERMS

- **Accuracy**
  1 d.p., one decimal place (0.1, 1.3, etc.); 2 s.f., two significant figures (23, 1.3, etc.).

- **Upper bound**
  Maximum possible value, taking into account the given accuracy.

- **Lower bound**
  Minimum possible value, taking into account the given accuracy.

Exam-style questions

4.01　The height, h metres, of a telegraph pole is 12 metres correct to the nearest metre. Complete the statement about the value of h:

$$\leqslant h <$$

4.02　A triangle has base 8 cm and a perpendicular height of 6 cm, both given to the nearest cm. Find the least possible area of the triangle.

4.03　At a school sports day, the winning time for the 100 m race was given as 12.2 s. Using t seconds for the time, express the range of values in which t must lie as an inequality.

4.04　A boy's mass was measured to the nearest 0.01 kg. If his mass was recorded as 58.93 kg, give the upper and lower bounds of his mass.

4.05　The time it takes the Earth to rotate around the Sun is given as 365.25 days to five significant figures. What are the upper and lower bounds of this time?

Learning outcomes

By the end of this unit, you should be able to:

■ give appropriate upper and lower bounds to solutions of simple problems given data to a specified accuracy

4.02 Accuracy in problems

If the numbers in a problem are written to a specified degree of accuracy, then the solutions to the problems involving those numbers will also give a range of possible answers.

4.03 Worked example

The circle below has a radius of 8 cm, measured to the nearest centimeter. Find the upper and lower bounds of its circumference.

Circumference of circle = $2\pi r$

Since the radius could be anywhere in the range $7.5\,\text{cm} \leqslant r < 8.5\,\text{cm}$, the circumference will also have a range of values:

Upper bound of circumference = $2 \times \pi \times 8.5 = 53.4\,\text{cm}$

Lower bound of circumference = $2 \times \pi \times 7.5 = 47.1\,\text{cm}$

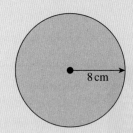

4.04 Worked example

Calculate the upper and lower bounds for the area of the rectangle shown if its dimensions are accurate to 1 decimal place.

Area of rectangle = length × width
Range of length = $10.45 \leqslant l < 10.55$
Range of width = $7.45 \leqslant w < 7.55$
Upper bound of area is the maximum value the area could be: $10.55 \times 7.55 = 79.65\,\text{cm}^2$
Lower bound of area is the minimum value the area could be: $10.45 \times 7.45 = 77.85\,\text{cm}^2$

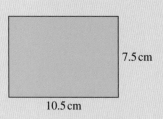

7.5 cm

10.5 cm

4.05 Worked example

Calculate the lower and upper bounds for the calculation $\frac{54\,000}{6000}$ if each of the numbers is given to 2 significant figures.

Range of numerator n is $53\,500 \leqslant n < 54\,500$
Range of denominator d is $595 \leqslant d < 605$

Therefore:

Upper bound $= 54\,500 \div 595 = 91.60$
Lower bound $= 53\,500 \div 605 = 88.43$ (2 d.p.)

Progress check

4.06 A rectangle measures 100 cm by 70 cm, correct to 2 significant figures. Calculate the upper and lower bounds of its area.

4.07 The mass of a cube of side 8 cm is given as 100 grams. The side is accurate to the nearest mm and the mass accurate to the nearest gram. Calculate the maximum and minimum possible values for the density of the material (density = mass/volume).

4.08 The masses to 1 d.p. of three books are 0.8 kg, 1.2 kg and 0.6 kg. What are the lower and upper bounds of their combined mass?

4.09 The radius of a circle is given as 3.00 cm to 2 d.p. Express as an inequality the lower and upper bounds for

   a the circumference of the circle   b the area of the circle

4.10 The mass of 25 apples is given as 22 kg correct to 2 s.f. Calculate the upper and lower bounds for the average mass of one apple.

Exam-style questions

4.06 The distance between Singapore and Sydney is 6300 km correct to the nearest 100 km. A businessman travelled from Singapore to Sydney and then back to Singapore. He did this six times in a year. Between what limits is the total distance he travelled?

4.07 Selina's height was measured and recorded at 1.64 metres to 2 d.p. Give the upper and lower bounds of her height, using appropriate inequalities.

4.08 A cuboid has side length 6 cm (measured to the nearest whole number). Find the maximum and minimum possible values of its volume.

4.09 In 2005 there were 9 million bicycles in Beijing, correct to the nearest million. The average distance travelled by each bicycle in one day was 6.5 km correct to one decimal place. Work out the upper bound for the **total** distance travelled by all the bicycles in one day.
Source: Cambridge IGCSE Mathematics 0580 Paper 21 Q6 June 2009.

4.10 The surface area of a sphere is $4\pi r^2$. If the radius is 3.1 cm, accurate to 1 d.p., find the lower bound of the surface area. (Use π from your calculator.)

Ratio, proportion and rate

Learning outcomes

By the end of this unit you should be able to:

■ understand and use ratio, direct and inverse proportion and common measures of rate

■ use scales in practical situations

■ calculate average speed

5.01 Ratio

A ratio is used when we want to compare two or more quantities. For example, if $400 is to be shared between three people, Jim, Fred and John, in the ratio 4 : 3 : 1, respectively, the total amount of money is split into 8 equal parts (4 + 3 + 1), of which Jim will get 4 parts, Fred 3 parts and John 1 part as shown below:

$$\$200 \quad : \quad \$150 \quad : \quad \$50$$
$$\uparrow \qquad\qquad \uparrow \qquad\qquad \uparrow$$
$$\text{Jim} \quad : \quad \text{Fred} \quad : \quad \text{John}$$

We can check that all of the money has been accounted for by adding each of the amounts:

$$\$200 + \$150 + \$50 = \$400$$

Simplifying ratios

Many ratios are the same but shown differently, for example 1 : 2 is the same as 2 : 4. The second amount is twice the size of the first amount in each case.

In order to simplify ratios, we have to find common divisors of each part of the ratio. The ratio 3 : 9 simplifies to 1 : 3 since both three and nine divide by three exactly:

$$3 \quad : \quad 9$$
$$\uparrow \qquad\qquad \uparrow$$
$$1 \quad : \quad 3$$

Note that the ratios must be in the same units before you simplify them to their lowest terms. For example, to simplify the ratio 10 cm : 40 mm we first make the units the same, so it becomes 100 mm : 40 mm. Then we can divide both terms by 20 to get the simplified ratio 5 : 2.

Progress check

5.01 Simplify the ratio 4 : 12 : 16.

Calculating ratios

There are two main types of ratio calculations:

i direct proportion
ii inverse proportion

With **direct proportion**, as the share increases then the amount also increases.

The example at the start of the unit showed that Jim's amount of money was four times the value of John's, because Jim's share was four times the value of John's share.

With **inverse proportion**, as the share increases the actual amount decreases.

For example, if 8 people can dig a hole in 4 hours, how long would it take 2 people to dig the same hole?

We now have the number of people reduced by a factor of 4 so therefore the time will increase by a factor of 4 to become 16 hours.

The following examples involve **direct proportion**.

5.01 Worked example

Share $200 in the ratio $3 : 2$.

When calculating with ratios we can use either of the two methods shown:

First method

The first amount is 3 parts out of a total of 5 parts of the $200 and the second amount is 2 parts out of 5 parts of the $200:

$$\frac{3}{5} \times \$200 = \$120$$

$$\frac{2}{5} \times \$200 = \$80$$

Second method

Find the value of one part of the total by dividing the total money to be shared by the total number of parts, and then multiply each ratio by this singular amount:

$$\text{One part} = \$200 \div 5 = \$40$$
$$3 \times \$40 = \$120$$
$$2 \times \$40 = \$80$$

The answer from both methods is $\$120 : \$80$.

It is up to you which method you prefer, but either method can be extended to include more than two shares, as shown in the following example.

5.02 Worked example

$400 is distributed between four people in the ratios $2 : 3 : 4 : 7$. Find the amount of money each person gets.

Using the first method, the total of parts is $2 + 3 + 4 + 7 = 16$, so:

$$\frac{2}{16} \times \$400 = \$50 \qquad \text{(2 parts of the total)}$$

$$\frac{3}{16} \times \$400 = \$75 \qquad \text{(3 parts of the total)}$$

$$\frac{4}{16} \times \$400 = \$100 \qquad \text{(4 parts of the total)}$$

$$\frac{7}{16} \times \$400 = \$175 \qquad \text{(7 parts of the total)}$$

Now make a simple check: $\$50 + \$75 + \$100 + \$175 = \$400$ (which is the correct total).

5.03 Worked example

An aircraft is cruising at 720 km/h and covers 1000 km. How far would it travel in the same period of time if the speed increased to 800 km/h?

We know that if an aircraft increases its speed when the time has remained constant, then its distance will also increase.

By comparing ratios:

Speed $720 : 800$

      $\downarrow$ $\downarrow$

Distance $1000 : x$

So:

$$\frac{x}{800} = \frac{1000}{720}$$

$$x = \frac{800 \times 1000}{720} = 1111.1 \text{ km}$$

TIP

Note how the
second method
has been used
for this type of
problem.

In another type of ratio question the value of one of the amounts is given and from
this information you have to work out the value of the other amounts.

5.04 Worked example

A sum of money is split between two people in the ratio 2 : 3. If the smaller
amount is $100, what is the value of the larger amount and the overall total sum of
money?

If we know that two parts of the total = $100, then we can calculate the
value of one part:
one part = $100 ÷ 2 = $50
three parts = 3 × $50 = $150

Total sum of money = $100 + $150 = $250

The following examples involve **inverse proportion**.

5.05 Worked example

If 8 people can pick the apples from some trees in 6 hours, how long will it take
12 people?

We know that the time taken to pick the apples will be less for 12
people than for 8 people, and that the time will decrease by the factor $\frac{12}{8}$.
So time taken = $6 \div \frac{12}{8}$ = 4 hours

5.06 Worked example

A tap issuing water at a rate of 1.2 litres per minute fills a container in 4 minutes.
How long would it take to fill the same container if the rate was decreased to 1
litre per minute?

If the flow is decreased by a factor of $\frac{1}{1.2}$ then the time should increase by the
same factor.

So time = $4 \div \frac{1}{1.2}$ = 4.8 minutes

Progress check

5.02   Share $300 in the ratio 2 : 3 : 5.

5.03   If 2 people can dig a hole in 4 hours, how long would it take 8 people
(assuming that they work at the same rate) to dig the same size hole?

5.04   A sum of money is split between three people in the ratio 3 : 5 : 8. If the
smallest share is $150, how much is the largest share?

5.02 Using scales in practical situations

Scales are used primarily in maps and model work. A typical map scale is given below:

| : 25 000

Actual length   Scaled length

In this case, one unit on the scaled or map length is equal to 25 000 units in actual or real length.

5.07 Worked example

A model car is a $\frac{1}{40}$ scale model. Express this as a ratio. If the length of the real car is 5.5 metres, what is the length of the model car? (Give your answer in centimetres.)

Ratio = 1 : 40 (One unit on the model length is equal to 40 units on the actual car length.)

Length of model car = $5.5 \times \frac{1}{40}$ = 0.1375 metres = 13.75 cm

5.08 Worked example

The scale of a map is 1 : 40 000. If two villages are 8 cm apart on the map, how far apart are they in real life?

Real-life distance = 8 cm $\times$ 40 000 = 320 000 cm = 3.2 km

---

5.03 Calculating average speed

Speed can be displayed in several ways: metres/second, km/h, cm/second, km/second. The units used depend on how fast or slow an object travels. For example, something very fast, such as the speed of light, would be displayed as 300 000 km/s, whereas a slow-moving object such as a snail would be represented in mm/s. Below are some useful conversion examples.

5.09 Worked example

A car is travelling at 25 m/s. What speed does this represent in km/h?

Divide by 1000 to change metres into km. Multiply by 60 and 60 again to change seconds to hours:
25 m/s = 0.025 km/s = 90 km/h

5.10 Worked example

The speed of sound is 1188 km/h. Write this in:

a metres per second   **b** mm per minute

a Multiply by 1000 to change kilometres into metres. Divide by 60 and by 60 again to change hours into seconds:

1188 km/h = 1 188 000 m/h = 330 m/s

b Multiply by 1000 and by 1000 again to change kilometres into millimetres. Divide by 60 to change hours into minutes:

1188 km/h = 1 188 000 000 mm/h = 19 800 000 mm/min

In order to calculate the speed, we need to know the distance and the time. We can use the formula triangle shown in Figure 5.01 to help us:

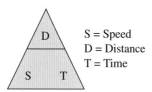

S = Speed
D = Distance
T = Time

Fig. 5.01 Distance/speed/time triangle

$$\text{Speed} = \frac{\text{Distance}}{\text{Time}}$$

$$\text{Distance} = \text{Speed} \times \text{Time}$$

$$\text{Time} = \frac{\text{Distance}}{\text{Speed}}$$

It is useful to know all three formulae. When performing calculations with speed, distance and time, always check that the units are the same.

5.11 Worked example

If a cyclist travels 25 km in a time of 5 hours, find the average speed.

Speed = Distance ÷ Time = 25 ÷ 5 = 5 km/h

5.12 Worked example

Find the time taken for a car travelling at 120 km/h to cover 360 km.

Time = Distance ÷ Speed = 360 ÷ 120 = 3 hours

5.13 Worked example

What distance would a bus cover if it travelled for 4 hours at an average speed of 100 km/h?

Distance = Speed × Time = 100 × 4 = 400 km

5.14 Worked example

If a car travels at 125 km/h for 25 minutes, what distance would it cover?

Change 25 minutes into hours by dividing by 60.

Distance = Speed × Time = $125 \times \frac{25}{60}$ = 52.1 km

5.15 Worked example

If a snail took 2 hours 24 minutes to climb to the top of a plant of height 35 centimetres, what was its average speed in millimetres per second?

2 hours 24 minutes = $2\frac{24}{60}$ hours = 2.4 hours

Divide by 60 and 60 again to change hours into seconds, and change 35 cm into 350 mm:

Speed = Distance ÷ Time = 35 ÷ 2.4 ÷ 60 ÷ 60 = 350 ÷ 2.4 ÷ 60 ÷ 60 = 0.04 mm/s

5.16 Worked example

An object travels 25 km in a time of 4 hours 45 minutes. Find its average speed.

4 hours 45 minutes = $4\frac{45}{60}$ hours = 4.75 hours

Speed = Distance ÷ Time = 25 ÷ 4.75 hours = 5.26 km/h

Or we could use the **time key** on the calculator (Unit 7). The sequence of key presses is:

25 ÷ 4 [° ′ ″] 45 [° ′ ″] [=] to give the answer 5.26 km/h

Note that some calculators may use the second function key to obtain the correct decimal format.

Progress check

5.05 A train travels at an average speed of 1200 km/h. What distance would it cover in 3 hours 20 minutes?

- Simplifying ratios
  Always simplify the ratios by dividing by the highest common factor.

- Direct proportion
  The share increases in proportion to the ratio increase.

- Inverse proportion
  The share decreases in proportion to the ratio increase, and vice versa.

Exam-style questions

5.01 Andre changed $600 into euros when the exchange rate was €1 = $1.34. He later changed all the euros back into dollars when the exchange rate was €1 = $1.38. How many dollars did he receive?

5.02 Two similar jugs have heights in the ratio 3 : 4.

    a If the height of the smaller jug is 15 cm, calculate the height of the larger jug.

    b If the surface area of the smaller jug is 1000 cm², calculate the surface area of the larger jug.

5.03 A school has 210 boys and 240 girls.

    a Find the ratio of boys to girls in its simplest form.

    b The ratio of students to teachers is 9 : 1. Find the number of teachers.

5.04 The scale of a map is 1 : 25 000. Two towns are 10 cm apart on the map. How far apart are they in real life?

5.05 Convert 100 km/h into metres per second.

Learning outcomes

By the end of this unit you should be able to:

- ■ understand and use direct and inverse variation in algebraic terms and in finding unknown quantities

- ■ increase and decrease a quantity by a given ratio

5.04 Expressing direct and inverse variation in algebraic terms

Table 5.01 shows an example of **direct variation**.

Table 5.01 Direct variation

x	0	1	2	3	5	10
y	0	2	4	6	10	20

As the value of x increases, the value of y also increases or, reading from right to left, as x decreases y also decreases.

In algebraic terms we can say $y = kx$: y is directly proportional to x.
k is the constant of proportionality, i.e. the constant we have to multiply x by to get y.

Table 5.02 shows an example of **inverse variation**.

Table 5.02 Inverse variation

x	1	2	3	4	5	6
y	1	0.5	0.3333…	0.25	0.2	0.16666…

This time, as the value of x increases, the value of y decreases, and vice versa.

In algebraic terms we can say $y = \frac{k}{x}$: y is inversely proportional to x, and again k is the constant of proportionality.

Now let's try a few examples.

5.17 Worked example

y is directly proportional to x. If $y = 6$ when $x = 2$, find:

a the constant of proportionality   **b** the value of y when $x = 9$

> **a** If y is directly proportional to x then we can say $y = kx$. To find the value of k, we have to rearrange the equation:
>
> $k = \frac{y}{x} = \frac{6}{2}$ (substituting the given values of x and y into the equation)
>
> $k = 3$
>
> **b** Now that we know the value of k, the y value when $x = 9$ can be found using $y = kx$:
>
> $y = 3 \times 9 = 27$

5.18 Worked example

If y is inversely proportional to x and $y = 4$ when $x = 2.5$, find y when $x = 20$.

First we need to find k, which we can find by rearranging the inverse proportion equation: $y = \frac{k}{x}$:

$$k = yx = 4 \times 2.5 = 10$$

Now to find y we use the original equation when $x = 20$:

$$y = \frac{k}{x} = \frac{10}{20} = 0.5$$

5.19 Worked example

If a stone is dropped off the edge of a cliff, the height (h metres) of the cliff is proportional to the square of the time (t seconds) taken for the stone to reach the ground. A stone takes 5 seconds to reach the ground when dropped off a cliff 125 metres high.

a Write down a relationship between h and t, using k as the constant of proportionality.

b Calculate the constant of variation.

c Find the height of a cliff if a stone takes 3 seconds to reach the ground.

a As h is proportional to t^2 we can say $h = kt^2$.

b To find k, we rearrange the equation above and substitute the given values:

$$k = \frac{h}{t^2} = \frac{125}{5^2} = 5$$

c For the height, use the original equation:

$$h = kt^2 = 5 \times 3^2 = 45 \text{ metres}$$

5.05 Increase and decrease a quantity by a given ratio

Sometimes an amount has to be changed according to a given ratio.

5.20 Worked example

Decrease 60 by the ratio $2 : 3$.

$$60 \times \frac{2}{3} = 40$$

5.21 Worked example

A rectangle of width 12 cm and length 16 cm is enlarged in the ratio 3 : 2. Find its new dimensions.

The rectangle has increased by a factor of $\frac{3}{2}$, so:

new width $= 12\,\text{cm} \times \frac{3}{2} = 18\,\text{cm}$

new length $= 16\,\text{cm} \times \frac{3}{2} = 24\,\text{cm}$

Progress check

5.06 Increase $50 in the ratio 3 : 2.

5.07 If y is directly proportional to x and $y = 5$ when $x = 10$, find y when $x = 20$.

5.08 If y is inversely proportional to x, and $y = 3$ when $x = 6$, find y when $x = 2$.

5.09 A triangle of base 15 cm and perpendicular height 25 cm is enlarged in the ratio of 5 : 3. Find its new dimensions.

5.10 The length, y, of a solid is inversely proportional to the square of its width, x.

    a Write down a general equation for x and y.
    b Show that when $x = 2$ and $y = 8$, the equation becomes $x^2 y = 32$.

TERMS

• Direct variation
The value of x increases in proportion to the value of the y increase.

• Inverse variation
The value of x decreases inversely to the y increase, and vice versa.

Exam-style questions

5.06 A spray can is used to paint a wall. The thickness of the paint on the wall is t. The distance of the spray can from the wall is d. t is inversely proportional to the square of d. $t = 0.2$ when $d = 8$. Find t when $d = 10$.

5.07 A company makes two models of television. Model A has a rectangular screen that measures 44 cm by 32 cm. Model B has a larger screen with these measurements increased in the ratio 5:4.

a Work out the measurements of the larger screen.

b Find the **fraction** $\dfrac{\text{Model } A \text{ screen area}}{\text{Model } B \text{ screen area}}$ in its simplest form.

Source: Cambridge IGCSE Mathematics 0580 Paper 2 Q14a, b June 2006.

Percentages

CORE CURRICULUM

6.01 Calculating a percentage of a quantity

Percentage means 'out of a hundred', so when we are required to find a given percentage of an amount, we are really being asked to find a certain 100th of that value.

6.01 Worked example

Find 25% of $400.

We are finding 25 hundredths of the $400.

$$\frac{25}{100} \times \$400 = \frac{25 \times 40}{100} = \$100$$

6.02 Worked example

A survey was carried out in a school to find the nationality of its students. Of the 220 students in the school, 65% were Kuwaiti, 20% were Egyptian and the rest were European. Find the number of students of each nationality.

$$\text{Kuwaiti} = \frac{65}{100} \times 220 = 143$$

$$\text{Egyptian} = \frac{20}{100} \times 220 = 44$$

$$\text{European} = \frac{15}{100} \times 220 = 33$$

We can check the result by adding each category of student: $143 + 44 + 33 = 220$, our original total.

6.03 Worked example

Find the new selling price of a shirt originally costing \$20 that has been reduced by 10% in a sale.

$$\text{Reduction} = \frac{10}{100} \times \$20 = \$2$$

The words discount and deduction are also frequently used to describe a reduction. They all mean the same thing, so **subtract** the value.

New selling price = \$20 − \$2 = \$18

Alternative method:

100% is the whole amount, so a reduction of 10% means that we are now finding 90% of the previous whole amount:

$$90\% \text{ of } \$20 = \frac{90}{100} \times \$20 = \$18$$

Progress check

6.01 In a mathematics class of 50 students, 40% were girls. Calculate the number of girls in the class.

6.02 Expressing one quantity as a percentage of another

To express one quantity as a percentage of another, first write the first quantity as a fraction of the second and then multiply by 100.

6.04 Worked example

In two recent mathematics exams, Lewis scored 56 out of 80 in the first exam and 48 out of 60 in the second exam. In which exam did he score the higher percentage?

$$\text{First exam} = \frac{56}{80} \times 100 = 70\%$$

$$\text{Second exam} = \frac{48}{60} \times 100 = 80\%$$

Therefore his highest score was in the second exam.

6.05 Worked example

Four candidates stood in an election:

Candidate A received 24 500 votes
Candidate B received 18 200 votes
Candidate C received 16 300 votes
Candidate D received 12 000 votes

Express each of these as a percentage of the total votes cast.

Total votes = 24 500 + 18 200 + 16 300 + 12 000 = 71 000

$$\text{Candidate A} = \frac{24\,500}{71\,000} \times 100 = 34.5\%$$

$$\text{Candidate B} = \frac{18\,200}{71\,000} \times 100 = 25.6\%$$

$$\text{Candidate C} = \frac{16\,300}{71\,000} \times 100 = 23.0\%$$

$$\text{Candidate D} = \frac{12\,000}{71\,000} \times 100 = 16.9\%$$

All answers are given to one decimal place.
Make a simple check by adding all the percentages and ensuring that we get 100% in total, i.e. all votes are accounted for.

Progress check

6.02 In two recent science examinations, Mathilde scored 24 out of a possible 30 marks while Jocelyn scored 42 out of a possible 48 marks. Comment on their percentage marks.

6.03 Calculating percentage increase or decrease

Sometimes the original value and the new value are given and we have to calculate the increase or decrease as a percentage. We can use the formula below to calculate these:

$$\% \text{ increase or decrease} = \frac{\text{actual increase or decrease}}{\text{original value}} \times 100$$

100% is the full amount, so a 20% increase represents 120% of the original amount, whereas a 20% decrease represents 80% of the original amount.

6.06 Worked example

A car dealer buys an old car for $1000 and sells it for $1200. Calculate the profit he makes as a percentage increase.

From above:

$$\% \text{ increase} = \frac{\text{actual increase}}{\text{original value}} \times 100$$

$$= \frac{1200 - 1000}{1000} \times 100 = 20\%$$

Progress check

6.03 Find the new selling price of a pair of shoes, originally costing $30, that have been reduced by 20% in a sale.

6.04 An employee receives a pay rise of 25%. If he originally earned €500 per week, calculate his new weekly wage.

6.05 A car salesman buys a new car for £12 000 and sells it several years later for £8 000. Calculate the loss he has made as a percentage decrease.

TERMS

• **Percentage**
Out of a hundred.

• **Percentage increase/decrease**
Actual increase or decrease divided by the original amount, times 100.

Exam-style questions

6.01 Caroline scored 22 out of 34 in a recent history test. Calculate her percentage score.

6.02 A shop increases the price of a television set by 8%. If the original price was $300, what is the new price?

6.03 In a sale a shop reduces its prices by 12%. What is the sale price of a desk previously costing £2000?

6.04 Express the first quantity as a percentage of the second:

a 25 minutes: 2 hours   b 500 kg: 3 tonnes
c 15 seconds: 4 minutes   d 50 cm: 2 m

6.05 Each day the population of a type of insect increases by approximately 10%. How many days will it take to double?

> ### Learning outcomes
>
> By the end of this unit you should be able to:
>
> - perform calculations using reverse percentages, e.g. finding the cost price given the selling price and the percentage markup.

6.04 Reverse percentages

This time we are given the selling price and the percentage increase or decrease and we have to work out the cost price. There's a simple formula we can use to work this out:

$$\text{cost price} = \frac{\text{selling price}}{\% \text{ change}}$$

If the change was an increase it would be added to 100; if a decrease it would be subtracted.

6.07 Worked example

This year a farmer's crop yielded 22 000 tonnes. If this represents a 10% increase on last year, what was the yield last year?

Using the formula:

$$\text{original yield} = \frac{\text{new yield}}{110\%}$$

$$= \frac{22\,000}{110/100}$$

$$= 20\,000 \text{ tonnes}$$

Note how the cost price is the same as the original yield and the selling price is the same as the new yield. The 100% has been changed to 110% as the yield underwent a percentage increase.

6.08 Worked example

A car manufacturer produced 24 000 cars in the month of April, which was a decrease of 4% from the previous month. Calculate the number of cars produced in March.

$$\text{Original production} = \frac{\text{new production}}{96\%}$$

$$= \frac{24\,000}{96/100}$$

$$= 25\,000 \text{ cars}$$

This time we have subtracted 4% from 100% as the production suffered a percentage decrease.

Note, for an increase (profit, tax, surcharge, etc.) we **add** the percentage change to 100%. For a decrease (reduction, discount, depreciation) we **subtract** the percentage change from 100%.

Progress check

6.06 A town has 3200 families who own a car. If this represents 25% of the families in the town, how many families are there in total?

6.07 A motorcycle is sold for €15 600. This represents a profit of 30% to the seller. What did the motorcycle originally cost the seller?

6.08 A three-year-old car is worth £5600. If it has depreciated by 30% over 3 years, calculate its new price.

6.09 A computer manufacturer is expected to have produced 42 000 units by the end of this year. If this represents a 5% increase on last year, calculate the number of units produced last year.

6.10 In an examination, Mario needs to obtain 75% to obtain an A grade. If the test contains 40 questions, how many questions does he need to answer correctly?

TERMS

- **Loss, reduction, discount, depreciation**
  Represent a decrease.

- **Reverse percentages**
  Find the original amount, given the new amount and the percentage change.

Exam-style questions

6.06 Lin scored 18 marks in a test and Jon scored 12 marks. Calculate Lin's mark as a percentage of Jon's mark.

6.07 In 2004 Colin had a salary of $7200.

   a This was an increase of 20% on his salary in 2002. Calculate his salary in 2002.
   b In 2006 his salary increased to $8100. Calculate the percentage increase from 2004 to 2006.

6.08 At the end of the year a factory has produced 38 500 television sets. If this represents a 10% increase in productivity on last year, calculate the number of sets that were made last year.

6.09 In a test Juliette gained 90% by answering 135 questions correctly. How many questions did she answer incorrectly?

6.10 This year a dairy farmer's yield was 10 000 litres of milk. If this represents a 25% increase on last year, what was the yield last year?

Use of calculator, measures and time

CORE CURRICULUM

Learning outcomes

By the end of this unit you should be able to understand and use:

- an electronic calculator

- appropriate degrees of accuracy

- unit conversion of mass, length, area, volume and capacity in practical situations

- 24-hour and 12-hour clocks, dials and timetables

7.01 Using a calculator

Although there are literally thousands of different types of calculators, with a variety of functions, displays and operating procedures, the most important things to remember when buying your calculator are:

- It should be scientific, i.e. it has all the required functions for IGCSE. Ask your teacher for recommendations.
- It should be straightforward to use, with clear instructions enclosed. Familiarise yourself with the instructions immediately after purchase and practise the examples given.

Even with the huge variety of calculators available, all of the more common types use the same basic keys to find specific answers. The most common keys are shown in Figure 7.01.

Fig. 7.01 Common calculator functions

shift / inv	This enables the second function on some keys to be used.
x^2, x^3	Will either square or cube the input.
x^y	Power key, will raise the input to the selected power. For example, 2 x^y 5 = 32
$\sqrt{\ }$, $\sqrt[3]{\ }$	Will calculate the square root or cube root of the input.
$a^b/_c$	Fraction key. For example, 3 $a^b/_c$ 5 = $3/5$
sin, cos, tan	Trigonometric functions.
EXP	Standard form: expresses the input as a power of 10. For example, 4 . 2 EXP 3 = $4.2 \times 10^3 = 4200$
MR, Min	Memory keys. Allow numbers to be recalled from and inserted into the calculator memory.
STO, RCL	Memory keys, found on more modern calculators. Allow multiple memory locations.
° ′ ″	Time key: allows units of time to be entered. See Section 7.03.

Shift or Inverse function

Modern calculators are extremely powerful, able to perform far more functions than older models. Many of these extra functions are allocated to existing keys and can be accessed by pressing the Shift/Inverse button. A good example would be the sin, cos, tan keys which also hold the $\sin^{-1}$, $\cos^{-1}$, $\tan^{-1}$ functions, usually shown above the key in a different colour.

Memory functions

Memory functions such as Min or STO insert number(s) into memory; MR or RCL recall number(s) from memory. These functions eliminate the need to write the numbers down part way through the calculation, which saves time and avoids rounding errors.

7.01 Worked example

Evaluate: $\dfrac{34.5 - 28.6}{1.295 \times 3.689753}$

We will use two methods.

Using memory keys:

$\boxed{1}\ \boxed{\cdot}\ \boxed{2}\ \boxed{9}\ \boxed{5}\ \boxed{\times}\ \boxed{3}\ \boxed{\cdot}\ \boxed{6}\ \boxed{8}\ \boxed{9}\ \boxed{7}\ \boxed{5}\ \boxed{3}\ \boxed{\text{STO}}$

$\boxed{\text{A}}\ \boxed{\text{AC}}\ \boxed{3}\ \boxed{4}\ \boxed{\cdot}\ \boxed{5}\ \boxed{-}\ \boxed{2}\ \boxed{8}\ \boxed{\cdot}\ \boxed{6}\ \boxed{=}\ \boxed{\div}\ \boxed{\text{RCL}}\ \boxed{\text{A}}\ \boxed{=}$

$= 1.235$ (to 3 d.p.)

Using bracket keys:

$\boxed{(}\ \boxed{3}\ \boxed{4}\ \boxed{\cdot}\ \boxed{5}\ \boxed{-}\ \boxed{2}\ \boxed{8}\ \boxed{\cdot}\ \boxed{6}\ \boxed{)}\ \boxed{\div}\ \boxed{(}\ \boxed{1}\ \boxed{\cdot}\ \boxed{2}$

$\boxed{9}\ \boxed{5}\ \boxed{\times}\ \boxed{3}\ \boxed{\cdot}\ \boxed{6}\ \boxed{8}\ \boxed{9}\ \boxed{7}\ \boxed{5}\ \boxed{3}\ \boxed{)}\ \boxed{=}$

$= 1.235$ (to 3 d.p.)

7.02 Worked example

Find: $\dfrac{4^3 \times 2^5 \times \sqrt{16}}{3.2 \times 10^{-4} + \dfrac{3}{4}\pi}$

Note that both standard form and π are required for this calculation. It will be quicker to use brackets again. Note the key selections:

$\boxed{(}\ \boxed{4}\ \boxed{x^3}\ \boxed{\times}\ \boxed{2}\ \boxed{x^y}\ \boxed{5}\ \boxed{\times}\ \boxed{\sqrt{\ }}\ \boxed{1}\ \boxed{6}\ \boxed{)}\ \boxed{\div}\ \boxed{(}\ \boxed{3}\ \boxed{\cdot}$

$\boxed{2}\ \boxed{\text{EXP}}\ \boxed{-}\ \boxed{4}\ \boxed{+}\ \boxed{3}\ \boxed{a^b/_c}\ \boxed{4}\ \boxed{\times}\ \boxed{\text{Shift}}\ \boxed{\pi}\ \boxed{)}\ \boxed{=}$

$= 0.256$ (3 d.p.)

7.03 Worked example

Find $\sin^{-1} -0.6$.

> $\sin^{-1}$ is the second function; the 0.6 can be made negative by using the [(-)] key:
>
> [Shift] [Sin⁻¹] [(] [(-)] [0] [.] [6] [)] [x^2] [=]
>
> $= 33.4°$
>
> Note that the [(-)] key is often a source of incorrect answers. If the negative term is raised to a power then the bracket key needs to be used before and after the term, otherwise the calculator will raise the term to the power and then make the result negative.

Progress check

7.01 Using your calculator, give the following to 2 decimal places:

a $\sin 30°$ b $\cos 25°$ c 8.45^3 d $\sqrt{63}$ e $\sqrt[3]{20} \times \dfrac{3}{8}$

7.02 Measures

Below are the standard units of mass, length and capacity, together with their conversions to smaller or larger units.

Mass (weight)

The units of mass are the tonne (t), kilogram (kg), gram (g) and milligram (mg).

The conversions are as follows:

I tonne	=	1000 kilograms
I kilogram	=	1000 grams
I gram	=	1000 milligrams

This flow diagram shows the conversions.

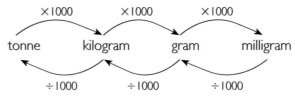

When you change, for example, tonnes to kilograms, you multiply the tonnes figure by 1000 to get the equivalent kilograms figure. To change kilograms to tonnes you divide by 1000.

Length

The units of length are the kilometre (km), metre (m), centimetre (cm) and millimetre (mm).

The conversions are as follows:

1 kilometre	=	1000 metres
1 metre	=	100 centimetres
1 centimetre	=	10 millimetres

This flow diagram shows the conversions.

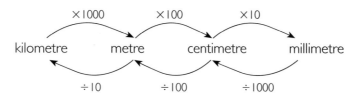

For example, to change kilometres to metres you multiply the kilometre figure by 1000 to get the equivalent metres figure. To change metres to kilometres you divide by 1000.

Capacity

The word capacity is used to measure volumes of liquid. The units of capacity are the litre (l), centilitre (cl) and the millilitre (ml).

The conversions are as follows:

1 litre	=	100 centilitres
1 centilitre	=	10 millilitres

This flow diagram shows the conversions.

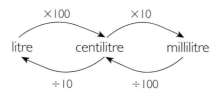

When changing litres to centilitres you multiply the litres figure by 100 to get the equivalent centilitres figure. To change centilitres to litres you divide by 100.

7.04 Worked example

Convert each of the following lengths to metres:

a 2.8 km   **b** 672 cm   **c** 28 400 mm

Using the flow diagram:

a km → metres = ×1000, so 2.8 km = 2.8 × 1000 = 2800 m
b cm → metres = ÷100, so 672 cm = 672 ÷ 100 = 6.72 m
c mm → metres = ÷10 ÷100, so 28 400 mm = 28 400 ÷ 10 ÷ 100
$$= 28.4 \, m$$

7.05 Worked example

How many 25 ml doses can be obtained from a bottle containing 1.7 litres of medicine?

In a problem where the two numbers are in different units, we must first change one of them to the other unit.

litres → ml = ×10 ×100 = 1.7 × 10 × 100 = 1700 ml

Number of 25 ml doses = 1700 ÷ 25 = 68

7.06 Worked example

15.4 tonnes of a medicine are to be made into tablets. If each tablet weighs 7 mg, calculate the number of tablets that can be made.

The units are different, so change the 15.4 tonnes into mg:

tonnes → mg = 15.4 × 1000 × 1000 × 1000 = 15 400 000 000 mg

Number of tablets = 15 400 000 000 ÷ 7 = 2 200 000 000

Note that we could have changed the 7 mg into tonnes and then divided as before to get the same answer.

Area and volume

Calculations involving areas and volumes of different shapes are looked at in detail in Unit 23, but you should be able to recognise which formulae refer to area and which refer to volume.

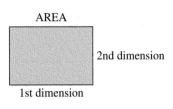

Fig. 7.02 Area: two dimensions

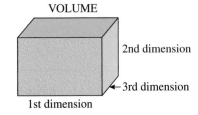

Fig. 7.03 Volume: three dimensions

As **area** involves two dimensions multiplied together, e.g. length × width for a rectangle (see Figure 7.02), the answer is always given as units squared (e.g. cm^2, mm^2).

With **volume** there are three dimensions multiplied together, e.g. length × width × height for a cuboid, so the answer is always given as units cubed (e.g. cm^3, m^3).

Here are useful area and volume formulae:

Area (involves 2 dimensions)

$\frac{1}{2}bh$	Area of a triangle
$2\pi r^2 + 2\pi rh$	Surface area of a cylinder
$4\pi r^2$	Surface area of a sphere
$\frac{1}{2}(a + b)h$	Area of a trapezium

Volume (involves 3 dimensions)

$\frac{4}{3}\pi r^3$	Volume of a sphere
$\frac{1}{3}\pi r^2 h$	Volume of a cone
$\pi r^2 h$	Volume of a cylinder

Progress check

7.02 Convert the following quantities to the units in brackets:

     a 100 cm (metres)   b 2 tonnes (grams)   c 1.5 litres (millilitres)

7.03 Time

The 12- and 24-hour clock

There are two ways of showing the time, by using the 12- or 24-hour clock. With the 12-hour clock there are two periods, each of 12 hours, during each day. The period between midnight and noon is called a.m. (*ante meridiem*, meaning before midday) and the period between noon and midnight is called p.m. (*post meridiem*, meaning after midday).

With the 24-hour clock there is one 24-hour period starting at midnight and finishing at midnight the following day. This type of clock system is generally used for bus and train timetables and is always given as **four figures.**

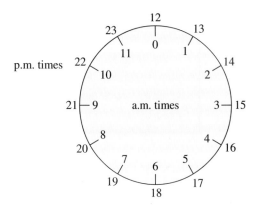

Fig. 7.04 12- and 24-hour times

The clock in Figure 7.04 shows that once the first 12-hour duration has finished (the a.m. times), then the 24-hour time continues using 13 to represent 1 o'clock p.m., 14 to represent 2 o'clock p.m., and so on until it completes its cycle of 24 hours.

For example, 2.30 p.m. = 1430 hours, 8.45 p.m. = 2045 hours.

Changing 12-hour time to 24-hour time

Both a.m. time and the 24-hour clock time start simultaneously at midnight. To convert, we simply replace the a.m. with hours or (h) and insert a zero before the digits, if required, to make it four figures.

7.07 Worked example

Change 4.25 a.m. and 10.45 a.m. into 24-hour clock times.

    4.25 a.m. = 0425 hours   (remember to add zero)
    10.45 a.m. = 1045 hours   (no need to add zero – the a.m. time already
                               has four digits)

When we change a p.m. time to 24-hour clock time, we must take into account the previous 12-hour cycle.

7.08 Worked example

Change 8.50 p.m. into 24-hour clock time.

    8.50 p.m. = 0850 hours + 12 hours = 2050 hours (add 12 hours for the
    previous a.m. cycle)

Changing 24-hour time to 12-hour time

This is simply a reversal of the previous method. If we have a time greater than 1200 hours, then it must have travelled through the a.m. time period. So we subtract 1200 hours to get the correct 12-hour p.m. time.

Table 7.01 gives some more examples.

7.09 Worked example

Change 0858 hours and 1835 hours to 12-hour clock time.

    0858 hours = 8.58 a.m.   (must be a.m. since it is less
                                 than 1200 hours)
    1835 hours = 1835 − 1200 = 6.35 p.m.   (subtract the first cycle of
                                  12 hours)

Table 7.01   12- and 24-hour times

12-hour	24-hour
4.25 a.m.	0425 hours
4.25 p.m.	1625 hours
8.15 a.m.	0815 hours
9.35 p.m.	2135 hours

Calculating with time

We will deal with the calculator method shortly, but you should also be able to perform the necessary calculations without using a calculator.

Remember the conversions: 1 day = 24 hours, 1 hour = 60 minutes, 1 minute = 60 seconds.

7.10 Worked example

Add 3 hours 25 minutes to 2 hours 45 minutes.

First set out the calculation as shown:

Hours	Minutes
3	25
2	45 +
5	70

We can't leave the time as 5 hours 70 minutes so we have to carry one hour, i.e. 60 minutes, over to the hours column. It then becomes 6 hours 10 minutes.

7.11 Worked example

Find the time difference between 10.45 a.m. and 8.34 p.m.

First change both times to 24 hour clock time: 10.45 a.m. = 1045 hours
8.34 p.m. = 2034 hours

Now subtract the smaller time from the larger time:

Hours	Minutes
20	34
− 10	45

The minutes column can't be subtracted normally because 45 is bigger than 34, so we have to borrow one hour from the 20 and add it to the 34 minutes. It now becomes 1994 hours. Then we subtract as normal:

19 (20 − 1)	94 (34 + 60)
− 10	45
9	49

Note that occasionally the minutes will subtract normally without having to borrow an hour.

Calculator method:
The ◦′″ key shown above enables calculations with hours, minutes and seconds to be done. The example above could have done by pressing the following keys on your calculator:

to give the answer 9° 49′ 0″, which is the same as 9 hours, 49 minutes and 0 seconds.

Timetables

This is a timetable of the Cheltenham to Teddington bus, which runs from Monday to Saturday weekly. (All times shown in the table are in 24-hour clock time.)

	First bus	Second bus	Third bus						Starting point
Cheltenham	0705	0735	0830	0930	0955	1020	1125	1200	1230
Cleeve Estate	0717	0747	0842	0942	1007	1032	1137	1212	1242
Bishop's Cleeve	0725	0755	0850	0950	1015	1040	1145	1220	1250
Gretton	0735	—	—	—	—	1050	—	—	—
Alstone	—	—	0909	—	—	—	—	—	—
Teddington	—	—	0914	—	—	—	—	—	—
Cheltenham	1255	1335	1455	1455	1605	1700	1730	1800	1930
Cleeve Estate	1307	1347	1507	1507	1617	1712	1742	1812	1942
Bishop's Cleeve	1315	1355	1515	1515	1625	1720	1750	1820	1850
Gretton	1325	1405	—	1525	1635	1730	1800	1830	—
Alstone	1340	—	—	—	1645	—	—	1840	—
Teddington	1345	—	—	—	1650	—	—	1845	—

Finishing point

From the timetable we can see that the first bus commences at 0705 hours, continues through the towns of Cleeve Estate and Bishop's Cleeve, and finally reaches Gretton at 0735 hours. The second bus leaves Cheltenham at 0735 hours and finishes at Bishop's Cleeve at 0755, and so on.

We also notice that some buses call at certain villages, while others do not, so this must be kept in mind when planning a journey. Now for a few examples:

7.12 Worked example

What time does the 0930 bus from Cheltenham arrive in Bishop's Cleeve? Calculate its journey time.

By inspection of the timetable, the 0930 is the fourth bus which arrives at 0950 in Bishop's Cleeve.

To calculate the journey time, simply subtract the start time from the finishing time:
0950 − 0930 = 20 minutes

7.13 Worked example

I want to travel from Bishop's Cleeve to Alstone.

a How long does the 1315 bus take for the journey?
b How long does the 1625 bus take?
c What is the difference in the time taken?

> **a** From the timetable we can see that the 1315 bus from Bishop's Cleeve is the 10th bus, and it arrives at Alstone at 1340. Therefore, by subtracting the times we get:
> 1340 − 1315 = 25 minutes
>
> **b** From the timetable, the 1625 bus arrives at 1645, which is a journey of
> 1645 − 1625 = 20 minutes
>
> **c** Difference in time taken = 25 − 20 = 5 minutes

Reading dials

Figure 7.05 shows the dials of an electricity meter, each dial showing its actual numerical value. Altogether, they show the amount of electricity used in units of kilowatt-hours (kWh).

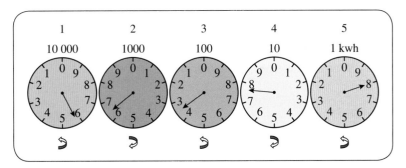

Fig. 7.05 Dials on an electricity meter

dial 1 = 5 × 10 000
dial 2 = 6 × 1000
dial 3 = 3 × 100
dial 4 = 7 × 10
dial 5 = 8 × 1

Therefore total amount of electricity used to date = 56 378 kWh.

Note that we read the dials alternately anticlockwise then clockwise. Remember that if the pointer comes between two numbers, choose the lower number for the actual value.

Progress check

7.03 Complete the following table:

12-hour	24-hour
2.45 a.m.	
	1835 hours
3.50 p.m.	
	0110 hours
12.25 .m.	

7.04 Add 3 hours 26 minutes to 4 hours 38 minutes.

7.05 Find the time difference between 7.42 a.m. and 2.45 p.m.

TERMS

- a.m.
  Ante-meridiem, from 12 o'clock midnight until 12 o'clock midday.

- p.m.
  Post-meridiem, from 12 o'clock midday until 12 o'clock midnight.

- **STO** / **RCL**
  Store and recall memory keys on scientific calculator.

-
  Power keys.

-
  Time key: represents hours, minutes and seconds.

- kilo
  1000 × metric standard unit, e.g. kilogram, kilometre.

- centi
  1/100th of metric standard unit, e.g. centimetre, centilitre.

- milli
  1/1000th of metric standard unit, e.g. millimetre, milligram.

Exam-style questions

7.01 A cyclist left Adelaide on Monday 23 May at 0945 to travel to Sydney. The journey took 84 hours. Write down the day, date and time that the cyclist arrived in Sydney.

7.02 A rectangular sheep pen measures 4.5 metres by 2.8 metres. Calculate its perimeter in centimetres.

7.03 Use your calculator to work out $\dfrac{1-(\sin 60°)^2}{2(\sin 40°)}$ to 2 decimal places.

7.04 Sophia drinks 2.5 litres of water each day. A full glass holds 250 millilitres of water. How many full glasses of water does Sophia drink each day?

7.05 A motorcyclist travels 250 km in 4 hours. Calculate his average speed in metres/second.

Money, personal, household and small business finance

CORE CURRICULUM

Learning outcomes

By the end of this unit you should be able to understand and use:

- calculations with money

- conversions between different currencies

- personal and household finance involving earnings, simple interest, discount, profit and loss

- data from tables and charts

8.01 Exchange rates

Every country has its own monetary system, for example Japan has the yen, Britain the pound, America the dollar. If there is to be trade and travel between any two countries there has to be a rate at which the money of one country can be converted into the money of another country. This is called the rate of exchange. Table 8.01 shows some typical exchange rates.

Table 8.01 US dollar foreign exchange rates at October 2012

Country	Rate of Exchange
Australia	0.97 dollars
Qatar	3.64 riyals
Sweden	6.64 kronor
Eurozone	0.77 euros
Japan	78.98 yen
Thailand	30.77 bahts
Canada	0.98 dollars
Switzerland	0.93 Swiss francs

Table 8.01 shows exchange rates for the American dollar. For every $1 we get 0.77 euros, for $2 we get 1.44 euros, and so on. Here are a few examples using the exchange rates from Table 8.01.

8.01 Worked example

Change $300 into Japanese yen.

Dollars	1	300
Yen	78.98	x

So $\dfrac{x}{300} = \dfrac{78.98}{1}$

$x = \dfrac{300 \times 78.98}{1} = 23694$ yen

8.02 Worked example

Change 2760 bahts into American dollars.

Dollars	1	x
Bahts	30.77	2760

So $\dfrac{x}{2760} = \dfrac{1}{30.77}$

$x = \dfrac{2760 \times 1}{30.77} = \$89.70$

Note that the accuracy to which you give your answer should be appropriate for the currency you're dealing in. For example, answers in US dollars and UK pounds need only be given to two decimal places since the smallest denominations available are cents and pence, respectively (2nd decimal place).

Progress check

8.01 In the Grand Bazaar in Cairo, a visitor sees two carpets priced at 800 Egyptian pounds. If €1 = 7.93 Egyptian pounds, calculate how much this represents in euros.

8.02 2.7 Australian dollars can be exchanged for €1.72. Calculate how many Australian dollars you would receive for €350.

8.02 Personal and household finance

There are many words related to personal and household finance. The more common ones are listed below.

Salary	Payment made to a person for doing a period of work. Salaries are usually paid monthly.
Wages	Again, payment made to a person for doing a period of work, but usually paid weekly.
Overtime	Extra hours of work, for which the person is usually paid an increased amount.
Piecework	Where the person is paid a fixed amount for each article or piece of work that they complete.

Commission	Where the worker is paid a percentage of the total amount sold. Salesmen, shop assistants and representatives are usually paid on commission.
General Sales tax	A tax levied by a government and placed upon the price of certain products and services.
Pension fund	A percentage of the employee's salary is paid into a pension fund in order to provide income after retirement.
Profit	A profit is made when the selling price is greater than the cost price (i.e. you make money).
Loss	A loss is made when the selling price is less than the cost price (i.e. you lose money).
Discount	A reduction of an amount, usually given as a number or as a percentage figure.

Here are some examples on a few of the above terms.

8.03 Worked example

An employee in a clothes factory earns $200 for a 40-hour week. Find:

a his hourly rate   **b** his overtime rate if overtime is paid at time and a half.

a Hourly rate = $200 ÷ 40 = $5 per hour

b Overtime rate = $5 × $1\frac{1}{2}$ = $7.50 per hour

8.04 Worked example

Harsha earns $8500 per annum. She pays 9% of her salary in pension contributions. How much does she pay per annum?

Amount paid = $\frac{9}{100}$ × $8500 = $765

8.05 Worked example

Jamie's salary is $14000 per annum and his total tax-free allowances are $4500.

a Work out his taxable income.
b If income tax is levied at 25%, calculate the amount of tax payable.

a Taxable income is the amount of earnings he must pay tax on after his tax-free allowances have been deducted.
Taxable income = $14000 − $4500 = $9500

b Tax payable = $\frac{25}{100}$ × $9500 = $2375

Profit and loss

A profit occurs when a small business sells the product for more than they paid for it. i.e. the selling price is higher than the cost price.

Loss occurs when the small business has had to sell the item for less than what they paid for it.

8.06 Worked example

a A second-hand car salesman buys a vehicle for $2000 then sells it a month later making 10% profit. Find the price he sold it for.

b A motorcycle is bought for $3000, but is sold several years later at a 20% loss. Find its selling price.

    a Profit = 10% of $2000 = $200

       Therefore selling price is $2200

    b Loss = 20% of $3000 = $600

       Therefore selling price = $2400

For examples on profit, loss and discount, see Unit 6.

Progress check

8.03 Eleonore's hourly rate is $6.80. Last week she worked her regular 40 hours and then 5 hours overtime, paid at time and a half. If 25% income tax is deducted, calculate her take-home pay.

8.04 A market trader sells tools and small electrical goods. Find his profit if he sells 15 torches at €2.45, given that the cost price of one torch is €2.10.

Simple interest

When money is invested with a bank, interest is paid to the investor for lending the money. The amount of interest paid depends on:

a The amount invested, or **principal**.
b The percentage **rate** of interest.
c The **time** period.

The simple interest formula is $I = \frac{PTR}{100}$, where I is the interest, P the principal, T the time and R the rate (%).

8.07 Worked example

Find the interest payable on $500 invested for 2 years at 6% per annum.

$$\text{Using the formula: } I = \frac{PTR}{100} = \frac{500 \times 2 \times 6}{100} = \$60$$

8.08 Worked example

Find the percentage simple interest rate per annum if $1200 is the interest on $3000 invested for 4 years.

$$\text{Rearranging the formula: } R = \frac{100I}{PT} = \frac{100 \times 1200}{3000 \times 4} = 10\%$$

Progress check

8.05   Find the simple interest paid in the following cases:

Principal ($)	Rate (%)	Time (years)	Interest ($)
300	6	4	
425	10	5	
6500	3	7	

8.06   Calculate how long it would take to earn £150 simple interest at 6% with a principal amount of £500.

Compound interest

With compound interest, the interest earned over each time period is added to the original amount. The next time period will have the same percentage rate of interest but the principal amount has now increased, hence giving a higher return.

The effect of compound interest can be calculated using simple interest calculations.

8.09 Worked example

Ahmed deposits $3000 in a bank offering 10% per annum compound interest. Calculate he much will receive after 3 years.

After the 1st year:

10% of $3000 = $300

we then add this to initial amount at the start of the second year

$3000 + $300 = $3300

After the 2nd year:

10% of $3300 = $330

we then add this to initial amount at the start of the third year

$3300 + $330 = $3630

After the 3rd year:

10% of $3630 = $363

we then add this to initial amount at the start of the third year

$3630 + $363 = $3993

8.10 Worked example

If the principal amount is $2000, the time period is 4 years and the rate of interest is 6%, what is the total amount of money returned?

The compound interest paid by a bank to the investor is 1.262, so:

Total money returned = 1.262 × $2000 = $2524

Stationery $150
Sports $300
Furniture $600
Household goods $450
Clothing $500

Fig. 8.01 A pie chart showing the total sales of a department store for one day

We can also extract information from other forms of charts such as a pie chart. The pie chart in Figure 8.01 shows that the highest sales were in the furniture section as this has the largest sector in the chart, followed by clothing, household goods, sports equipment and stationery.

8.11 Worked example

Find as a percentage the amount of sports equipment sold compared to the total sales.

From Figure 8.01:

Sports equipment = $300, total sales = $2000

% sports = $\frac{300}{2000}$ × 100 = 15%

TERMS

- **Principal**
  Initial amount deposited.

- **Taxable income**
  Amount of earnings an employee pays tax on.

- **Overtime**
  Hours worked beyond the standard working week, usually paid at a significantly higher hourly rate.

- **Commission**
  Employee receives a percentage of total selling cost of items produced.

- **Piecework**
  Employee is paid a fixed amount for each article they produce.

- **Simple interest**
  Interest received on principal investment, usually on an annual basis.

Exam-style questions

8.01 Alfredo changes 500 euros into Chinese yuan at a rate of 1 euro = 9.95 Chinese yuan. How many Chinese yuan did he receive?

8.02 Rihanna pays $276 in tax, which is $\frac{4}{11}$ of the money she earns. How much does Rihanna earn?

8.03 Nicolas needs to borrow $4000 for 3 years. The bank offers him a choice:

Offer A	Offer B
Interest rate 8.5% per year.	Interest rate 8% per year.
Pay the interest at the end of each year	Pay all the interest at the end of three years

Nicholas recognises that offer A is simple interest and offer B is compound interest.

a If he takes offer A, what is the total amount of interest he will pay?
b If he takes offer B, how much **interest** will he pay? Give your answer correct to 2 decimal places.

Source: *Cambridge IGCSE Mathematics 0580 Paper 11 Q23a, b June 2008.*

8.04 A holiday in Europe was advertised at a cost of €245. The exchange rate was $1 = €1.06. Calculate the cost of the holiday in dollars, giving your answer correct to the nearest cent.

Source: *Cambridge IGCSE Mathematics 0580 Paper 21 Q5 June 2008.*

8.05 Beatrice invests $100 at 7% per year **simple interest**.

a Show that after 20 years Beatrice has $240.
b How many dollars will Beatrice have after 40 years?

Source: *Cambridge IGCSE Mathematics 0580 Paper 4 Q8e June 2008.*

EXTENDED CURRICULUM

Learning outcomes

By the end of this unit you should be able to understand and use:

☐ compound interest formula

8.03 The compound interest formula

The compound interest formula is:

Value of investment $= P \left(1 + \frac{r}{100}\right)^n$, where $P =$ amount invested, $r =$ percentage interest rate, and $n =$ number of years of compound interest.

8.12 Worked example

Find the final value when $800 is invested for 2 years at 5% per annum compound interest.

Using the formula:

$$\text{Value} = 800 \left(1 + \frac{5}{100}\right)^2 = \$882$$

Exam-style questions

8.06 Michelle invests $350 for 3 years at 8% per year compound interest. Find the final value of her investment.

Graphs in practical situations

CORE CURRICULUM

Learning summary

By the end of this unit you should be able to:

- interpret and use graphs in practical situations, including travel graphs and conversion graphs
- draw graphs from given data

9.01 Graphs with two dimensions

Graphs with two dimensions have two axes which allow you to compare two variables; the line of the graph shows you the relationship between the variables. Figures 9.01, 9.02 and 9.03 show some graphs with two dimensions.

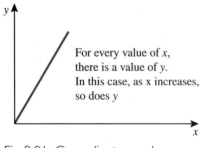

Fig. 9.01 Co-ordinate graph

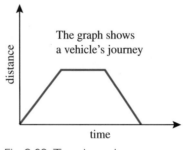

Fig. 9.02 Travel graph

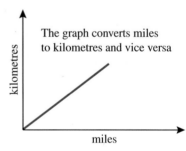

Fig. 9.03 Conversion graph

9.02 Interpreting and using graphs in practical situations

The two most common practical graphs are:

- **travel graphs**, where the vertical axis shows the distance travelled and the horizontal axis shows the time taken for each part of the journey.
- **conversion graph**, where the vertical axis shows one variable and the horizontal axis shows the other variable, and the line of the graph gives the conversion.

Travel graphs

The graph in Figure 9.04 shows a train's journey from Granada to Madrid, a distance of 200 miles.

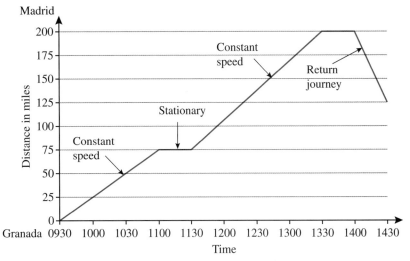

Fig. 9.04 Granada to Madrid train journey

We can draw the following conclusions from Figure 9.04:

- The train left Granada at 0930 hours.
- It continued at a constant speed until 1100 hours (straight line graph).
- It was stationary from 1100 to 1130 hours.
- It continued at a constant speed again from 1130 to arrive in Madrid at 1330 hours.
- The return journey began at 1400 hours back to Granada.

Progress check

9.01 The graph shows the journey made by a car travelling from home to its destination, 400 km away.

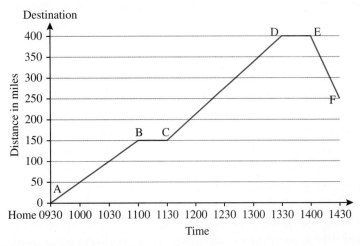

From the graph:
a Interpret the car's motion from points:
    i A to B   ii B to C   iii C to D   iv E to F
b Find the time taken for the car to travel from point A to B.
c Find the average speed of the car in this time.
d Find the total amount of time that the car was stationary.

Conversion graphs

The graph in Figure 9.05 shows the conversion of ounces (imperial weight) to grams (metric).

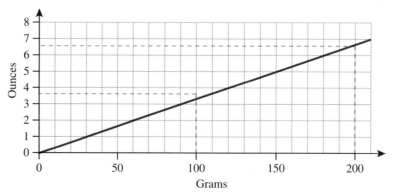

Fig. 9.05 Ounces to grams conversion graph

Figure 9.05 is a constant (linear) graph, e.g. 1 ounce ≈ 28 grams, 2 ounces ≈ 56 grams. The number of grams is always, approximately, the ounces figure multiplied by 28. We can use the graph to find any corresponding value of ounces or grams, e.g.:

    3.5 ounces = approx. 100 grams
    6.5 ounces = approx. 188 grams

9.03 Drawing graphs from given data

When drawing a graph, bear in mind the following guidelines:

- **Decide which axis is to show which variable.** For conversion graphs it doesn't really matter since it will be a straight line graph anyway. However, for distance–time graphs we normally put distance on the vertical axis and time on the horizontal axis.
- **Select a suitable scale** for your graph. The graph should cover all required points and be neither too large (too much detail) nor too small (not enough detail).
- **Label your axes**, e.g. distance on the vertical axis and time on the horizontal axis.
- Give your graph a **title**.

9.01 Worked example

Given that 80 km = 50 miles, draw a conversion graph up to 80 km. Using your graph:

a How many miles is 50 km? **b** Estimate the speed in km/h equivalent to 40 mph.

We only need two points to be able to draw our straight line graph.

We have the final point, 80 km = 50 miles, so we need a starting point.

By calculation, 10 miles = $\frac{80}{50} \times 10 = 16$ km.

As it is a conversion graph it doesn't matter which axis we use for miles or km, so let's make the vertical axis the kilometres variable and the horizontal axis the miles variable.

Remember that the graph should be drawn on graph paper so that the points can be plotted more accurately. We then label the axis and give the graph a title. See the complete graph in Figure 9.06.

a Using the graph, 50 km = approx. 32 miles

b As speed is consistent with the graph, 40 mph = approx. 64 km/h

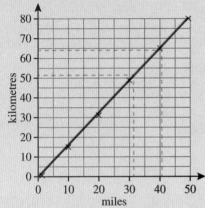

Figure 9.06 Miles/kilometres conversion graph

Progress check

9.02 Given that 1 inch is approximately 2.5 cm, draw a conversion graph up to 10 inches. Use your graph to estimate:

a how many centimetres in 5 inches b how many inches in 18 cm.

TERMS

- Travel graph
  Shows an object's journey over a period of time.

- Conversion graph
  Used to convert one variable to another, e.g. miles to kilometres.

- Vertical axis
  The y-axis.

- Horizontal axis
  The x-axis.

Exam-style questions

9.01 The graph shows a train's progress over 200 km.

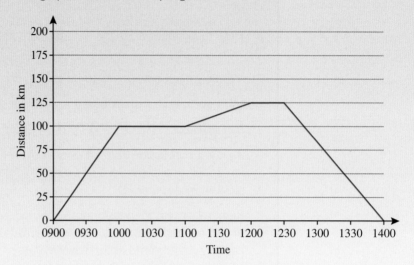

Use the graph to answer the following:

a After how many minutes did it make its first stop?
b What was its average speed over the first part of the journey?
c How can you tell the train travelled at a slower constant speed from 1100 hours to 1200 hours?
d What was its average speed on the return journey?

9.02 Given that 1 foot is 12 inches, draw a conversion graph up to 8 feet. Use your graph to estimate:

a how many inches in 7 feet   b how many feet in 40 inches.

9.04 Speed–time graphs

In speed–time graphs, the vertical axis shows the speed and the horizontal axis shows the time. Figure 9.07 shows an example with the relevant parts explained.

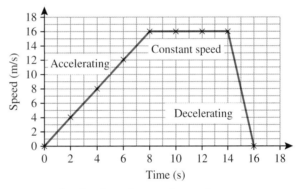

Accelerating = increase in speed.

Decelerating = decrease in speed.

Constant speed = no change in speed.

Fig. 9.07 Speed–time graph

From Figure 9.07 we can draw the following conclusions:

- From 0 seconds (rest) to 8 seconds the vehicle increases its speed from 0 m/s to 16 m/s at a constant acceleration.
- From 8 seconds to 14 seconds the vehicle maintains a constant speed of 16 m/s (no acceleration).
- From 14 seconds to 16 seconds the vehicle decreases its speed from 16 m/s to 0 m/s (back to rest) at a constant deceleration.

In summary:

- A straight horizontal line represents constant speed.
- A positive gradient indicates acceleration; a negative gradient indicates deceleration.
- The steepness of the gradient indicates the rate of acceleration/deceleration (the steeper the slope, the faster the increase/decrease in speed).

Calculating the distance travelled from the area under a speed–time graph

The area under a speed–time graph gives the total distance travelled. Consider the example shown in Figure 9.08.

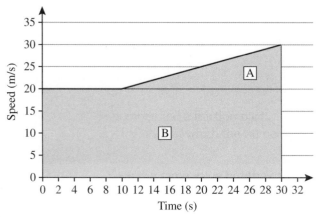

Fig. 9.08 Area under a speed–time graph

The bold line in Figure 9.08 shows the speed–time graph.

In order to calculate the area under the graph we have to split it into two distinct shapes: shape A is a triangle, shape B is a rectangle.

Now we can work out the areas of each of the shapes and add them to get the total area:

$$\text{Area A} = \frac{\text{base} \times \text{height}}{2} = \frac{20 \times 10}{2} = 100\,\text{m}$$

$$\text{Area B} = \text{length} \times \text{width} = 30 \times 20 = 600\,\text{m}$$

$$\text{Total area} = 100\,\text{m} + 600\,\text{m} = 700\,\text{m}$$

Therefore the total distance travelled by the vehicle is 700 metres.

Calculating the acceleration and deceleration

We can calculate both of these from the formula:

$$\text{Acceleration/deceleration} = \frac{\text{change in speed}}{\text{time taken}}$$

So if we wanted to calculate the acceleration for the second part of the journey in Figure 9.08, i.e. from 10 seconds to 30 seconds:

$$\text{Acceleration} = \frac{\text{change in speed}}{\text{time taken}} = \frac{30 - 20}{30 - 10} = \frac{10}{20} = 0.5\,\text{m/s}^2$$

Note that we know that we are calculating acceleration since the graph shows a positive gradient. It is possible to get the same answer by splitting the area under a speed–time graph into a different arrangement of shapes, provided we know the formulae for the areas of these shapes (e.g. a trapezium or a square).

9.05 Exponential growth and decay

Graphs displaying population growth are usually curved in nature (the gradient increases as time increases).

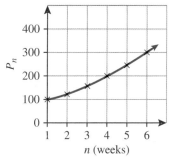

Fig. 9.09 Population growth of rabbits over seven weeks

Figure 9.09 shows the population growth of rabbits over a seven-week period. We can see that the initial population of mice was 100, but after 7 weeks the population reached approximately 360 rabbits.

Graphs showing decay are also usually curved in nature but this time the gradient decreases as time increases.

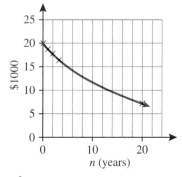

Fig. 9.10 Reduction in value of a car

Figure 9.10 shows an example of a decay graph. It shows the value in thousands of dollars of a car over a 22-year period. The car's initial value was $20 000, but after 22 years it was worth approximately $6000.

Progress check

9.03 The graph shows a car's speed over a period of ten hours.

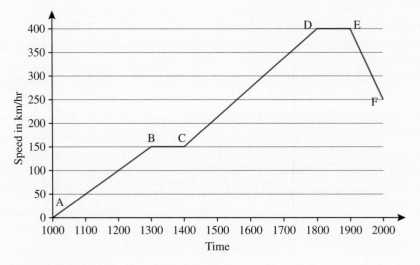

From the graph:

a Interpret the car's motion from points:
   i A to B
   ii B to C
   iii C to D
   iv E to F
b Find the acceleration of the vehicle from point A to point B.
c Find the distance travelled by the vehicle in this time.
d Find the total amount of time that the vehicle was travelling at constant speed.

9.04 A car accelerated from 0 to 50 m/s in 9 seconds. How far did it travel in this time?

9.05 A motorcycle decelerates from 50 km/h to 10 km/h in 2 minutes. How far did it travel in this time?

9.06 For the vehicle journey shown in the graph, find:

a The distance travelled in the first 20 seconds.
b The acceleration over the first 20 seconds.
c The total distance travelled.

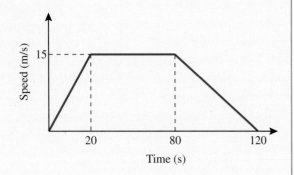

• Acceleration
  Increase in speed over a certain time.

• Deceleration
  Decrease in speed over a certain time.

• Area under speed–time graph
  Used to calculate the distance travelled by the object.

Exam-style questions

9.03 For the vehicle journey shown in the graph, find:

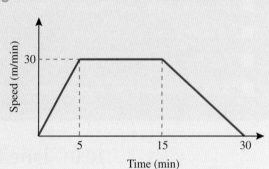

a The distance travelled in the first 5 minutes.
b The acceleration over the first 5 minutes.
c The total distance travelled.

9.04 When taking off, an aircraft accelerates from 0 to 100 m/s in a distance of 500 metres. How long did it take to cover this distance?

9.05 A coach decelerated from 60 km/h to 0 km/h in 30 seconds. How many metres did it travel in this time?

9.06 The diagram shows part of a journey by a truck.

a The truck accelerates from rest to 18 m/s in 30 seconds. Calculate the acceleration of the truck.
b The truck then slows down in 10 seconds for some road works and travels through the road works at 12 m/s. At the end of the road works it accelerates back to a speed of 18 m/s in 10 seconds. Find the **total** distance travelled by the truck in the 100 seconds.

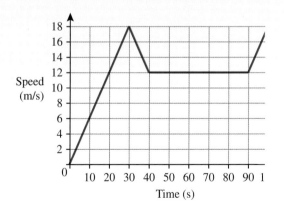

Source: Cambridge IGCSE Mathematics 0580 Paper 2 Q21a, b June 2007.

Graphs of functions

CORE CURRICULUM

Learning outcomes

By the end of this unit you should be able to:

- construct tables of values for linear, quadratic and reciprocal functions

- draw and interpret such graphs

- find the gradient of a straight line graph

- solve linear and quadratic equations approximately by graphical methods

10.01 Linear graphs of the form $y = ax + b$ (where a and b are integers)

This type of graph is a straight line graph. Any function which involves x^1, or in other words just x, must be a straight line graph.

10.01 Worked example

Draw the graph of the function $y = 2x + 1$, using values of x from -3 to $+3$.

Step 1 Construct a table using the x-values given.

For example, when $x = -3, y = 2(-3) + 1 = -5$; when $x = -1$, $y = 2(-1) + 1 = -1$; when $x = 1, y = 2(1) + 1 = 3$. Hence:

x	-3	-2	-1	0	1	2	3
$y = 2x + 1$	-5	-3	-1	1	3	5	7

Step 2 Plot the graph, using the values from the table. Looking at the table, the x-values range from -3 to $+3$ and the y-values range from -5 to $+7$. See Figure 10.01.

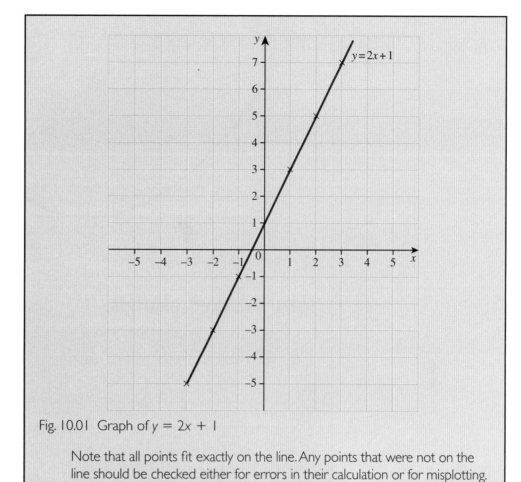

Fig. 10.01 Graph of $y = 2x + 1$

Note that all points fit exactly on the line. Any points that were not on the line should be checked either for errors in their calculation or for misplotting.

10.02 Quadratic graphs of the form $y = \pm x^2$

This type of graph is a parabolic graph. Any graph which involves x^n where n is greater than 1 is a curved graph. As the examples show, plotting them involves the same basic steps as before.

10.02 Worked example

Draw the graph of x^2 using values of x from -3 to $+3$.

Step 1 Construct a table using the x-values given.

For example, when $x = -3, y = (-3)^2 = 9$; when $x = -1, y = (-1)^2 = 1$; when $x = 2, y = (2)^2 = 4$.

x	-3	-2	-1	0	1	2	3
$y = x^2$	9	4	1	0	1	4	9

Step 2 Plot the graph using the x and y values from the table – see Figure 10.02.

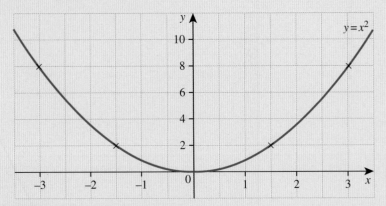

Fig. 10.02 Graph of $y = x^2$

10.03 Worked example

Draw the graph of $-x^2$ using x values from -3 to $+3$.

Draw the table and hence plot the graph:

x	-3	-2	-1	0	1	2	3
$y = -x^2$	-9	-4	-1	0	-1	-4	-9

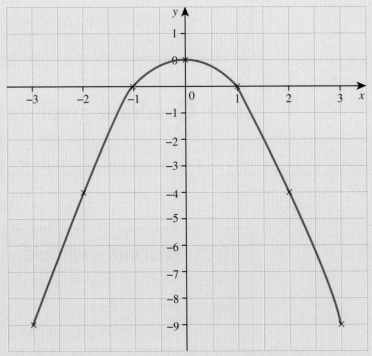

Fig. 10.03 Graph of $y = -x^2$

We can see from the graph that the shape is similar to the graph of $y = x^2$, but it is upside down. The effect of the negative sign is to invert the graph.

10.03 Use of function notation in graphs: $f(x) = ax + b$

Very often the notation $f(x) = ax + b$ is used instead of $y = ax + b$. So we are now calculating the $f(x)$ value for varying values of x instead of the y-values. In effect the vertical axis will now represent $f(x)$, rather than y.

The method for constructing and solving this type of question is the same as before.

10.04 Worked example

Draw the graph of $f(x) = 2x^2 + 3x - 1$, using x-values from -3 to $+1$.

Draw the table and put in the $f(x)$ values. The graph is shown in Figure 10.04.

x	-3	-2	-1	0	1
$2x^2$	18	8	2	0	2
$3x$	-9	-6	-3	0	3
-1	-1	-1	-1	-1	-1
$f(x) = 2x^2 + 3x - 1$	8	1	-2	-1	4

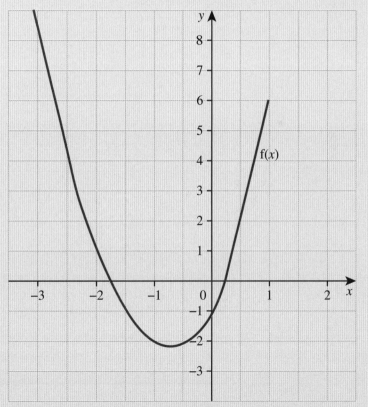

Fig. 10.04 Graph of $f(x) = 2x^2 = 3x - 1$

Note that the shape of the graph is very similar to the x^2 graph but it has been shifted to the left. The other values that have been added to the x^2 term are responsible for this.

10.04 Reciprocal graphs of the form $y = \frac{a}{x}$ (where $x \neq 0$)

Reciprocal graphs are also curved graphs. The final shape of the graph depends on the values applied to x. They are sometimes symmetrical graphs, as the next example shows.

10.05 Worked example

Draw the graph of $y = \frac{5}{x}$ using values of x from -3 to $+3$.

Draw the table and calculate the y-values. The graph is shown in Figure 10.05.

x	-3	-2	-1	0	1	2	3
$y = \dfrac{5}{x}$	-1.67	-2.5	-5	—	5	2.5	1.67

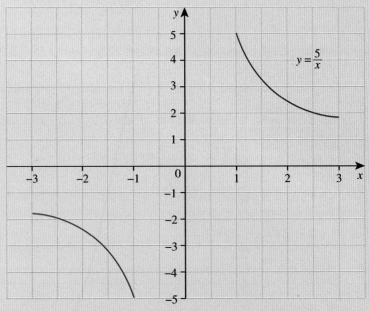

Fig. 10.05 Graph of $y = \dfrac{5}{x}$

Note that we have a symmetrical graph, the line of symmetry being the line $y = -x$. The end of the curves will never actually touch the x or y axes because $1 \div 0$ is infinity.

The process is the same for any $\frac{a}{x}$ graph, although the final shape of the graph will alter according to the actual function values.

10.05 The gradient of a graph

The gradient is the slope of the graph. It tells us how much the graph rises or falls for each unit change in x. The gradient can be positive or negative depending on which direction the graph is sloping and it can be steep or shallow depending on the function.

The general formula for finding the gradient is:

$$\text{Gradient} = \frac{\text{change in } y}{\text{change in } x}, \text{ where } x \text{ is the horizontal size and } y \text{ the vertical size.}$$

10.06 Worked example

The line AB has end points A(2, 3) and B(4, 9). Find its gradient.

We first sketch the setup in Figure 10.06. Note that there is no need for a scale.

$$\text{Gradient} = \frac{y \text{ change}}{x \text{ change}} = \frac{6}{2} = 3$$

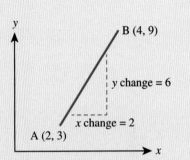

Fig. 10.06 Sketch of the line AB

Types of gradient

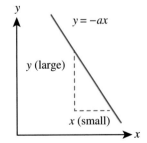

Fig. 10.07 A positive steep gradient

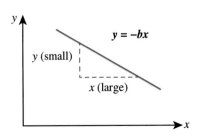

Fig. 10.08 A positive shallow gradient

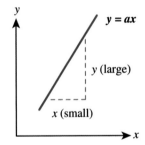

Fig. 10.09 A negative steep gradient

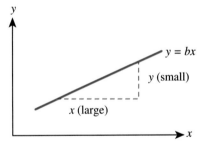

Fig. 10.10 A negative shallow gradient

Finding the gradient of a graph

In order to find the gradient of any straight line graph, we choose any point along its length, form a right-angled triangle and simply read off the corresponding changes in x and y. Then we use the formula for the gradient, gradient = (change in y) ÷ (change in x).

10.07 Worked example

Find the gradient for the graph of $y = 2x + 1$.

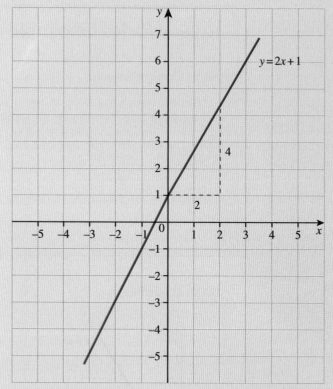

Fig. 10.11 Calculating the gradient of $y = 2x + 1$

Step 1 Consult Figure 10.11. We start the triangle at co-ordinates (0, 1) and go across 2 units in the x direction. Then we have to go up for 4 units in order to touch the graph again.

Step 2 Using the formula:

$$\text{Gradient} = \frac{\text{change in } y}{\text{change in } x} = 4 \div 2 = 2$$

Now we have found the gradient to be 2 for the graph of $y = 2x + 1$, we know that for every one unit the graph moves horizontally, it will move two units vertically. It also tells us that it is a positive gradient in the x-direction, i.e. both x and y increase in value when moving from left to right. If there were a negative sign in front of the 2, then the gradient would be negative.

10.08 Worked example

Find the gradient for the graph of $y = -3x + 2$.

First we construct our table of values and plot the graph (see Figure 10.12).

x	-2	-1	0	1	2
$y = -3x + 2$	8	5	2	-1	-4

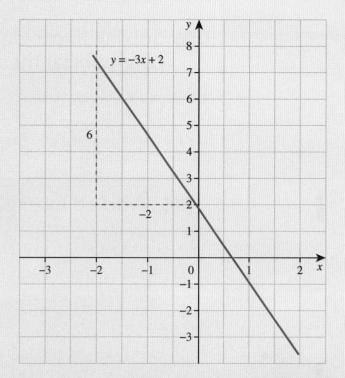

Fig. 10.12 Calculating the gradient of $y = -3x + 2$

Step 1   We start the triangle at the point $(0, 2)$ and go across (-2) units in the x direction. Then we have to go up six units in order to touch the graph again.

Step 2   Using the formula:

Gradient $= y \div x = 6 \div (-2) = -3$

We have found the gradient to be -3 for the graph of $y = -3x + 2$. This tells us that for every one unit in the x direction the graph moves horizontally, it will move three units vertically. It also tells us that it is a negative gradient, i.e. x and y vary inversely in value when moving from left to right (as x increases, y decreases and vice versa).

10.06 Solving linear equations ($y = ax + b$) by graphical methods

We know that any equation of the form x^1 (or simply x) is linear and that it is a straight line graph.

Once you have drawn the graph of an equation, it is very easy to solve it by simple observation of the graph.

10.09 Worked example

Use the graph of $y = x + 3$ to solve the equation $0 = x + 3$. Use x-values of -3 to $+3$ and check that the solution is correct.

In effect the question is asking for the x-value that will give $y = 0$.

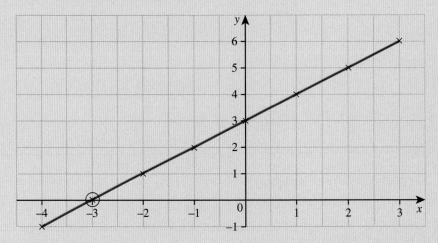

Fig. 10.13 Graph of $y = x + 3$

$y = 0$ is the x-axis, and we can see that the graph crosses the x-axis at $x = -3$, the point circled in Figure 10.13.

Therefore the solution from the graph for $0 = x + 3$ is $x = -3$.

Now we can check. Substituting our $x = -3$ value from the graph:

$x + 3 = 0$

$(-3) + 3 = 0$

$0 = 0$

Both sides of the equation balance, therefore the solution is correct.

10.07 Solving quadratic equations $(y = ax^2 + b)$ by graphical methods

We know that graphs involving x^2 terms are curved, parabolic in shape. The index value above the x also tells us how many possible solutions of x there are for the equation, so in this case there must be two solutions for x. The method of solving quadratic equations using graphs is the same as for linear equations, except that the graph will now have two solutions for x (the graph will intersect the appropriate line in two places, not just one).

10.10 Worked example

Solve the quadratic function $-3 = x^2 - 4$ using a graphical method, using x-values of -3 to $+3$. Check that the solution is correct using any other method.

We will draw the graph of $y = x^2 - 4$, and then, by observation of the graph, find where it intersects the line $y = -3$.

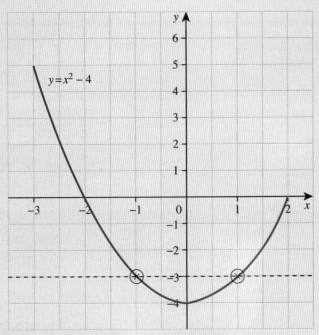

Fig. 10.14 Intersection of $y = x^2 - 4$ and $y = -3$

The dashed line $y = -3$ in Figure 10.14 intersects the graph of $y = x^2 - 4$ at two points (circled):
$x = 1$ and $x = -1$, which are the required solutions.

Now we can check. Substituting our $x = -1, 1$ from Figure 10.14:
$(-1)^2 - 4 = -3$ and $(1)^2 - 4 = -3$.

In both cases, both sides of equation balance, so the solutions are correct.

Progress check

10.02 a Draw a graph of $y = x^2 - 4x + 3$ for $-2 \leqslant x \leqslant 5$.

b Use your graph to solve the equation $x^2 - 4x + 3 = 0$.

10.03 a Plot the graph of $y = \frac{2}{x}$ for $-4 \leqslant x \leqslant 4$.

b Showing your method clearly, use your graph to solve the equation $\frac{2}{x} = x + 1$.

TERMS

• **Gradient**
The slope or steepness of a line.

• **Linear (graphs)**
Straight line graphs; can be written in the form $y = mx + c$.

Exam-style questions

10.01 For each of the functions below:

a plot a graph, and
b calculate the gradient of the function.

i $y = 4x - 3$ ii $y = -2x + 6$

10.02 Plot a graph of the following functions between the given limits of x:

a $y = -x^2 - 2x - 1$ for $-3 \leqslant x \leqslant 3$
b $y = x^2 + 2x - 5$ for $-5 \leqslant x \leqslant 3$

10.03 a The equation of a straight line is $y = mx + c$. Which letter in this equation represents the gradient?

b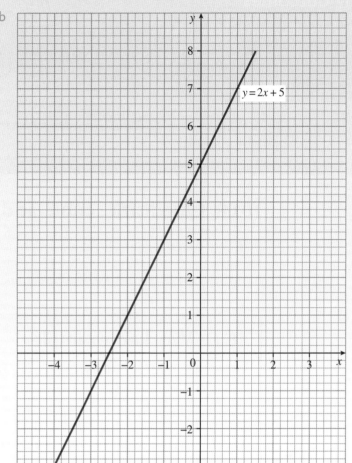

Write down the equation of the line shown on the grid.

c Complete the table of values for $y = 12 - x^2$:

x	−4	−3	−2	−1	0	1	2	3	4
y	−4	3		11		11	8		−4

d On the grid above, draw the graph of $y = 12 - x^2$.

e Write down the co-ordinates of the points of intersection of the straight line with your curve.

EXTENDED CURRICULUM

Learning outcomes

By the end of this unit you should be able to:

- construct tables of values and draw graphs of quadratic, cubic, reciprocal and exponential functions

- estimate gradients of curves by drawing tangents

- solve associated equations approximately by graphical methods

10.08 Quadratic, cubic and reciprocal graphs

There are countless forms that these graphs can take but the method of constructing the table and then plotting the graph is essentially the same as for the work covered in the earlier part of this unit. We will look at two more examples to illustrate this.

10.11 Worked example

Draw the graph of the function $y = (3 + 2x)(3 - x)$ for values of x from -2 to 4. Use your graph to solve $0 = (3 + 2x)(3 - x)$.

Construct the table and plot the graph. Remember that a $-x^2$ graph should be an inverted parabola and that the graph should cut the x-axis in two places in order to obtain the two solutions.

x	-2	-1	0	1	2	3	4
$y = (3 + 2x)(3 - x)$	-5	4	9	10	7	0	-11

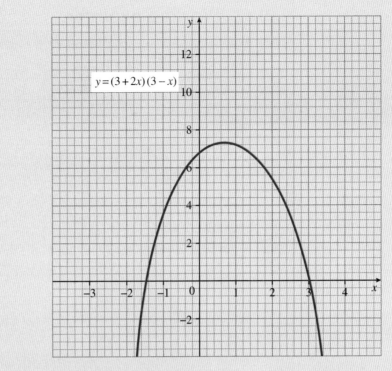

Fig. 10.15 Graph of $y = (3 + 2x)(3 - x)$

We can see from Figure 10.15 that it does in fact have two solutions, $x = -1.5$ and $x = 3$, and that it is an inverted parabola.

10.09 Finding the gradient of a curved graph

Because a curved graph has a constantly changing gradient, both in size and direction, we need to know at which point on the graph to measure the gradient. We then draw a tangent to this point and use it to construct our right-angled triangle. When we have this, it is a simple matter of using the formula to calculate the gradient.

10.12 Worked example

The following table shows some values for the function $y = \dfrac{x^3}{12} - \dfrac{6}{x}$. Values of y are given to one decimal place.

x	0.6	1	1.5	2	2.5	3	3.5	4	4.5	5
y	p	-5.9	-3.7	-2.3	-1.1	0.3	1.9	3.8	q	r

a Find the values of p, q and r.

b Use the values in your table to draw the graph.

c Find, from your graph, correct to one decimal place, the value of x for which $\dfrac{x^3}{12} - \dfrac{6}{x} = 0$.

d Draw the tangent to the curve at the point where $x = 1$, and hence estimate the gradient of the curve at that point.

  a By simple substitution of the x-values into the function

$$p = (0.6)^3/12 - 6/0.6 = 0.018 - 10 = -9.9$$
$$q = (4.5)^3/12 - 6/4.5 = 7.594 - 1.33... = 6.3$$
$$r = (5)^3/12 - 6/5 = 10.4 - 1.2 = 9.2$$

  b Now we plot the graph – see Figure 10.16.

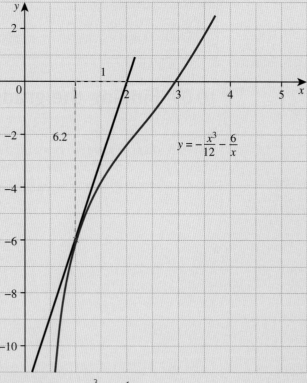

$$y = -\frac{x^3}{12} - \frac{6}{x}$$

6.2

Fig. 10.16 Graph of $y = \dfrac{x^3}{12} - \dfrac{6}{x}$

c We see from the graph in Figure 10.16 that it crosses the x-axis (where $y = 0$) at the point $x = 2.9$, so this is the solution.

d Draw the tangent to the graph at $x = 1$ and construct the triangle, as shown in Figure 10.16.
Read off the x and y co-ordinates and find the gradient.

$$\text{Gradient} = \frac{\text{change in } y}{\text{change in } x} = \frac{6.2}{1} = 6.2$$

Note that the changes in x and y are approximate and have been rounded to the nearest whole number.

10.10 Solving exponential graphs ($y = a^x$)

10.13 Worked example

Plot the graph of $y = 2^x$ and use it to solve the equation $2^x = 6 - 2^x$.

Using a table of values for both functions, the graphs are plotted in Figure 10.17.

x	0	0.5	1	1.5	2	2.5	3
$y = 2^x$	1	1.41	2	2.83	4	5.67	8
$y = 6 - 2^x$	6	5	4	3	2	1	0

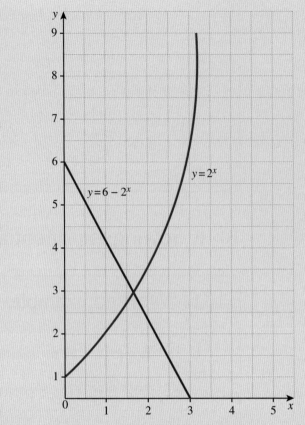

Fig. 10.17 Graphs of $y = 2^x$ and $y = 6 - 2^x$

From Figure 10.17 we can see that the point of intersection is approximately 1.54.
Therefore this is the solution to the equation $2^x = 6 - 2^x$.

Progress check

10.04 For each of the functions below:

    a plot a graph, and
    b calculate the gradient of the function at the specified point.

    i $y = x^3$ ii $y = 2x^2$ iii $y = x^3 - 3x^2$

10.05 Plot the function $y = 2x^3 - x^2 + 3$ for $-2 \leqslant x \leqslant 2$.

    Showing your method clearly, use the graph to solve the equations:

    i $2x^3 - x^2 + 3 = 0$ ii $2x^3 - 7 = 0$

- **Quadratic (graphs)**
  Graphs that are parabolic in shape (U or ∩ shaped).

- **Cubic (graphs)**
  Curved graphs, usually three possible solutions.

- **Reciprocal (graphs)**
  Curved graphs, involving x in the denominator.

Exam-style questions

10.04 For each of the functions below:

a   Plot a graph for $-3 \leqslant x \leqslant 3$.
b   Calculate the gradient of the function at the specified point.

  i $y = x^3$ (gradient where $x = 1$)   ii $y = 2x^2$ (where $x = 0.5$)
  iii $y = x^3 - 3x^2$ (where $x = -0.5$)

10.05 Copy and complete the table below for the function $y = x^3 + x - 2$ for $-2 \leqslant x \leqslant 2$.

x	-2	-1.5	-1	-0.5	0	0.5	1	1.5	2
$y = x^3 + x - 2$	-12	-6.9			-2	-1.4	0	2.88	

Showing your method clearly, use your graph to solve:

a $x^3 + x - 2 = -1$ b $x^3 = 7 - x$

Straight line graphs

CORE CURRICULUM

Learning outcomes

By the end of this unit you should be able to:

■ find the equation of a straight line graph in the form $y = mx + c$

■ determine the equation of a straight line parallel to a given line.

11.01 Finding the equation of a straight line

Any linear equation can be written in the form $y = mx + c$. We can break down this equation into its separate parts as shown:

$$y = \qquad mx \qquad + \qquad c$$
y-value = (gradient × x-value) + y-intercept

We've already looked at how we calculate the gradient either by graph observation or by using two sets of co-ordinates.

To find the c value we need to look at the graph and read off the point at which it crosses the y-axis. Look at the example below.

11.01 Worked example

Find the equation of the straight line shown in Figure 11.01.

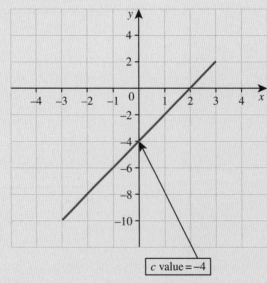

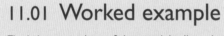
c value = −4

Fig. 11.01 Straight line graph

First we find the gradient by using the triangle method:

$$\text{Gradient} = \frac{\text{change in } y}{\text{change in } x} = \frac{6}{3} = 2$$

Then we find the point where the graph crosses the y-axis. In this case the c value $= -4$.

Therefore the equation of the graph is:
$y = 2x + (-4)$
$y = 2x - 4$

Straight lines with negative gradients

In Unit 10 we noted that lines with a negative gradient will decrease in y-values as the x-value increases, and vice versa. The method of calculating the gradient is the same.

11.02 Worked example

Calculate the gradient of the line in Figure 11.02.

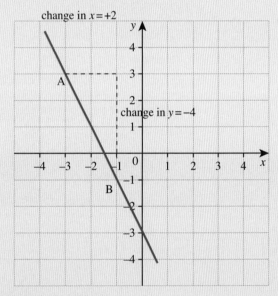

Fig. 11.02 Straight line graph

Take any two points on the line in Figure 11.02 and label them A and B.
To get from A to B, we need to move $+2$ in the x direction and -4 in the y direction.

$$\text{Gradient} = \frac{\text{change in } y}{\text{change in } x} = \frac{-4}{2} = -2$$

11.02 Finding the equation of a straight line parallel to a given line

If two lines are parallel their gradients will be equal. We can then use any point on the line to find its c value (y-intercept).

11.03 Worked example

A line AB is known to be parallel to another line with equation $y = 2x + 1$. Given that point A has co-ordinates (2, 1), find the equation of line AB.

Line AB is parallel to $y = 2x + 1$, so the equation of AB is of the form $y = 2x + c$

By substituting the co-ordinates (2, 1) into $y = 2x + c$, and rearranging for c:

$(1) = 2(2) + c, c = -3$

Equation of AB: $y = 2x - 3$

Progress check

11.01 State the gradient and the y-intercept of the following:

    a $y = x + 3$ b $y = -3x - 5$ c $2y - x = 6$

11.02 Line CD is parallel to another line with equation $y = 3x + 2$.

    If point D has co-ordinates (8, 22), find the equation of line CD.

11.03 Find the equation of a line which:

    a Passes through (0, 7) and has a gradient of 3
    b Passes through (2, 11) and has a gradient of 3

11.04 Find the equation of the following straight lines.

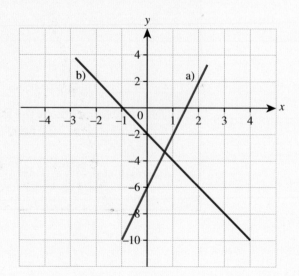

• Gradient
  Slope of a line, usually the coefficient of x. A larger coefficient indicates a steeper slope.

• Intercept
  The point where a line crosses another line or arc. The c value tells us the y-intercept.

• Parallel
  Lines in the same direction, always the same distance apart, so equal gradients.

Exam-style questions

11.01 State the gradient and the y-intercept of the following:

  a $y = 2x - 5$ b $y = -5x + 6$ c $4y - 3x = 12$

11.02 Line XY is parallel to another line with equation $y = -2x + 5$. If point X has co-ordinates $(6, -7)$, find the equation of line XY.

11.03 Find the equation of a line which:

  a Passes through $(0, -9)$ and has a gradient of 2
  b Passes through $(4, 3)$ with a gradient of -1

11.04 Two straight lines labelled A and B are shown below.

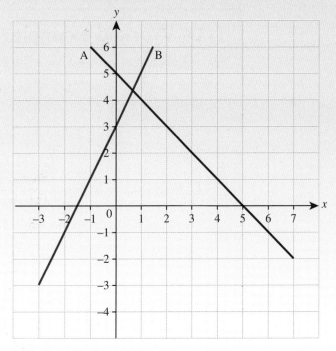

  a Find the gradient of line A.

  b The equation of line B can be written as $y = mx + c$. Find the values of m and c.

  c i On the diagram draw the line which is parallel to B and passes through the point $(1, -1)$.
     ii Write down the equation of this line.

Learning outcomes

By the end of this unit you should be able to:

- calculate the gradient of a straight line from the co-ordinates of two points on it

- calculate the length of a straight line segment and the co-ordinates of its midpoint from the co-ordinates of its end points

- find the equation of a line perpendicular to another line

- find the equation of a line perpendicular to one passing through a set of co-ordinates.

11.03 Calculating the gradient of a straight line from its co-ordinates

In Section 11.01 we looked at calculating the gradient of a straight line graph by inspection of the graph itself and using the formula. However, it is just as easy to find if we have two sets of co-ordinates on the line.

11.04 Worked example

Find the gradient of a straight line AB with co-ordinates A(4, 2) and B(7, 14).

From the given co-ordinates of A and B we can calculate the corresponding changes in x and y:

Change in $x = 7 - 4 = 3$

Change in $y = 14 - 2 = 12$

Use the formula, gradient $= \dfrac{\text{change in } y}{\text{change in } x} = \dfrac{12}{3} = 4$

This can be illustrated in the sketch in Figure 11.03.

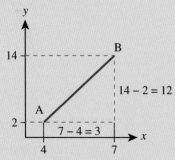

Fig. 11.03 Calculating the gradient from two points

Note that this line has a positive gradient.

Similarly we can use the formula

$$\text{Gradient} = \frac{y_2 - y_1}{x_2 - x_1}$$

where:

x_1 is the first x co-ordinate (A)
x_2 is the second x co-ordinate (B)
y_1 is the first y co-ordinate (A)
y_2 is the second y co-ordinate (B)

11.04 Calculating the length and midpoint of a straight line segment from the co-ordinates

We can make use of Pythagoras' theorem to calculate the length of a straight line by simply making a rough sketch of it. First let us remind ourselves of the theorem.

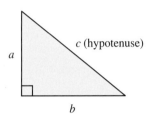

Fig. 11.04 Pythagoras' theorem

$c^2 = a^2 + b^2$ or $c = \sqrt{a^2 + b^2}$, where c is the longest side (hypotenuse) and a, b are the two shorter sides.

The **midpoint** of a line is found by calculating the average of the x and y co-ordinates.

Now look at the following example and how we use these formulae.

11.05 Worked example

Find the length and midpoint of line CD which has co-ordinates C (2, 1) and D (−6, −5).

We start with a sketch of the line – see Figure 11.04.

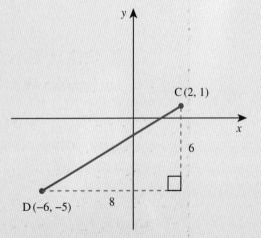

Fig. 11.05 Finding length and midpoint of a line

From Figure 11.05, use the line itself as the longest side (hypotenuse) of the triangle, then the changes in x and y become the lengths of the shorter sides.

Use the formula:

Length of CD $= \sqrt{a^2 + b^2} = \sqrt{8^2 + 6^2} = 10$ units

The midpoint is found by using the formula: $\left[\dfrac{x_1 + x_2}{2}, \dfrac{y_1 + y_2}{2} \right]$, so for the above

line the midpoint is: $\left[\dfrac{2 + (-6)}{2}, \dfrac{1 + (-5)}{2} \right] = (-2, -2)$.

11.05 Gradients of perpendicular lines

Perpendicular lines have gradients which are negative reciprocals of each other:

$y = 2x$ is perpendicular to $y = -\frac{1}{2}x$; $y = 3x$ is perpendicular to $y = -\frac{1}{3}x$.

11.06 Worked example

Find the equation of a line perpendicular to one passing through the co-ordinates A(1, 2) and B(9, 18).

Figure 11.06 shows a sketch of the line.

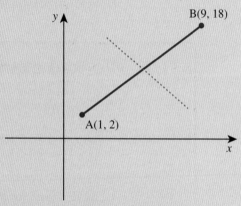

Fig. 11.06 Finding a perpendicular line

The midpoint of line AB is (8, 10), and the gradient is 2 (see the example above).

This means that line AB has the equation $y = 2x + c$.

The equation of the line perpendicular to AB must be of the form $y = -\dfrac{1}{2}x + c$.

Using the midpoints we can find c thus:

$(10) = -\dfrac{1}{2}(8) + c$, so $c = 14$

Therefore, the equation of line required is $y = -\dfrac{1}{2}x + 14$

Progress check

11.05 Calculate the gradient of the line joining the following pairs of points:

a $(1, 1), (3, 5)$ b $(3, 4), (-2, 4)$ c $\left(\frac{1}{2}, 1\right), \left(\frac{3}{4}, 2\right)$

11.06 Find the length and midpoint of the following straight line segments:

a $(2, 6), (6, -2)$ b $(-2, 6), (2, 0)$ c $(-3, -5), (-5, -1)$

TERMS

- Midpoint (of a line)
  The position of the point directly in the middle of the line, found by calculating the mean of the x and y co-ordinates, respectively.

- Length (of a line)
  The magnitude of a line segment. Found by using Pythagoras' theorem on the x and y changes.

- Segment (of a line)
  Part of a straight line.

Exam-style questions

11.05 With the aid of axes if necessary, calculate the length of the line segment between each of the following pairs of points:

a $(0, 3), (-3, 6)$ b $(3, 6), (-3, -3)$ c $(-2, 2), (4, -4)$

11.06 Given the co-ordinates of the end points for the following line segments, calculate their midpoints and gradients:

a $(2, -3), (8, 1)$ b $(1, 2), (9, -2)$ c $(4, 2), (-4, -2)$

11.07 Find the co-ordinates of the midpoint of the line joining the points A $(2, -5)$ and B $(6, 9)$.

Source: Cambridge IGCSE Mathematics 0580 Paper 21 Q7 June 2009.

11.08 The equation of a straight line can be written in the form $3x + 2y - 8 = 0$.

a Rearrange this equation to make y the subject.
b Write down the gradient of the line.
c Write down the co-ordinates of the point where the line crosses the y axis.

Source: Cambridge IGCSE Mathematics 0580 Paper 2 Q18a, b, c June 2007.

11.09 Find the equation of a line perpendicular to one passing through the co-ordinates $(2, 3)$ and $(4, 9)$.

Algebraic representation and formulae

CORE CURRICULUM

Learning outcomes

By the end of this unit you should be able to understand and use:

- letters to represent numbers and express basic arithmetic processes algebraically

- substitution of numbers for letters

- simplification of expressions

- changing the subject of a formula

In algebra we use letters and symbols to represent numbers. We can use algebra to obtain or display a general formula and hence use this formula to solve problems. There are certain rules we must follow in algebra.

First let's look at general algebra notation:

$x + y$ A certain quantity x is added to a different quantity y.

$3x$ 3 multiplied by x. For example, if $x = 2$, $3x = 3 \times (2) = 6$.

$4a - 3b$ 4 multiplied by a minus 3 multiplied by b.

y^2 y to the power of two or $y \times y$. For example, if $y = 3$, $y^2 = (3)^2 = 9$.

$3c^2 + 4d^3$ $3 \times c \times c + 4 \times d \times d \times d$ (3 multiplied by c squared added to 4 multiplied by d cubed).

Whenever possible algebra should be written in its shortest possible terms – it should be simplified. The process of simplifying algebraic expressions is called **collecting like terms**.

12.01 Collecting like terms (simplification)

When adding or subtracting algebraic expressions, you can only **simplify** or combine terms that have the same letter and power of that letter. The final simplified answers should be in alphabetical order with the highest power first (if applicable).

$x + 2x = 3x$ x has a certain value. If we have one of x added to two xs we get three xs altogether.

$3y - 2y = y$ This time we are subtracting two ys from three ys.

$$3x + 2y + 2x + 4y = 5x + 6y$$

The x terms can be added to each other and the y terms can also be simplified, but we cannot combine the x and y terms because they are different letters: x represents one quantity and y represents a different quantity.

$$y^2 + 2y^2 + 3y^3 = 3y^3 + 3y^2$$

We can add the first two terms as the letter and power are the same, but the third term has a higher power so it cannot be added to the others.

Note that the simplified answers have been arranged in alphabetical order with the highest powers in order from left to right.

12.02 Multiplying and dividing algebraic terms

When multiplying terms, first multiply the numbers then the letters together:

$$3a \times 4b = 3 \times 4 \times a \times b = 12ab$$

$$5c^2 \times 3c^4 = 5 \times 3 \times c \times c \times c \times c \times c \times c = 15c^6$$

$$2c^2 \times 3d^4 \times 2e^2 = 2 \times 3 \times 2 \times c \times c \times d \times d \times d \times d \times e \times e = 12c^2d^4e^2$$

When dividing terms, change the terms to their unsimplified form and then cancel where possible:

$$6a^4 \div 2a^2 = \frac{\cancel{6}^3 \times \cancel{a} \times \cancel{a} \times a \times a}{\cancel{2} \times \cancel{a} \times \cancel{a}} = 3 \times a \times a = 3a^2$$

A quicker method would be to divide the numbers in your head and use the indices rules for the letters. For example, $x^5 \div x^2 = x^{5-2} = x^3$.

$$10x^5 \div 5x^4 = 2x^1 = 2x$$

$$4x^3y^2 \div x^2y = 4xy$$

Make sure you revise the rules of indices (Unit 15) to speed up the process of simplification with powers.

Progress check

12.01 Simplify the following:

    a $2x + 4x$ b $3q - q$ c $2a + 3b - 4a + 7b$ d $8a^6 \div 2a^2$

12.03 Forming simple algebraic statements

We can choose any letter we like to represent the quantities, but x is used most frequently in algebra.

- the sum of two numbers: $x + y$ (where x is the first number and y is the second number.)

- seven times a number x: $7x$

- half of a number x: $\dfrac{x}{2}$

- the sum of two numbers x and y divided by a third number z: $\dfrac{x+y}{z}$

- the total cost x of two apples costing a pence and three bananas costing b pence: $x = 2a + 3b$

12.04 Substitution in algebra

With substitution, we are told the value of the letters and hence we can calculate the actual value of an expression.

12.01 Worked example

If $x = 2$, $y = 3$ and $z = 4$, find the value of these expressions:

a $3x$ b $2y^2$ c $2x - z$

a $3x = 3 \times (2) = 6$ (since $3x$ means three multiplied by the value of x)
b $2y^2 = 2 \times (3)^2 = 2 \times 9 = 18$
c $2x - z = 2 \times (2) - (4) = 4 - 4 = 0$

Note that the value of a letter could be negative and/or a fraction. The process of changing the letters to their number value is still the same.

Progress check

12.02 If $x = 2$, $y = 3$ and $z = 5$, find the value of the expressions:

a $2x + y$ b $2z^2$ c $4y^2 + 3z^3 - 2x^4$

12.05 Transforming simple formulae

There are many mathematical formulae in current use, but what if the formula gives one variable and we need to find another variable somewhere else in the same formula? In these cases we have to rearrange the formula for our required term. Take, for example, the formula used to find the area of a rectangle. Suppose we know the area of a rectangle and want to know its width, as in Figure 12.01.

area   =   length   ×   width

subject of formula   required term

The formula is used to calculate area when we know the values of length and width. We say that area is the **subject** of this formula. For the rectangle in Figure 12.01 we know the area and the length but not the width, so we have to rearrange the formula to make the width the subject.

To change the subject of the formula we leave the required term where it is and, step by step, move terms away from it so that it is isolated on one side and becomes the new subject of the formula.

This is the same as solving an equation for a required unknown.

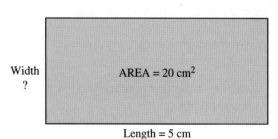

Fig. 12.01 Finding the width of a rectangle of known area

12.02 Worked example

Manipulate the formula $x = cy - d$ so that y is the subject.

$x = cy - d$	We need to eliminate the $-d$ first.
$x + d = cy - d + d$	Add d to both sides.
$x + d = cy$	There are no ds left on the right-hand side.
$\dfrac{x+d}{c} = \dfrac{cy}{c}$	Divide both sides by c.
$\dfrac{x+d}{c} = y$	y is now the subject.

When we move a term from one side to the other, we are effectively inverting its operation:

change sides			=	change operation		
$+$	$\rightarrow$	$-$		$-$	$\rightarrow$	$+$
$\times$	$\rightarrow$	$\div$		$\div$	$\rightarrow$	$\times$
x^2	$\rightarrow$	$\sqrt{x}$		$\sqrt{x}$	$\rightarrow$	x^2

Now we will solve the rectangle problem on the previous page:

Area = Length × Width

We can simplify this further by using the first letter for each term.

$A = LW$

To isolate the W we need to move the L to the other side, remembering to use the inverse operation of 'multiply by L', which is 'divide by L'.

$\dfrac{A}{L} = W$

Now W is the subject of the formula.

Substituting the values of $A = 20$ and $L = 5$, we can find the required width:

$W = \dfrac{20}{5} = 4\,\text{cm}$

12.03 Worked example

For each of the following formulae, rearrange to make the letter in **bold** the subject:

a $x = \dfrac{b}{y}$ **b** $S = \dfrac{ta}{p}$ **c** $E = m\mathbf{v}^2$

a $x = \dfrac{b}{y}$

$xy = b$ — First move y to the other side to remove the fraction.

$y = \dfrac{b}{x}$ — Isolate y by moving the x to the other side, remembering to use the inverse of multiply by x, which is divide by x.

b $S = \dfrac{ta}{p}$ — Eliminate the fraction by moving the p to the other side.

$Sp = ta$ — The inverse operation is multiply by p.

$\dfrac{Sp}{t} = a$ — Isolate a by moving the 'multiply by t' to the other side so it becomes 'divide by t'.

c $E = mv^2$

$\dfrac{E}{m} = v^2$ — Move the multiply by m to the other side to become divide by m.

$\sqrt{\dfrac{E}{m}} = v$ — Remove the square by moving it to the other side where it becomes a square root.

The whole process becomes much quicker with practice. Make sure that you use the correct inverse when you move a term from one side of the equation to the other.

The method of rearranging formulae is called **transposition** and is extremely powerful, as we will see when we look at solving equations in Unit 16. It is used in many other topics throughout the syllabus.

Progress check

12.03 In the following questions, make the letter in **bold** the subject of the formula:

a $m + \mathbf{n} = p$ **b** $2x + \mathbf{y} = c$ **c** $3\mathbf{x} - 2y = w$ **d** $5y - 9 = 3\mathbf{x}$

12.04 Make p the subject:

a $\dfrac{4}{p} = r$ **b** $p(q + r) = 2$ **c** $3p^2q = 2x$

- **Subject (of formula)**
  The main term that is found by using the formula.

- **Transposition**
  The process of making another term the subject of the formula.

- **Simplification**
  Collection of like terms to simplify the final result.

Exam-style questions

12.01 If $y = 5uv - 2v$, find the value of y when $u = -4$ and $v = 2$.

12.02 Make x the subject of the formula $2x + 5y = w$.

12.03 If $a = 3, b = -8$ and $c = 2$, find the value of the following:

a $\dfrac{8a}{b}$ b $4c^2 + 2a^3$ c $\dfrac{c^5}{2b}$

12.04 Manipulate the formula so that x is the subject:

$$\frac{2x + 3y^2}{5} = w$$

EXTENDED CURRICULUM

12.06 Constructing equations

In order to construct an equation, follow the three simple rules below:

- Represent the quantity to be found by a **symbol** (x is usually used).
- Form the **equation** which fits the given information.
- Make sure that both sides of the equation are in the same **units**.

12.04 Worked example

Express algebraically: five times a number x minus three times a number y.

$5x - 3y$ Five times x is $5x$ and three times y is $3y$.

12.05 Worked example

A girl is m years old now. How old was she three years ago?

$m - 3$ Three years before her present age will be m minus 3 years.

12.06 Worked example

I think of a number. If I subtract 9 from it and multiply the answer by 4, the result is 32. What is the number I thought of?

Let the unknown number be x.

If I subtract nine from it, it becomes $x - 9$. I then multiply it by four, so $x - 9$ goes inside brackets because the whole expression is multiplied by four. The thirty-two goes on the right-hand side of the equation. Then solve as a linear equation.

$$4(x - 9) = 32$$
$$4x - 36 = 32$$
$$x = 17$$

12.07 Worked example

The sides of a triangle are x cm, $(x - 5)$ cm and $(x + 3)$ cm. If the perimeter is 25 cm, find the length of the three sides.

The perimeter of the triangle is the sum of all three sides, so we simply add the three lengths.

$x + (x - 5) + (x + 3) = 25$ cm

$3x - 2 = 25$ cm

$x = 9$ cm   (one side)

When we have the first dimension, we can find the remaining two sides using substitution.

$(x - 5) = 4$ cm   (second side)

$(x + 3) = 12$ cm   (third side)

Note that we have gone one step further with examples 12.06 and 12.07 and solved for x. Solving equations will be looked at in greater detail in Unit 16.

Progress check

12.05 Express algebraically: Four times a number y minus two times a number w.

12.06 I think of a number. If I subtract 4 from it and multiply the answer by 3, the result is 9. What is the number I thought of?

12.07 Jocelyn is x years old. Her brother is 8 years older and her sister is 12 years younger than she is. If their total age is 50 years, how old are they?

TIP

It is unlikely that a formula will contain all six operations. If one is not present, go on to the next applicable operation in the list.

12.07 Transforming more complicated formulae

Although the method of 'change sides, change operation' is still primarily used for more complicated formulae, we need to transform the formulae in the following sequence:

1 Remove square roots or other roots.
2 Remove fractions.
3 Clear brackets.
4 Collect together the terms containing the required subject.
5 Factorise if necessary.
6 Isolate the required subject.

12.08 Worked example

Make y the subject of $M = 5(x + y)$.

$M = 5x + 5y$ Expand the brackets

$M - 5x = 5y$ Move the $5x$ to the other side to become $-5x$

$\dfrac{M - 5x}{5} = y$ Move 'multiply by 5' to other side to become 'divide by 5'

12.09 Worked example

Make x the subject of $y = \dfrac{7}{4 + x}$.

Remove fractions: move 'divide by $(4 + x)$' to the other side to become 'multiply by $(4 + x)$'.

$(4 + x)y = 7$

$4y + xy = 7$ Then expand the brackets

$xy = 7 - 4y$ Move $+4y$ to other side, it becomes $-4y$

$x = \dfrac{7 - 4y}{y}$ Move 'multiply by y' to the other side, where it becomes 'divide by y'

$x = \dfrac{7}{y} - 4$ Simplify

12.10 Worked example

Make x the subject of $y = \dfrac{2 - 5x}{2 + 3x}$.

$(2 + 3x)y = 2 - 5x$ Remove the fraction by taking $(2 + 3x)$ to other side

$2y + 3xy = 2 - 5x$ Expand the brackets

$5x + 3xy = 2 - 2y$ Collect the terms involving x on one side; move other terms to the other side

$x(5 + 3y) = 2 - 2y$ Factorise for x

$x = \dfrac{2 - 2y}{5 + 3y}$ Move $(5 + 3y)$ to the other side

Remember, the correct sequence must be followed: if an operation doesn't apply then move to the next in the sequence.

Progress check

12.08 Make p the subject of the formula $A = \pi r \sqrt{p+q}$.

12.09 The angles of a triangle are x, $2x$ and $(x + 40)$ degrees.

    a   Construct an equation in terms of x.
    b   Solve the equation.
    c   Calculate the size of each of the angles.

TERMS

• **Equation**
An expression involving a result and an unknown letter.

• **Expansion**
The process of multiplying out the brackets.

• **Factorisation**
Collecting common factors; the reverse of expanding brackets.

Exam-style questions

12.05 Make d the subject of the formula $c = \dfrac{5d + 4w}{2w}$.

12.06 The interior angles of a pentagon are $9x$, $5x + 10$, $6x + 5$, $8x - 25$ and $10x - 20$ degrees. If the sum of the interior angles of a pentagon is $540°$, find the size of each of the angles.

12.07 A rectangle is y cm long. The length is 3 cm more than the width. The perimeter of the rectangle is 54 cm. Calculate the length and width of the rectangle.

12.08 The sum of three numbers is 66. The second number is twice the first and six less than the third. Find the numbers.

12.09 Himesh is 32 years older than his son. Ten years ago he was three times as old as his son was then. Find the present age of each.

Algebraic manipulation

CORE CURRICULUM

Learning outcomes

By the end of this unit you should be able to understand and use:

■ algebraic calculations with directed numbers

■ expansion of brackets and factorising

In Unit 2 we learnt that directed numbers are numbers with either a positive or negative sign. When using these numbers in algebra, it is important that we follow the same rules as we would for normal directed number calculations:

(positive number)	$\times$ / $\div$	(positive number)	=	(positive answer)
(negative number)	$\times$ / $\div$	(negative number)	=	(positive answer)
(positive number)	$\times$ / $\div$	(negative number)	=	(negative answer)
(negative number)	$\times$ / $\div$	(positive answer)	=	(negative answer)

So $3y \times (-2y) = -6y^2$ and $-3y \qquad \times -2y = 6y^2$.

13.01 Expanding brackets

When removing brackets, every term inside the bracket must be multiplied by whatever is outside the bracket.

13.01 Worked example

Expand the brackets and simplify where possible:

a $3(x + 2)$ **b** $2a(3a + 4b - 3c)$ **c** $3(x - 4) + 2(4 - x)$

a $3(x + 2) = 3x + 6$	The expression means three lots of x and three lots of two.
b $2a(3a + 4b - 3c) = 6a^2 + 8ab - 6ac$	$2a$ must be multiplied by every term inside the bracket.
c $3(x - 4) + 2(4 - x) = 3x - 12 + 8 - 2x$	Expand the first bracket and then the second.
$= x - 4$	Collect together like terms and simplify.

13.02 Worked example

Simplify the following expression:

$2(2a + 2b + 2c) - (a + b + c) - 3(a + b + c)$

$= 4a + 4b + 4c - a - b - c - 3a - 3b - 3c$ — Expand each bracket in turn to give all nine terms.

$= 4a - a - 3a + 4b - b - 3b + 4c - c - 3c$ — Collect together the like terms to form one simplified expression.

$= 0$

Progress check

13.01 Expand the brackets and simplify:

a $2(x + 3)$ b $3(3x - 2)$
c $2a(3a + 2b)$ d $3(3x + 1) - 2(4x - 3)$

13.02 Simplify the following expressions:

a $2x(3x^2 + 4x^3)$ b $3(4a + 2b - 3c) - 2(2a - 5b - 4c)$

13.02 Factorisation

Factorising is the reverse of expanding brackets. We start with a simplified expression and put it back into brackets. When factorising, the largest possible factor (number or letter) is removed from each of the terms and placed outside the brackets.

13.03 Worked example

Factorise each of the following expressions:

a $6x + 15$ **b** $10a + 15b - 5c$ **c** $8x^2y - 4xy^2$

a $6x + 15$ — 3 is the highest number that will divide into both 6 and 15.

$= 3(2x + 5)$ — Highest number factor is 3.

There is no common letter, so only 3 goes outside the bracket.

b $10a + 15b - 5c = 5\left(\dfrac{10a}{5} + \dfrac{15b}{5} - \dfrac{5c}{5}\right)$ — 5 is the highest number that will divide into

$= 5(2a + 3b - c)$ — 10, 15 and −5.

c $8x^2y - 4xy^2 = 4xy\left(\dfrac{8x^2y}{4xy} - \dfrac{4xy^2}{4xy}\right)$ — 4xy is the highest common factor.

$= 4xy(2x - y)$

13.04 Worked example

Factorise $4r^3 - 6r^2 + 8r^2s$.

$$= 2r^2\left(\frac{4r^3}{2r^2} - \frac{6r^2}{2r^2} + \frac{8r^2s}{2r^2}\right)$$

Highest common factor is $2r^2$.

$$= 2r^2(2r - 3 + 4s)$$

Progress check

13.03 Factorise each of the following:

a $8x + 16$

b $9a + 6b - 15c$

c $24x^2 - 38x^3$

d $16x^2y - 4x^3y^2$

13.04 Factorise:

a $6r^2 - 9r + 12r^3$

b $x^2 + 5x$

c $2kx + 6ky + 4kz$

TERMS

- **Factor**
A letter or number that divides exactly into another letter or number.

- **Expanding brackets**
Multiplying out the brackets to give separate terms.

- **Factorisation**
Collecting together common factors, putting expression back into brackets.

Exam-style questions

13.01 Expand the brackets and simplify, where possible:

a $a(b + c)$

b $3c(a - b - c)$

c $k^2m^2(m - n)$

d $3x(2x + 4x^2)$

13.02 Simplify the following expressions:

a $3(2a + 4b - 3c) - 3(4a + 2b - 5c)$

b $3x + 2(x + 1)$

c $5x(x + 2) + 3x$

13.03 Factorise each of the following expressions:

a $6y^2 + 3y^3$

b $3a^2b + 2ab^2$

c $6a^2 + 4ab - 2ac$

13.04 Factorise:

a $x^2y + xy^2$

b $2abx + 2ab^2 - 2a^2b$

c $3ab^3 - 3a^3b + 3a^3b^3$

Learning outcomes

By the end of this unit you should be able to:

- ☐ manipulate harder algebraic expressions and fractions

- ☐ factorise using difference of two squares, quadratics and grouping methods

13.04 Expanding products of algebraic expressions

These expressions are more complicated, in particular because they use double brackets. When expanding double brackets, all terms in the first bracket must be multiplied by all terms in the second bracket.

13.05 Worked example

Expand the following and simplify your answer:

a $(x + 3)(x + 2)$ **b** $(2y + 1)(2y - 2)$ **c** $(4x + 4y)^2$

a $\underbrace{(x \quad + \quad 3)}_{\text{1st term} \quad \text{2nd term}}$ $\underbrace{(x \quad + \quad 2)}_{\text{1st term} \quad \text{2nd term}}$ $= x^2 + 2x + 3x + 6$

       B1   B2 $= x^2 + 5x + 6$

All terms in one bracket must be multiplied by each term in the other bracket:

   1st (B1) $\times$ 1st (B2) $= x^2$

   1st (B1) $\times$ 2nd (B2) $= 2x$

   2nd (B1) $\times$ 1st (B2) $= 3x$

   2nd (B1) $\times$ 2nd (B2) $= 6$

b $(2y + 1)(2y - 2) = 4y^2 - 4y + 2y - 2$

                    $= 4y^2 - 2y - 2$ Same rules as above, simplifying the answer where possible.

c $(4x + 4y)^2 = (4x + 4y)(4x + 4y)$ The whole of the bracket is

            $= 16x^2 + 16xy + 16xy + 16y^2$ squared so we have to write out the bracket twice and multiply

            $= 16x^2 + 16y^2 + 32xy$ out each term.

Progress check

13.05 Expand the following and simplify your answer:

     a $(y + 4)(y + 5)$ **b** $(a - 7)(a + 5)$ **c** $(3x + 4)(x - 2)$

13.06 Expand and simplify: $(4x + 3y)^2 + (2x - 4y)^2$

13.05 Harder factorisation

There are three basic methods we have to learn:

- factorisation by grouping   (usually involves 4 terms)
- difference of two squares   (involves 2 terms)
- factorisation of quadratic expressions (involves 3 terms).

These methods are demonstrated in the following examples.

Factorisation by grouping

13.06 Worked example

Factorise the following expressions:

a $ax + bx + ay + by$ **b** $6x + xy + 6z + zy$ **c** $2x^2 - 3x + 2xy - 3y$

a $ax + bx + ay + by = a(x + y) + b(x + y)$

$$= (a + b)(x + y)$$

Since $(x + y)$ is a factor of both terms we can place $a + b$ inside the other bracket.

b $6x + xy + 6z + yz = 6(x + z) + y(x + z)$

$$= (6 + y)(x + z)$$

Now $(x + z)$ is a factor of both terms, so we can place $6 + y$ inside the other bracket.

c $2x^2 - 3x + 2xy - 3y = 2x(x + y) - 3(x + y)$

$$= (2x - 3)(x + y)$$

$(x + y)$ is a common factor, so this goes in one bracket and $2x - 3$ goes in the other.

Difference of two squares

If we expand the expression $(x + y)(x - y)$, we get:

$$(x + y)(x - y) = x^2 - xy + xy - y^2 = x^2 - y^2$$

Both x^2 and y^2 are squared terms, so therefore $x^2 - y^2$ is known as the **difference of two squares**.

13.07 Worked example

Factorise the following:

a $4a^2 - 9b^2$　　　　**b** $144 - y^2$　　　　**c** $16x^4 - 81y^4$

a $4a^2 - 9b^2 = (2a)^2 - (3b)^2$

$= (2a + 3b)(2a - 3b)$

In this case the $2a$ term will represent the 'x' and the $3b$ term will represent the 'y'.

b $144 - y^2 = (12)^2 - y^2$

$= (12 + y)(12 - y)$

Now the 12^2 is the first squared term and the y^2 is the second squared term.

c $16x^4 - 81y^4 = (4x^2)^2 - (9y^2)^2$

$= (4x^2 + 9y^2)(4x^2 - 9y^2)$

The $(4x^2)^2$ term represents the first squared term and the $(9y^2)^2$ term represents the second squared term.

Note that each of the above answers can be checked by reversing the process, i.e. by expanding the brackets back to get the original question. The last equation becomes:

$$(4x^2 + 9y^2)(4x^2 - 9y^2) = 16x^4 - 36x^2y^2 + 36x^2y^2 - 81y^4$$

$$= 16x^4 - 81y^4$$

This is the original problem.

Factorisation of quadratic expressions

A quadratic expression is one which contains a **squared term** in it, such as $x^2 + 5x + 6$.

Any quadratic expression can be written as a product of two brackets.

13.08 Worked example

Factorise the following quadratic expressions:

a $x^2 + 7x + 12$　　　　**b** $x^2 - 2x - 63$　　　　**c** $3x^2 + 8x + 4$

a $x^2 + 7x + 12$

We know that the first term in each bracket must be x, since x multiplied by x is x^2. In order to find the other terms, follow the method below:

x^2　　　　$+7x$　　　　$+12$

sum of the　　product of the
2 numbers　　2 numbers

Products which make 12 are $4 \times 3, -4 \times -3, 2 \times 6, -2 \times -6,$
$1 \times 12, -1 \times -12.$

Sums of two numbers which make 7 are $4 + 3, 6 + 1, 5 + 2.$

As 4 and 3 are the only numbers that give the correct sum and the correct product, these must be the missing terms.

$$x^2 + 7x + 12 = (x + 4)(x + 3)$$

Note that the order of the numbers is not important.

b x^2 $\quad -2x \quad$ -63

$\qquad$ sum $\qquad$ product

Products which make -63 are 9 and -7, 7 and -9, 3 and -21, -21 and 3, -1 and 63, -63 and 1.

Of these, the two numbers whose sum makes -2 are 7 and -9.

As 7 and -9 give the correct sum and the correct product, these must be the correct terms.

$$x^2 - 2x - 63 = (x + 7)(x - 9)$$

c $\quad 3x^2 \qquad +8x \qquad +4$

product of $\qquad$ product of
x and $3x$ $\qquad$ two numbers

This type of question is more difficult because we only know that the product is 4 and that the first term in the brackets are x and $3x$, so we have to list the products of 4 and see which two numbers go in the brackets to give us the middle term of $8x$.

Products which make 4 are 2×2, -2×-2, 1×4, -1×-4.

By trial and error, the only two numbers that will give us $8x$ after expanding the brackets are 2 and 2.

$$3x^2 + 8x + 4 = (3x + 2)(x + 2)$$

Note that you should always check your answers at the end by multiplying out brackets to get back to the original problem.

Progress check

13.07 Factorise the following expressions:

    a $xh + xk + yh + yk$ $\qquad\qquad$ b $2mh - 2mk + nh - nk$
    c $6ax + 2bx + 3ay + by$

13.08 Factorise:

    a $x^2 + 7x + 10$ b $9a^2 - 16b^2$ c $3x^2 + 8x + 4$ d $4x^2 - y^2$

13.06 Manipulating algebraic fractions

The rules for algebraic fractions are the same as for normal fractions.

For example, when multiplying or dividing:

$$\frac{a}{c} \times \frac{b}{d} = \frac{ab}{cd} \qquad\qquad \frac{a}{b} \div \frac{c}{d} = \frac{a}{b} \times \frac{d}{c} = \frac{ad}{bc}$$

When adding or subtracting, if the denominators are the same we just add/subtract the numerators:

$$\frac{a}{5} + \frac{b}{5} = \frac{a+b}{5} \qquad\qquad \frac{x}{2} - \frac{y}{2} = \frac{x-y}{2}$$

However, when the denominators are different we have to manipulate one of the fractions so that the denominators become equal:

$$\frac{2}{y} + \frac{3}{2y} = \frac{4}{2y} + \frac{3}{2y} = \frac{7}{2y} \quad \text{(the first fraction must be multiplied by 2 to make}$$
$$\text{the denominators equal)}$$

However, in some cases one denominator is not a multiple of the other, so we then have to find a **common multiple** of all the denominators and make this the common denominator:

$$\frac{x}{4} + \frac{5y}{9} = \frac{9x}{36} + \frac{20y}{36} = \frac{9x+20y}{36} \quad \text{36 is a common multiple of 4 and 9.}$$

Even with more complex fractions, the method of finding a common denominator is still required.

Consider $\dfrac{1}{x-2} - \dfrac{2}{x-3}$.

Now a common denominator is the product of $x - 2$ and $x - 3$. We multiply $\dfrac{1}{x-2}$ by $\dfrac{x-3}{x-3}$ (which is equal to 1) and multiply $\dfrac{2}{x-3}$ by $\dfrac{x-2}{x-2}$ (which is also equal to 1).

Multiplying by 1 in each case means we have not changed the value of the fractions. The two fractions now have a common denominator and can be combined and then simplified.

$$\frac{1}{x-2} - \frac{2}{x-3} = \frac{1}{x-2} \times \frac{x-3}{x-3} - \frac{2}{x-3} \times \frac{x-2}{x-2}$$

$$= \frac{1(x-3) - 2(x-2)}{(x-2)(x-3)}$$

$$= \frac{x-3-2x+4}{(x-2)(x-3)}$$

$$= \frac{-x+1}{(x-2)(x-3)}$$

13.09 Worked example

Simplify the algebraic fraction $\dfrac{5m}{4y} - \dfrac{3m}{6y}$.

$$\frac{5m}{4y} - \frac{3m}{6y} = \frac{5m(6y)}{(4y)(6y)} - \frac{3m(4y)}{(4y)(6y)}$$

Express the fractions in terms of a common denominator: $(4y)(6y)$.

$$= \frac{30my - 12my}{(4y)(6y)}$$

Multiply out the numerators.

$$= \frac{18my}{24y^2}$$

$$= \frac{3m}{4y}$$

Simplify the fraction to its lowest terms.

13.10 Worked example

Simplify the following: $\dfrac{2r}{3x} + \dfrac{5r}{4x} - \dfrac{3r}{2x}$

$$\frac{2r}{3x} + \frac{5r}{4x} - \frac{3r}{2x} = \frac{8r}{12x} + \frac{15r}{12x} - \frac{18r}{12x}$$

$\times 4 \quad \times 3 \quad \times 6$ Common denominator is $12x$, so we multiply each fraction by the appropriate number and then simplify the numerators.

$$= \frac{5r}{12x}$$

Simplifying algebraic fractions involving quadratics

When you have an expression such as $\dfrac{x^2 - 2x}{x^2 - 5x + 6}$, factorise the numerator and denominator and then cancel where possible.

13.11 Worked example

Simplify the algebraic fraction $\dfrac{x^2 - 2x}{x^2 - 5x + 6}$.

$x^2 - 2x$ factorises to $x(x - 2)$, and $x^2 - 5x + 6$ factorises to $(x - 3)(x - 2)$.

$$\frac{x^2 - 2x}{x^2 - 5x + 6} = \frac{x\cancel{(x - 2)}}{(x - 3)\cancel{(x - 2)}}$$

Cancel the common terms.

$$= \frac{x}{x - 3}$$

13.12 Worked example

Simplify $\dfrac{x^2 + 4x}{x^2 + x - 12}$.

$x^2 + 4x$ factorises to $x(x + 4)$, and $x^2 + x - 12$ factorises to $(x + 4)(x - 3)$.

$$\frac{x^2 + 4x}{x^2 + x - 12} = \frac{x\,\cancel{(x + 4)}}{\cancel{(x + 4)}(x - 3)} \quad \text{Cancel the common terms.}$$

$$= \frac{x}{x - 3}$$

TERMS

- **Grouping method**
  Four terms involved, have to pair off factors.

- **Difference of two squares**
  Involves one squared term subtracted from another squared term.

- **Quadratic**
  Involves x^2, y^2; any term squared.

Exam-style questions

13.05 Expand the following and simplify your answer:

    a $(x + 8)(x - 2)$ b $(2x + 1)(x - 4)$

    c $(3x^2 - 2x)(2x^2 - x)$

13.06 Expand and simplify: $(2x - 3y)^2 - (3x - 4y)^2$

13.07 Factorise the following expressions:

    a $ms + 2mt^2 - ns - 2nt^2$ b $am - bm - an + bn$

    c $2ax + 2ay + bx + by$

13.08 Factorise:

    a $x^2 - 2x - 35$ b $25x^2 - 36b^2$

    c $8x^2 - 10x - 3$ d $2x^2 + 7x + 5$

Functions

EXTENDED CURRICULUM

Fig. 14.01 Representation of $f(x) = 3x - 5$

An expression such as $f(x) = 3x - 5$, in which the variable is x, is called a **function of x**. Its numerical value depends on the value of x.

The function above can be shown as a diagram – see Figure 14.01.

In Figure 14.01, the input is a certain value x, the function is a certain operation applied to x and the output is the result after the function has been applied.

There are four basic types of function problems you need to learn.

14.01 Finding the output of a function for a given input

In this type of problem the value of x is given and you have to substitute this value for x in the expression to find the corresponding output.

14.01 Worked example

If $f(x) = 2x + 7$, find the value of: a $f(3)$ b $f(-2)$

a $f(3) = 2(3) + 7 = 13$ Using simple substitution of the value 3 for x. In reality, the x input value was 3, we applied the function to it and got the output of 13.

b $f(-2) = 2(-2) + 7 = -4 + 7 = 3$

Progress check

14.01 For the function $f(x) = 5x + 1$, evaluate:

    a $f(2)$ b $f(0)$ c $f(-3)$ d $f(x + 1)$

14.02 If $g(x) = 3x^2 + 1$, write down the following in their simplest terms:

    a $f(3)$ b $f(x + 2)$ c $f(2x - 3)$ d $f(x - 3) + 10$

14.02 Finding the input for a given function output

In this type of problem the value of the output side of the equation is given and you have to find the value of x that was input.

14.02 Worked example

If $f(x) = 2x + 1$, solve $f(x) = 4$.

We can say $4 = 2x + 1$
Solve as a normal linear equation:
$4 - 1 = 2x$
$3 = 2x$
$1.5 = x$
So the x input must have been 1.5 in order to get an output of 4.

Progress check

14.03 If $f(x) = \dfrac{x+3}{2}$, solve: a $f(x) = 4$ b $f(x) = -3$

14.03 The inverse function $f^{-1}(x)$

This time we have to find the inverse of the function. Table 14.01 shows some functions and their inverses.

Table 14.01 Inverse functions

Function f(x)	Inverse function f⁻¹(x)
$x + 3$	$x - 3$
$4x$	$\dfrac{x}{4}$
$\dfrac{x+4}{5}$	$5x - 4$

To find the inverse function we can use either a flowchart method or an algebraic method.

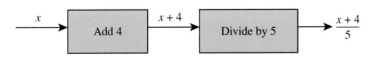

The flowchart method

To find the inverse of $f(x) = \dfrac{x+4}{5}$, first look

at the steps needed for x to become $f(x)$,

as shown in the upper half of Figure 14.02.

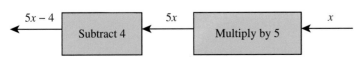

Fig. 14.02 The function $\dfrac{x+4}{5}$ and its inverse

Then to reverse the function we perform the reverse operations, as shown in the lower half of Figure 14.02.

Therefore the inverse is $f^{-1}(x) = 5x - 4$.

The algebraic method

We can write the function as $f(x) = \dfrac{x+4}{5}$. Then if we transpose the function to make x the subject we have:

$$f(x) = \frac{x+4}{5}$$
$$5f(x) = x + 4$$
$$5f(x) - 4 = x$$

Then simply change the $f(x)$ term back into x:

$$5x - 4 = f^{-1}(x)$$

Progress check

14.04 If $f(x) = \dfrac{x-2}{3}$, find $f^{-1}(x)$.

14.04 The composite functions, fg(x) and gf(x)

In this type of problem, more than one function is involved.

If $f(x) = 2x - 1$ and $g(x) = 3x + 2$, then we can find $fg(x)$:

As f is the first letter this becomes the main function. We then substitute the $g(x)$ function as the value of x in the $f(x)$ function:

$$\begin{aligned} fg(x) &= 2(3x + 2) - 1 \\ &= 6x + 4 - 1 \\ &= 6x + 3 \end{aligned}$$

Similarly, we could find the composite function $gf(x)$ by substituting the $f(x)$ function as the value of x in the $g(x)$ function:

$$\begin{aligned} gf(x) &= 3(2x - 1) + 2 \\ &= 6x - 3 + 2 \\ &= 6x - 1 \end{aligned}$$

The following examples use combinations of each type of function.

14.03 Worked example

If $f(x) = 3x - 5$ and $g(x) = 2x + 1$, find:

a $f(-2)$ b $g(4)$ c $g^{-1}(x)$ d $fg(3)$

a $f(-2) = 3(-2) - 5 = -6 - 5 = -11$

b $g(4) = 2(4) + 1 = 8 + 1 = 9$

Both (a) and (b) involved simple substitution of x into first the $f(x)$ function, then the $g(x)$ function.

c $g^{-1}(x) = y = 2x + 1$
$$y - 1 = 2x$$
$$\frac{y-1}{2} = x$$
$$g^{-1}(x) = \frac{x-1}{2}$$

We found the inverse of the g(x) function using the algebraic method. Try the flowchart method yourself to make sure the answer is correct.

d $fg(3) = 3(2x + 1) - 5$
$= 6x + 3 - 5$
$= 6x - 2$

The composite function was found, where $f(x)$ is the main function; this is $6x - 2$. Then we substitute the value of 3 into the function and get the final answer.

$= 6(3) - 2$
$= 16$

Progress check

14.05 If $f(x) = 3x - 1$ and $g(x) = 2x + 5$, find:

a $fg(x)$ b $gf(x)$ c $ff(3)$

• Inverse function
The function that will map the output back to the input.

• Composite function
The combination of one or more functions; the first letter is the main function.

Exam-style questions

14.01 $f(x) = x^3 - 3x^2 + 6x - 4$ and $g(x) = 2x - 1$. Find

a $f(-1)$,   b $gf(x)$,   c $g^{-1}(x)$.

Source: Cambridge IGCSE Mathematics 0580 Paper 21 Q18a, b,c June 2008.

14.02 The function $f(x)$ is given by $f(x) = 3x - 2$. Find, in their simplest form,

a $f^{-1}f(x)$ b $ff(x)$

14.03 $f(x) = 2x + 1, g(x) = x^2 - 1$ and $h(x) = 3^x$. Find the value of:

a $f\left(\dfrac{-1}{2}\right)$ b $g(-3)$ c $h(-3)$ d $f^{-1}(x)$ e $gf(x)$ f $fg(2)$

14.04 $f(x) = (x - 1)^3$ $g(x) = (x - 1)^2$ $h(x) = 3x + 1$

a Work out $fg(-1)$ b Find $gh(x)$ in its simplest form   c Find $f^{-1}(x)$

Source: Cambridge IGCSE Mathematics 0580 Paper 21 Q20 June 2010.

Indices

CORE CURRICULUM

Learning outcomes

By the end of this unit you should be able to understand and use:

☐ rules for positive, negative and zero indices

Indices mean **powers** or raised terms. The index figure above a term (number or letter) tells us how many times that term is multiplied by itself. For example:

$$4^2 = 4 \times 4 \qquad\qquad \text{Number 4 is multiplied by itself.}$$

$$y^4 = y \times y \times y \times y \qquad\qquad \text{Letter } y \text{ is multiplied by itself three times.}$$

15.01 Positive, negative and zero indices

Positive indices have positive powers, e.g. x^3.

Negative indices have negative powers, e.g. x^{-4}.

A negative power indicates the reciprocal of the term, e.g. $x^{-4} = \dfrac{1}{x^4}$.

Zero indices have zero powers, e.g. x^0. Any term with a zero index $= 1$, it does not matter whether it is a letter or a number. For example, $x^0 = 3^0 = 1$.

15.02 Rules for indices

When **multiplying** powers of the same term, we **add** the indices: $a^m \times a^n = a^{m+n}$.

e.g.
$$y^3 \times y^4 = y^{3+4} = y^7$$
$$3^2 \times 3^3 \times 3^4 = 3^{2+3+4} = 3^9$$

When **dividing** powers of the same term, we **subtract** the indices: $a^m \div a^n = a^{m-n}$.

e.g.
$$x^5 \div x^2 = x^{5-2} = x^3$$
$$4^6 \div 4^3 = 4^{6-3} = 4^3$$

Problems with indices usually involve one or more of the operations above, very often combining positive, negative and zero indices.

15.01 Worked example

Simplify the following expression: $6a^3 \times 4b^{-2} \times 3z^0$.

Multiply the numbers together to give 72. Write b^{-2} as $\dfrac{1}{b^2}$ and z^0 as 1:

$$6a^3 \times 4b^{-2} \times 3z^0 = 6a^3 \times 4 \times \frac{1}{b^2} \times 3 \times 1 = \frac{72a^3}{b^2}$$

Progress check

15.01 Simplify the following using indices:

a $3^4 \times 3^2$ b $6^3 \times 6^2 \times 3^3 \times 3^4$ c $\dfrac{(6^2)^3}{6^5}$ d $\dfrac{2^5 \times 4^{-3}}{2^{-1}}$

15.02 Without using a calculator, evaluate the following:

a $2^{-4} \times 2^{-2}$ b $\dfrac{3^5}{3^3}$ c $\dfrac{7^{-5}}{7^{-7}}$ d $\dfrac{3^{-5} \times 4^2}{3^{-6}}$

15.03 Exponential equations

These involve terms with unknown indices, e.g. $2^x = 8$, $3^{x+2} = 81$.

When solving for the missing index, the terms on both sides of the equation should be made equal.

15.02 Worked example

If $2^x = 4$, find the value of x.

First make the terms on each side the same, so change the 4 on the right-hand side to a power of 2.

$2^x = 2^2$ As the terms are now the same the indices can be equated.
$x = 2$

15.03 Worked example

If $4^x = 64$, find the value of x.

$4^x = 4^3$ Make the terms balance ($4^3 = 64$).
$x = 3$

15.04 Worked example

If $3^{(y+2)} = 27$, find the value of y.

$3^{(y+2)} = 3^3$ Change the 27 to a power of 3, i.e. 3^3.
$y + 2 = 3$ Rearrange the equation for y.
$y = 1$

15.05 Worked example

If $2^{(-x+3)} = 64$, find the value of x.

$2^{(-x+3)} = 2^6$ Change the 64 to a power of 2, i.e. 2^6.

$-x + 3 = 6$
$-x = 3$ Solve for x.
$x = -3$

Progress check

15.03 Find the value of x in each of the following:

a $2^{(2x+2)} = 128$
b $5^{(-x+2)} = 125$
c $3^{(-x+4)} = 81$

- Indices
  Powers or raised terms.

- Exponential equations
  Terms with unknown indices.

Exam-style questions

15.01 When $x = 5$ find the value of a $4x^2$, b $(4x)^2$.

Source: *Cambridge IGCSE Mathematics 0580 Paper 1 Q4 October/November 2004.*

15.02 Write down the value of $\left(1\frac{1}{2}\right)^{-2}$ as a fraction.

15.03 Find the value of x in each of the following:

a $8^{-3x} = \dfrac{1}{4}$
b $2^{(x+1)} = 32$
c $5^{(x-4)} = 125$

15.04 Find the value of y in $10^{(y+1)} = 1$.

15.05 Evaluate the value of x in $3^{(x+2)} = 81$.

15.04 Fractional indices

This time the indices are in the form of fractions, e.g. $4^{\frac{1}{2}}, 2^{\frac{2}{4}}, 3^{\frac{4}{3}}$. We need to remember two more rules for fractional indices:

When raising the power of a quantity to a power, multiply the indices: $(a^m)^n = a^{mn}$.

e.g.
$$(y^2)^3 = y^{2 \times 3} = y^6$$
$$(4^3)^2 = 4^{3 \times 2} = 4^6$$

To find the nth root of a quantity, divide the index of the quantity by n: $\sqrt[n]{a^m} = a^{\frac{m}{n}}$.

e.g.
$$\sqrt[3]{y^2} = y^{\frac{2}{3}}$$
$$\sqrt[4]{3^2} = 3^{\frac{2}{4}} = 3^{\frac{1}{2}}$$

15.06 Worked example

Evaluate the following without the use of a calculator:

a $16^{\frac{1}{4}}$ b $81^{\frac{1}{4}}$ c $32^{\frac{3}{5}}$ d $\dfrac{4^{\frac{5}{6}} \times 4^{\frac{1}{6}}}{4^{\frac{1}{2}}}$

a $16^{\frac{1}{4}} = \sqrt[4]{16} = 2$ The fourth root of $16 = 2$, i.e. $2 \times 2 \times 2 \times 2 = 16$

b $81^{\frac{1}{4}} = \sqrt[4]{81} = 3$ The fourth root of $81 = 3$, i.e. $3 \times 3 \times 3 \times 3 = 81$

c $32^{\frac{3}{5}} = 2^{5 \times \frac{3}{5}} = 2^3 = 8$ Change 32 to a power of 2, then cancel the indices to leave 2 cubed.

d $\dfrac{4^{\frac{5}{6}} \times 4^{\frac{1}{6}}}{4^{\frac{1}{2}}} = \dfrac{2^{\frac{2 \times 5}{6}} \times 2^{\frac{2 \times 1}{6}}}{2^{\frac{2 \times 1}{2}}}$ Change the 4s to powers of 2 and multiply each by their index, cancelling where possible.

$= \dfrac{2^{\frac{5}{3}} \times 2^{\frac{1}{3}}}{2} = \dfrac{2^2}{2}$ Simplify the top of the fraction by adding the indices (rule for multiplying indices).

$= 2$ Divide the numerator by denominator to get the final answer.

Note that when we have questions with numbers as the terms, we can check the answers with a scientific calculator, but always show the method.

Progress check

15.04 Evaluate the following without the use of a calculator:

a $343^{\frac{2}{3}}$ b $625^{\frac{3}{4}}$ c $5^{\frac{5}{6}} \times 5^{\frac{4}{5}}$ d $\dfrac{8^{\frac{4}{3}}}{8^{\frac{2}{3}}}$

15.05 Simplify: a $\dfrac{\left(4^3\right)^{\frac{-1}{2}} \times 2^{\frac{3}{2}}}{2^{\frac{-3}{2}}}$ b $\dfrac{2}{16^{\frac{-3}{4}}}$ c $\dfrac{9^{\frac{5}{2}}}{3^3}$ d $27\dfrac{27^{\frac{4}{3}}}{3^3}$

TERMS

• Fractional indices
Where the power is a fraction, e.g. $3^{\frac{4}{3}}$.

• Roots
The inverse of a power, e.g. $\sqrt{x}$ is the inverse of x^2.

Exam-style questions

15.06 Simplify   a $\left(\dfrac{p^4}{16}\right)^{0.75}$,   b $3^2 q^{-3} \div 2^3 q^{-2}$.

Source: *Cambridge IGCSE Mathematics 0580 Paper 21 Q16a, b June 2010.*

15.07 Simplify $(27x^3)^{\frac{2}{3}}$.

15.08 a $\sqrt{32} = 2^p$. Find the value of p.

b $\sqrt[3]{\dfrac{1}{8}} = 2^q$. Find the value of q.

Source: *Cambridge IGCSE Mathematics 0580 Paper 2 Q17a, b June 2007.*

15.09 Find the values of x, y and z in each of the following, where $w > 0$:

a $w^0 = x$ b $w^y = \dfrac{1}{w}$ c $w^z = \sqrt{w^3}$

Solution of equations and inequalities

CORE CURRICULUM

Learning outcomes

By the end of this unit you be able to:

- ☐ understand and solve linear equations

- ☐ understand and solve simultaneous equations

16.01 Solving linear equations

The method for solving a linear equation is basically the same as for transforming formulae, but we are now given enough information to completely solve it.

Consider the linear equation $x + 4 = 9$.

We can rearrange the formula so that x becomes the subject:
$$x = 9 - 4 = 5$$
which is the solution for x.

This method of 'change sides, change operation' (see Unit 12) is used when solving linear equations, although the equations do get a little more difficult.

16.01 Worked example

Solve the following linear equations:

a $3x + 4 = 19$ **b** $2(y - 3) = 6$ **c** $6x + 9 = 3x - 54$

a $3x + 4 = 19$
$3x = 19 - 4$ Move the '+ 4' to the other side to become '− 4'.
$3x = 15$
$x = 5$ Take the 'multiply by 3' to the other side to become 'divide by 3'.

b $2(y - 3) = 6$
$2y - 6 = 6$ Expand the brackets.
$2y = 6 + 6$ Take the '− 6' to the other side to become '+ 6'.
$y = 6$ Take the 'multiply by 2' to the other side to become 'divide by 2'.

c $6x + 9 = 3x - 54$ Take the '+ 3x' to the other side to become '− 3x'
$6x - 3x = -54 - 9$ and the '+ 9' to the other side to become '− 9', then simplify.
$3x = -63$ Move the 'multiply by 3' to the other side to become 'divide by 3'.
$x = -21$

16.02 Worked example

Solve the equation for x: $\dfrac{7+2x}{3} = \dfrac{9x-1}{7}$

$\dfrac{21(7+2x)}{3} = \dfrac{21(9x-1)}{7}$ Eliminate fractions by multiplying by the LCM (21).

$7(7 + 2x) = 3(9x - 1)$
$49 + 14x = 27x - 3$ Expand brackets and move the xs to one side
$49 + 3 = 27x - 14x$ and numbers to the other side, remembering
to invert the operations.

$52 = 13x$
$4 = x$

Progress check

16.01 Solve the following equations:

a $8 - 4x = 24$ b $18 - 3p = 6 + p$ c $4(x - 5) = 7(2x - 5)$

16.02 Solving simultaneous equations

This time we are looking for the values of two unknowns, usually x and y. There are two methods for solving simultaneous equations. Both are used in the following example.

16.03 Worked example

Find the values of x and y in the following simultaneous equations:

$2x + y = 14$ (i)
$x + y = 9$ (ii)

First method (elimination)

With this method we have to eliminate either the x or the y term by adding or subtracting the equations.
In the equations above we can eliminate the y terms by subtracting the second equation from the first:

$2x + y = 14$
$\underline{-\ x + y =\ \ 9}$
$x + 0 =\ \ 5$

Second method (substitution)

For this method you need to have a good grasp of algebra manipulation. We have to rearrange one of the equations to make either x or y the subject and then substitute into the other equation.
Choosing the second equation, making x the subject:

$x + y = 9$
$x = 9 - y$

Therefore $x = 5$.

Now we substitute the value for x we have just found into either of the equations. Using the first equation:

$2x + y = 14$
$2(5) + y = 14$
$10 + y = 14$
$y = 4$
So $x = 5$, $y = 4$.

Now we substitute this rearranged equation into the first equation:

$2(9 - y) + y = 14$
$18 - 2y + y = 14$
$18 - y = 14$
$18 - 14 = y$
$4 = y$

Now we have the y value we substitute this into the second equation to get the x value:

$x + y = 9$
$x = 5$

16.04 Worked example

Solve the following simultaneous equations:

$2x = 18 - 5y$ (i)
$x + 3y = 10$ (ii)

Using the substitution method, we will rearrange the second equation for x:

$x = 10 - 3y$ $3y$ has been moved to the other side to become $-3y$.
$2(10 - 3y) = 18 - 5y$ Now we substitute this expression for x into the
$20 - 6y + 5y = 18$ other equation
$20 - 18 = y$ to find the value of y.
$2 = y$

Once we have the value of y we can substitute it into the second equation to find the x value.

$x + 3(2) = 10$
$x = 4$

Now we'll check our values using the first equation:

$2(4) = 18 - 5(2)$
$8 = 8$ (correct)

Progress check

16.02 Solve the following simultaneous equations:

$3x + y = 9$
$5x - y = 7$

16.03 A grandfather is ten times older than his granddaughter. He is also 54 years older than her. How old is each of them?

Solving simultaneous equations which have different coefficients

We will now have to manipulate one or both of the equations so that one pair of coefficients is equal and then use the elimination method as before.

16.05 Worked example

Solve for x and y:

$$4x + y = 14 \quad \text{(i)}$$
$$6x - 3y = 3 \quad \text{(ii)}$$

We can make the coefficients of y equal by multiplying the first equation by 3:
$12x + 3y = 42 \quad \text{(iii)}$
Then, using the elimination method:

$$
\begin{array}{ll}
12x + 3y = 42 & \text{(iii)} \\
+\ 6x - 3y = 3 & \text{(ii)} \\
\hline
18x \quad\ \ = 45 &
\end{array}
$$

We add the manipulated equation (iii) to equation (ii). The ys are now eliminated.

$x = 2.5$

Substituting the value of x into equation (ii) finally gives us the value of y. Don't forget to check!
Using $x = 2.5$:
$6(2.5) - 3y = 3$
$15 - 3y = 3$
$y = 4$

16.06 Worked example

Solve for x and y:

$$5x - 3y = -0.5 \quad \text{(i)}$$
$$3x + 2y = 3.5 \quad \text{(ii)}$$

Multiply the first equation by 2 and the second equation by 3. This gives equal y coefficients:

$$10x - 6y = -1 \quad \text{(iii)}$$
$$9x + 6y = 10.5 \quad \text{(iv)}$$

By adding equations (iii) and (iv), the ys are eliminated and x can be found:
$19x = 9.5$
$x = 0.5$
Substituting our known value of x into the first equation finally gives us the value of y:
$5(0.5) - 3y = -0.5$
$2.5 - 3y = -0.5$
$y = 1$

Note that we could have eliminated the x coefficients first by making them both equal to 15 (equation (i) multiplied by 3 and equation (ii) multiplied by 5). We would have obtained the same values for x and y.

Progress check

16.04 Find x and y:

$5x + 4y = 21$
$x + 2y = 9$

16.05 The sum of two numbers is 17 and their difference is 3. Find the two numbers by forming two equations and solving them simultaneously.

- **Coefficients**
  The number in front of the variable; e.g. the coefficient of $2x$ is 2.

- **Simultaneous equations**
  Two linear equations where the values of x and y are the same in both.

- **Elimination method**
  The process of getting rid of one of one variable by algebraic manipulation.

- **Substitution method**
  Rearrange one equation to make either x or y the subject, then substitute this statement into the other equation.

Exam-style questions

16.01 Solve the simultaneous equations
$$8x + 2y = 13,$$
$$3x + y = 4.$$

Source: *Cambridge IGCSE Mathematics 0580 Paper 3 Q7e October/November 2004.*

16.02 Solve the equation $3x + 1 = 4(x - 1)$.

16.03 Solve the following linear equations:

a $\dfrac{p}{-2} = -3$ b $8m - 9 = 5m + 3$ c $4(x - 7) = 2(x - 5)$

16.04 Four of the exterior angles of an octagon are the same size. The other four are twice as big. If the sum of the exterior angles is 360°, calculate the size of the interior angles.

16.05 A right-angled triangle has a base length of x cm and a height of $(x - 1)$ cm. If its area is 15 cm², calculate the base length and height.

EXTENDED CURRICULUM

16.03 Solution of quadratic equations

There are three methods of solving quadratic equations:

- factorisation
- using the formula
- completing the square.

We mentioned in Unit 13 that a quadratic equation takes the form $ax^2 + bx + c$, where a, b and c are constants. We also looked at the factorising method, so this will not be examined again in detail. But we need to look at how we actually solve a quadratic equation once we have it in brackets form.

16.07 Worked example

Solve the equation $x^2 + 3x - 10 = 0$.

The squared term (x^2) tells us that the equation has two possible values. First we factorise:

$x^2 + 3x - 10 = 0 \rightarrow (x + 5)(x - 2) = 0$ (factorising method)

Therefore, if $(x + 5)(x - 2) = 0$
either $x + 5 = 0 \rightarrow x = -5$
or $x - 2 = 0 \rightarrow x = 2$.
Now perform a check:

If $x = -5$	If $x = 2$
$(-5)^2 + 3(-5) - 10 = 0$	$(2)^2 + 3(2) - 10 = 0$
$25 - 15 - 10 = 0$	$4 + 6 - 10 = 0$
$0 = 0$	$0 = 0$

Since the left-hand side of the equation is equal to the right-hand side, we know that the answers obtained for x are correct.

Progress check

16.06 Solve the following quadratic equations by factorising:

    a $x^2 + 3x - 10 = 0$ b $x^2 + 6x = -9$

We can solve quadratic equations either by using the completing the square method or by using the quadratic formula.

The quadratic formula

For a quadratic of the form $ax^2 + bx + c$, where a, b and c are constants:

$$x = \frac{-b \pm \sqrt{b^2 - 4ac}}{2a}$$

16.08 Worked example

Solve the equation $x^2 + 5x - 7 = 0$, giving your answers to 2 decimal places.

Comparing this to the standard quadratic equation $ax^2 + bx + c$, we see that $a = 1, b = 5, c = -7$.

We can then substitute these values of a, b and c into the formula above to find x:

$$x = \frac{-(5) \pm \sqrt{(5)^2 - 4 \times (1) \times (-7)}}{2 \times 1}$$

$$= \frac{-5 + \sqrt{25 + 28}}{2} \text{ or } \frac{-5 - \sqrt{25 + 28}}{2}$$

$$= \frac{2.28}{2} \text{ or } \frac{-12.28}{2}$$

$$= 1.14 \text{ or } -6.14$$

Again we have two possible values for x. Both need to be checked.
If $x = 1.14$:
$(1.14)^2 + 5(1.14) - 7 = 0$
$1.2996 + 5.7 - 7 = 0$
$6.996 - 7 = \text{approx. } 0$
Note that the left-hand side doesn't exactly equal zero due to rounding errors in our calculator, but it is very close.

If we don't have the b or c constant values in a particular equation, we would substitute zero for these terms in the formula.

Progress check

16.07 Solve the quadratic equation $x^2 + 7x + 3 = 0$, giving your answer to two decimal places.

16.04 Solving linear inequalities

We looked at simple inequalities in Unit 3 and will see graphical inequalities in Unit 16, so make sure that you are familiar with the symbols.

16.09 Worked example

Solve the inequalities: **a** $x + 3 < 7$ **b** $8 \leqslant x + 1$

a $x + 3 < 7$
$x < 7 - 3$
$x < 4$

Move '+ 3' to other side to become '− 3'. Simplify to obtain the solution
and other possible solutions for x that still satisfy the inequality.

So x could be 3, 2, 1, …

b $8 \leqslant x + 1$
$8 - 1 \leqslant x$
$7 \leqslant x$
So x could be 7, 8, 9, …

Move '+ 1' to other side to become '− 1', simplify, then solve for all
possible values of x.

When solving an inequality treat it as a normal equation, only considering the symbol at the last stage of your working.

16.10 Worked example

Solve the following inequality: $9 - 4x \geqslant 17$.

$9 - 4x \geqslant 17$
$-4x \geqslant 17 - 9$
$-4x \geqslant 8$
$x \leqslant -2$

The '+ 9' is moved to the other side where it becomes '− 9'.

'Multiply by −4' goes to the other side where it becomes 'divide by −4'.

Invert the inequality to eliminate the minus sign.

So x could be −2, −3, −4, …

Solving harder inequalities

Take, for example, the inequality $5 < 3x + 2 \leq 17$. Here, x has a range of values that satisfy the inequalities $3x + 2 > 5$ and $3x + 2 \leq 17$.

16.11 Worked example

Find the range of values of the integer x for the inequality $5 < 3x + 2 \leq 17$.

First part of inequality:		Second part of inequality:	
$5 < 3x + 2$	Move '+ 2' to the other side to become '− 2'.	$3x + 2 \leq 17$	Move '+ 2' to the other side to become '− 2'.
$5 - 2 < 3x$	Move 'multiply by 3' to the other side to become 'divide by 3'.	$3x \leq 17 - 2$	Move 'multiply by 3' to the other side to become 'divide by 3'.
$1 < x$	Solve for x.	$x \leq 5$	Solve for x.

Now we can see that x is both greater than 1 and equal to or less than 5. Shown as an inequality: $1 < x \leq 5$.

So the x values are $x = 2, 3, 4, 5$.

The process of solving inequalities is very similar to that of solving linear equations, but remember that when you have a negative x-value make it positive by moving it to the other side of the inequality.

When you have to find a range of values, as in Worked example 16.11, treat the problem as two separate inequalities, solve both and then use your answers to form one general solution.

Progress check

16.08 Find the range of values for which the following inequalities are satisfied:

a $4 < 2x \leq 8$ b $3 \leq 2x + 5 < 7$ c $15 \leq 3(x - 2) < 9$

TERMS

- **Linear**
  Expressions or equations involving x only, with only one possible solution.

- **Quadratics**
  Equations involving x^2, usually having two possible solutions.

- **Inequalities**
  Solutions within a range of possible values.

- **Factorisation**
  Process of collecting terms with common factors into brackets. Opposite of expansion of brackets.

Exam-style questions

16.06 Solve the simultaneous equations
$$2y + 3x = 8$$
$$x = 3y + 10$$

16.07 Solve the inequality $\dfrac{2x-5}{8} > \dfrac{x+4}{3}$.

Source: Cambridge IGCSE Mathematics 0580 Paper 21 Q13 June 2008.

16.08 Find the possible values of x, giving your answer to two decimal places, if $x^2 + 5x - 8 = 0$.

16.09 By factorising, give the possible values of x if $x^2 + 11x = -24$.

16.10 A packet of sweets contains chocolates and toffees.

    a There are x chocolates which have a total mass of 105 grams. Write down, in terms of x, the mean mass of a chocolate.

    b There are $x + 4$ toffees which have a total mass of 105 grams. Write down, in terms of x, the mean mass of a toffee.

    c The difference between the two mean masses in parts **a)** and **b)** is 0.8 grams. Write down an equation in x and show that it simplifies to $x^2 + 4x - 525 = 0$.

    d i Factorise $x^2 + 4x - 525$.   ii Write down the solutions of
$$x^2 + 4x - 525 = 0.$$

    e Write down the total number of sweets in the packet.

Source: Cambridge IGCSE Mathematics 0580 Paper 4 Q8 a-e June 2007.

Linear programming

Learning outcomes

By the end of this unit you should be able to:

- represent inequalities graphically and use this representation in the solution of simple linear programming problems

- understand the conventions of using broken lines for strict inequalities and shading unwanted regions

17.01 Representing inequalities graphically

In Unit 3 we looked at the symbols $>, <, \geqslant, \leqslant$:

$a > b$: a is greater than b $a < b$: a is less than b

$a \geqslant b$: a is greater than or equal to b $a \leqslant b$: a is less than or equal to b

Strict inequalities use the signs $>$ and $<$ only.

When drawing graphs of strict inequalities, the graph lines are drawn with broken lines. If the inequality uses $\leqslant$ or $\geqslant$, then the graphs are drawn with solid lines.

Consider $x \geqslant 1$, where x could be 1 or any value greater than 1, e.g. 2, 3, 4. We can demonstrate this graphically as shown in Figure 17.01.

We can see from Figure 17.01 that the shaded region shows the values of x which are greater than or equal to 1, and the graph of $x = 1$ is a solid line. This is because 1 is included in the inequality.

If we had to show the graph of $x > 1$, the line would be broken because the value of $x = 1$ is not included in the inequality.

Note that we can also show an inequality as the unshaded region. The question will tell us whether the region should be unshaded or shaded.

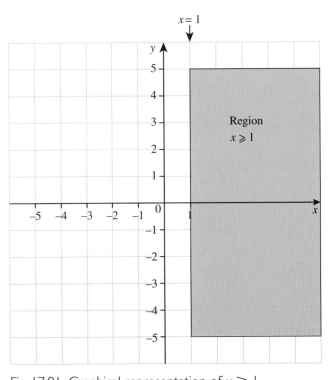

Fig. 17.01 Graphical representation of $x \geqslant 1$

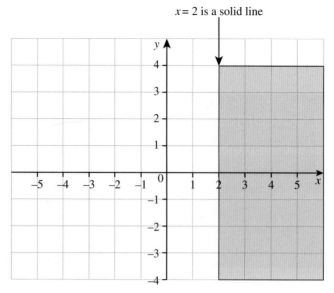

Fig. 17.02 Graphical representation of $x \leqslant 2$

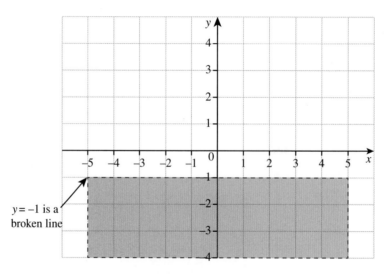

Fig. 17.03 Graphical representation of $y > -1$

The **unshaded** region in Figure 17.02 shows all the values of $x \leqslant 2$, while the **unshaded** region of Figure 17.03 shows the values of $y > -1$.

Now we will look at combining inequalities on the same axis.

17.01 Worked example

Leave unshaded the regions which satisfy the following inequalities simultaneously:

$$x \leqslant 2, y > -1, y \leqslant 3, y \leqslant x + 2$$

We draw each of the inequalities on the same set of axes, as shown in Figure 17.04.

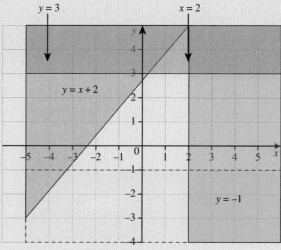

Fig. 17.04 Graphical representation of $x \leqslant 2, y > -1, y \leqslant 3, y \leqslant x + 2$

The unshaded region in the middle obeys all of the inequalities simultaneously.

Remember that the way the question is asked is very important: always check whether you need to identify the shaded or the unshaded region. Always show strict inequalities with broken lines and non-strict inequalities with solid lines.

Progress check

17.01 On the same pair of axes plot the following inequalities and leave unshaded the region which satisfies all of them simultaneously:

$y \geqslant 3x, y \leqslant 5, x + y > 4$

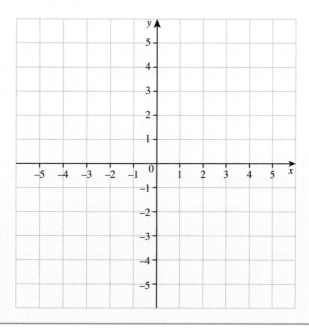

17.02 On the same pair of axes plot the following inequalities and leave unshaded the region which satisfies all of them simultaneously.

$x \leqslant 2, y > 1, y \leqslant 3, y \leqslant x + 2$

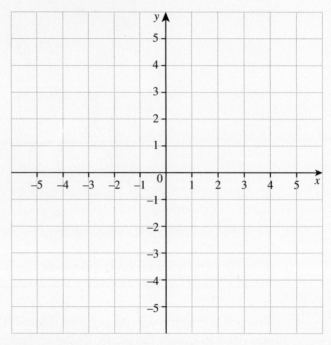

17.03 Kim is baking cookies and bread. She makes a cakes and b loaves. She bakes at least four cookies and at least two loaves but no more than ten cookies and loaves altogether.

a Write an inequality for each statement.
b Graph the inequalities, leaving the region which satisfies the inequalities unshaded.
c Using your graph, state one solution which satisfies all the inequalities simultaneously.

TERMS

• Strict inequalities
  Involve the $<$ and $>$ symbols, and do not include values on the line.

• Unshaded region
  The area left unshaded which satisfies all inequalities simultaneously.

Exam-style questions

17.01 a Draw the three lines $y = 4$, $2x - y = 4$ and $x + y = 6$ on the grid below.

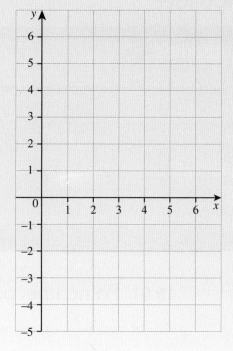

  b Write the letter R in the region defined by the three inequalities below.

$$y \leqslant 4 \qquad 2x - y \geqslant 4 \qquad x + y \geqslant 6$$

Source: *Cambridge IGCSE Mathematics 0580 Paper 21 Q20 a, b June 2009.*

17.02 a One of the lines in the diagram is labelled $y = mx + c$. Find the values of m and c.

  b Show, by shading all the **unwanted** regions on the diagram, the region defined by the inequalities

$$x \geqslant 1, \ y \leqslant mx + c, \ y \geqslant x + 2, \ y \geqslant 4$$

Write the letter **R** in the region required.

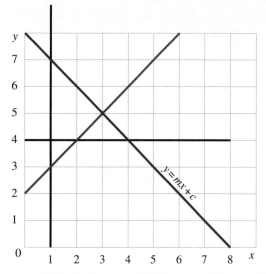

Source: *Cambridge IGCSE Mathematics 0580 Paper 2 Q20 June 2006.*

Geometric terms and relationships

CORE CURRICULUM

Learning outcomes

By the end of this unit you should be able to understand and use:

- calculations with angles
- angles at a point, a line, parallel lines and bearings
- right, acute, obtuse, reflex angles
- perpendiculars, similarity, congruence
- types of triangles, quadrilaterals, circles, polygons and solid figures

18.01 Point, line, parallel, bearing

Many of these terms are covered in more depth in Unit 21, but this is a quick summary.

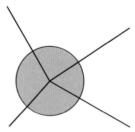

Fig. 18.01 Angles at a point

Angles at a point add up to 360° (see Figure 18.01).

Fig. 18.02 Angle at a straight line

When the angle between two lines is 180°, the lines form a straight line (see Figure 18.02).

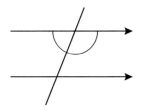

Fig. 18.03 Angles and parallel lines

Angles in parallel lines (see Figure 18.03) follow certain rules which are examined in detail in Unit 21.

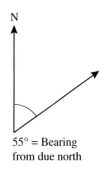

55° = Bearing
from due north

Fig. 18.04 Bearing

A bearing is a three-figure angular direction which is always measured from north in a clockwise direction (see Figure 18.04). It can also incorporate a distance by using a suitable scale.

Progress check

18.01 If point A is on a bearing of 165° and is 5 cm from point B, make an accurate drawing showing A and B.

18.02 Right angles, acute, obtuse and reflex angles

These are the names of the different types of angles.

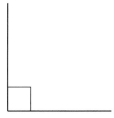

Fig. 18.05 Right angle

An angle of 90° is a right angle (see Figure 18.05).

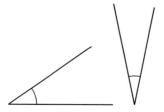

Fig. 18.06 Acute angles

An angle between 0° and 90° is an acute angle (see Figure 18.06).

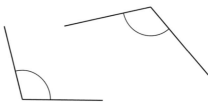

Fig. 18.07 Obtuse angles

An angle between 90° and 180° is an obtuse angle (see Figure 18.07).

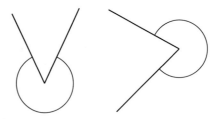

Fig. 18.08 Reflex angles

An angle greater than 180° is called a reflex angle (see Figure 18.08).

Progress check

18.02 Sketch the following angles:

    a acute   b obtuse   c reflex

18.03 Perpendicular lines

These are lines which are at 90° to each other, i.e. they cross each other at right angles.

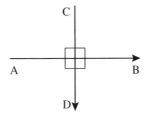

Fig. 18.09 Perpendicular lines

In Figure 18.09, line AB is perpendicular to line CD.

18.04 Similarity and congruence

If shapes are similar their corresponding angles are equal and the ratio of their corresponding sides is equal.

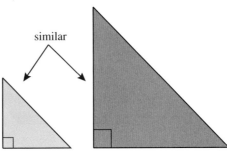

Fig. 18.10 Similar triangles

The second triangle in Figure 18.10 has corresponding angles the same as those in the first triangle, but it is exactly twice the size of the first triangle.

Congruent means identical to, i.e. the corresponding angles are equal and the corresponding sides are equal, like the shapes shown in Figure 18.11.

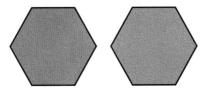

Fig. 18.11 Congruent hexagons

Progress check

18.03 Draw:

    a two similar isoceles triangles   b two congruent squares

18.05 Vocabulary of triangles and quadrilaterals

The various triangles (equilateral, isosceles, scalene, right-angled) and the different quadrilaterals (square, rectangle, parallelogram, trapezium, kite and rhombus) are considered in more detail in Unit 21.

18.06 Circles and polygons

These are studied in more detail in Unit 21.

18.07 Simple solid figures and their nets

These shapes are studied in detail in Unit 21, but now we need to look at some of their nets.

A **net** is an unfolded shape. Imagine that you have a solid shape and you need to unfold it. See Figure 18.12 for an example.

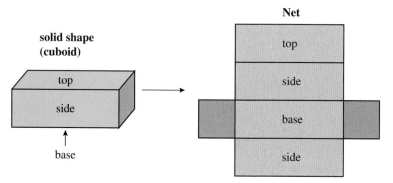

Fig. 18.12 A cuboid and its net

You can investigate this at home with any cuboid-shaped solid, such as a packet of cornflakes. An example of a different shape is shown in Figure 18.13.

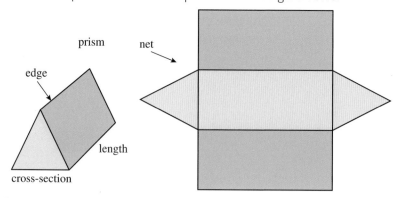

Fig. 18.13 A triangular prism and its net

When drawing the net always ensure it is the correct size, i.e. the length dimension of the solid corresponds to the length dimension of the net, and so on. It also helps to count the faces to make sure you have accounted for all of them. For example:

- a cube or cuboid has 6 faces
- a cylinder has 2 circular ends and a rectangular face
- a triangular prism has 5 faces.

Progress check

18.04 Make an accurate net of a cuboid with dimensions 5 cm by 4 cm by 3 cm. Label the base, top and sides.

18.05 Write down the number of faces, edges and vertices of a trapeziodal prism.

- **Acute**
  An angle between 0° and 90°.

- **Reflex**
  An angle between 180° and 360°.

- **Obtuse**
  An angle between 90° and 180°.

- **Similar**
  Shapes with equal corresponding angles; the ratio of corresponding sides is also equal.

- **Congruent**
  Identical shapes.

18.08 Similar shapes

Two shapes are similar if:

- all the corresponding angles are equal
- the ratio of corresponding sides equal.

The shapes in Figures 18.14 and 18.15 are similar.

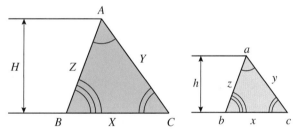

Fig. 18.14 Similar triangles

In the shapes shown in Figure 18.14, the corresponding angles are equal, i.e. $\angle A = \angle a$, $\angle B = \angle b$, $\angle C = \angle c$. The ratios of corresponding sides are also equal, i.e. $X = 2x$, $Y = 2y$, $Z = 2z$.

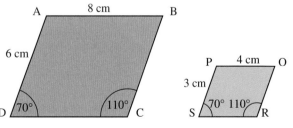

Fig. 18.15 Similar parallelograms

Again, in Figure 18.15 the corresponding angles are equal, i.e. ADC = 70°, PSR = 70°. Also, the ratios of the corresponding sides are equal, i.e. AB = 2PQ, AD = 2PS.

Exam-style questions

18.01 Give the correct name of each of the following angles:

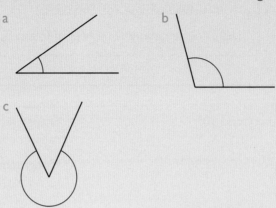

a   b

c

18.02 Draw an accurate net of the following shape:

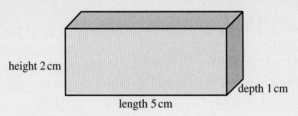

height 2 cm

depth 1 cm

length 5 cm

18.03 Write down the number of faces, edges and vertices of the shape in the previous question.

18.04 Describe the following bearing diagram:

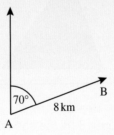

70°

8 km

B

A

18.05 The net of a shape is shown below. Draw the actual shape.

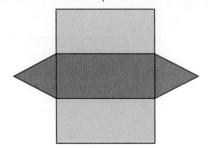

EXTENDED CURRICULUM

Learning outcomes

By the end of this unit you should be able to understand and use:

- [ ] areas and volumes of similar triangles, figures and solids

---

18.01 Worked example

Find the length x in the similar shapes shown in Figure 18.16.

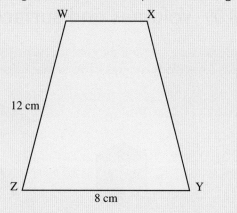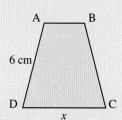

Fig. 18.16 Similar trapeziums

We can see from the shapes that WZ = 2AD, so we can say that:

$$2DC = ZY$$

$$DC = ZY \div 2 = 8\,cm \div 2 = 4\,cm$$

Alternatively,

$$\frac{DC}{ZY} = \frac{AD}{WZ}$$

$$DC = \frac{ZY \times AD}{WZ} = \frac{8\,cm \times 6\,cm}{12\,cm} = 4\,cm$$

18.09 Volumes and surface areas of similar solids

Two solids are similar if they are the same shape and the ratios of their corresponding linear dimensions are equal. Two similar solids are shown in Figure 18.17.

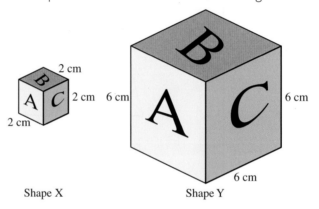

Fig. 18.17 Similar cubes

The linear dimensions of cube Y in Figure 18.17 are three times those of cube X.

If we know that solid shapes X and Y are similar, we can apply the following formulae:

$$\frac{\text{surface area of X}}{\text{surface area of Y}} = \frac{(\text{linear dimension of X})^2}{(\text{linear dimension of Y})^2}$$

$$\frac{\text{volume of X}}{\text{volume of Y}} = \frac{(\text{linear dimension of X})^3}{(\text{linear dimension of Y})^3}$$

We can calculate a missing area or volume or a missing side using the formulae above provided we have the other terms we need.

18.02 Worked example

In Figure 18.18, sphere X has a diameter of 12 cm, a surface area of 450 cm² and a volume of 900 cm³.

Sphere Y has a diameter of 6 cm. What are its surface area and volume?

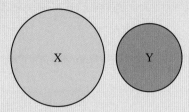

Fig. 18.18 Similar spheres

To find the surface area, use the formula:

$$\frac{\text{surface area of Y}}{\text{surface area of X}} = \frac{(\text{linear dimension of Y})^2}{(\text{linear dimension of X})^2}$$

$$\frac{\text{surface area of Y}}{450} = \frac{(12)^2}{(6)^2}$$

$$\text{surface area of Y} = \frac{450 \times (6)^2}{(12)^2} = 112.5 \text{ cm}^2$$

To find the volume, use the other formula:

$$\frac{\text{volume of Y}}{\text{volume of X}} = \frac{(\text{linear dimension of Y})^3}{(\text{linear dimension of X})^3}$$

$$\text{volume of Y} = \frac{900 \times (6)^3}{(12)^3} = 112.5 \text{ cm}^3$$

A linear dimension is any length. In this case the diameter could be used, but we could also use the height or base of a triangle, the length of a cuboid, etc.

18.03 Worked example

A circle of 14 cm radius has an area of 616 cm². What is the area of a circle with a radius of 7 cm?

$$\frac{\text{area of circle X}}{\text{area of circle Y}} = \frac{(\text{linear dimension of X})^2}{(\text{linear dimension of Y})^2}$$

$$\text{area of circle X} = \frac{616 \times (7)^2}{(14)^2} = 154 \text{ cm}^2$$

18.04 Worked example

A spherical cap has a height of 4 cm and a volume of 64 cm³. A similar cap has a volume of 512 cm³; find its height.

Rearranging the volume formula to give the linear dimension:

$$\frac{\text{volume of Y}}{\text{volume of X}} = \frac{(\text{linear dimension of Y})^3}{(\text{linear dimension of X})^3}$$

$$\text{linear dimension of Y} = \sqrt[3]{\frac{\text{volume of Y} \times (\text{linear dimension of X})^3}{\text{volume of X}}}$$

$$= \sqrt[3]{\frac{512 \times (4)^3}{64}}$$

height of Y = 8 cm

18.05 Worked example

The volume of a cone of height 14.2 cm is 210 cm³. Find the height of a similar cone whose volume is 60 cm³.

This problem uses the same rearranged formula as Worked example 18.04:

$$\text{height} = \sqrt[3]{\frac{60 \times (14.2)^3}{210}} = 9.35 \text{ cm}$$

Progress check

18.09 Two cubes X and Y are of different sizes. If n is the ratio of their corresponding sides, express in terms of n:

    a the ratio of their surface areas   b the ratio of their volumes.

18.10 The two packs of corn flakes A and B shown below are similar. The total surface area of pack B is four times that of pack A. Calculate:

    a the dimensions of pack B   b the mass of pack A if pack B has a mass of 600 kg.

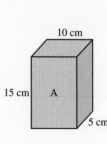
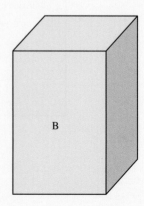

- **Corresponding**
  A side or angle on a shape at exactly the same position as a side or angle on a similar shape.

- **Dimension**
  A side length or magnitude.

- **Surface area**
  The total area of all the faces on a shape.

Exam-style questions

18.06 The cuboids A and B are similar. Calculate the volume of cuboid B.

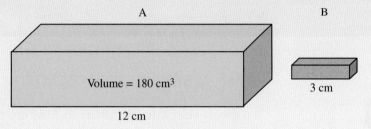

18.07 The two cylinders X and Y are similar. If the height of cylinder Y is 10 cm, calculate the height of cylinder X.

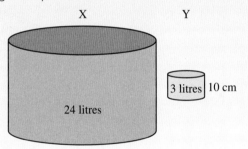

18.08 An equilateral triangle has an area of 24 cm². If the lengths of its sides are reduced by 15%, calculate the area of the reduced triangle.

18.09 An island has an area of 100 km². What would be its area on a map of scale 1 : 20 000?

18.10 Two similar vases have heights which are in the ratio 3 : 2.

 a The volume of the larger vase is 1080 cm³. Calculate the volume of the smaller vase.

 b The surface area of the smaller vase is 252 cm². Calculate the surface area of the larger vase.

Geometrical constructions

CORE CURRICULUM

Learning outcomes

By the end of this unit you should be able to:

- measure and construct lines, angles, bisectors and simple shapes using ruler, protractor and set of compasses

- use scale drawings

19.01 Using a protractor

You should be able to use a ruler to draw and measure lines to a specific length and also to construct and measure angles using a protractor. Take care, however, to read the correct scale on a protractor. This is how to draw an angle of 26°.

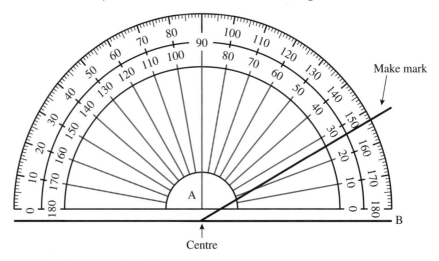

Fig. 19.01 Drawing an angle with a protractor

Looking at Figure 19.01, first we draw the base line AB (size not important).

Place the centre of the protractor on one end of the line (point A), lining up the zero of the protractor with line AB.

As the zero is on the inside scale, read in an anticlockwise direction until you reach 26° on the inside scale. At this point, make a mark.

Remove the protractor, and draw a straight line from point A through this mark.

19.02 Constructing a triangle using ruler and compasses

We'll construct the triangle shown in Figure 19.02.

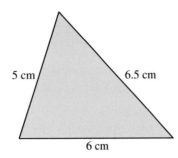

Fig. 19.02 Triangle to construct

Step 1
Draw the base of the triangle using a ruler and a pencil (6 cm).

Step 2
1. Choose another side, e.g. 6.5 cm. Set the compasses to 6.5 cm (Figure 19.03a) and draw an arc above the base of the triangle.
2. Set the compasses to 5 cm and draw an arc above the base from the other end (Figure 19.03b).
3. Join the point of intersection to the two ends of the base line (Figure 19.03c).

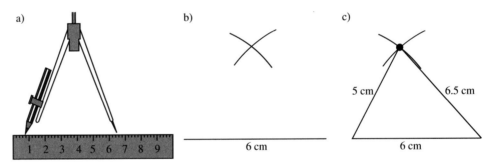

Fig. 19.03 Constructing a triangle

The construction of other simple geometrical figures will be similar. Always choose a base line to start from. If you are given angles to draw, use a protractor unless they are 90° angles, in which case you could use compasses again (see Section 19.03 below).

Progress check

19.01 Construct, using a ruler and compasses, a triangle of lengths 7 cm, 8 cm and 9 cm. Show all construction arcs.

19.03 Constructing angle bisectors

Bisect means cut in half. First draw the angle using a protractor, then follow these steps.

Step 1
With compass set to any value, place the point at the corner of the angle and draw arc so that it cuts both lines (Figure 19.04a).

Step 2
Keeping the compasses at the same setting, put the point of the compasses on the previous arc cuts and draw two more arcs in the centre of the angle (Figure 19.04b).

Step 3
Draw the line from the corner of the angle to where the arcs cross (Figure 19.04c).

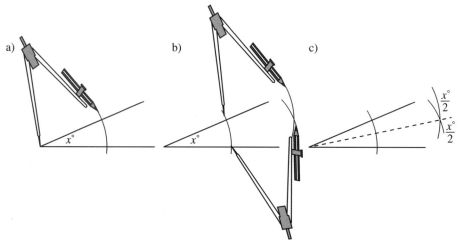

Fig. 19.04 Bisecting an angle

Progress check

19.02 Using a protractor, draw an angle of 55°. Bisect the angle using a pair of compasses.

19.04 Constructing perpendicular bisectors

A perpendicular bisector is a line which crosses another line at 90°, cutting it in half. Use the following steps, as shown in Figure 19.05.

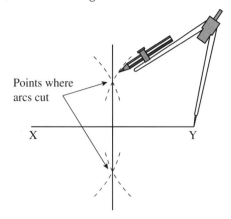

Points where arcs cut

X   Y

Fig. 19.05 Constructing a perpendicular bisector

Step 1
Draw the line you are going to bisect (XY).

Step 2
Set the compasses to approximately three quarters of the length of XY.

Step 3
Place the point of the compasses on one end of the line, e.g. point X. Draw an arc above and below XY.

Step 4
Without changing the compasses' setting, place the point of the compasses on the other end (point Y). Draw an arc above and below XY to cut the previous arcs.

Step 5
Join up the two points where the arcs cross.

Progress check

19.03 Draw a line AB, 8 cm long. Construct the perpendicular bisector of this line using a pair of compasses.

19.05 Scale drawings

Drawings are made to scale to show accurate representations of larger or smaller images at a manageable size. When you are presented with a scale drawing you are given the scale used and from this you can make accurate calculations. Unit 5 explains how to calculate real lengths from scaled lengths and vice versa. When you have the lengths, it is a simple case of drawing using the techniques covered in this unit.

19.06 Drawing squares and rectangles

Only 90° angles and straight lines are used to draw squares and rectangles, which means that these can be constructed with a ruler and a set of compasses or even a set square.

19.01 Worked example

Use a set square and a ruler to draw a rectangle with edge lengths of 4 cm and 3 cm.

First use a ruler to draw a line, AB, 4 cm long.
Then place the edge of the set square along the line AB so that the edge of the rectangle will start at point A, as shown in Figure 19.06.

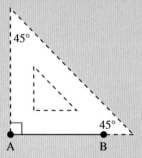

Fig. 19.06 Using a set square

From A, draw a line along the edge of the set square. Mark a point C on this line 3 cm from A.
Repeat at point B to reach a point D.
Join C to D with a ruler to complete the rectangle, as shown in Figure 19.07.
Measure the length of CD as a check.

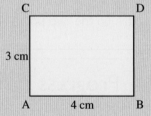

Fig. 19.07 The completed rectangle

19.02 Worked example

Construct the shape shown in Figure 19.08, using a ruler, set square and compasses.

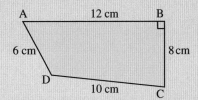

Fig. 19.08 Shape to construct

Draw line AB of length 12 cm with the ruler, ensuring that enough space is left below it.

Construct the 90° angle at B using the set square and drawing a line of 8 cm to point C.

From point C, set the compasses to 10 cm and draw an arc to the left of the shape.

From point A, set the compasses to 6 cm and draw an arc to intersect the previous arc. This will be point D (see Figure 19.09).

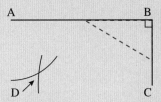

Fig. 19.09 Constructing the shape

Join A to D and D to C. Check that the dimensions are correct.

Progress check

19.04 Construct the following shape, using a ruler, set square and compasses:

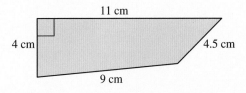

Exam-style questions

19.01 Construct, using a ruler and compasses, a triangle of lengths 5 cm, 4 cm and 7 cm. Show all construction arcs.

19.02 Using a protractor, draw an angle of 120°. Bisect the angle using a pair of compasses.

19.03 Draw a line XY, 7 cm long. Construct the perpendicular bisector of this line using a pair of compasses.

19.04 Construct the following shape, using a ruler, set square and compasses:

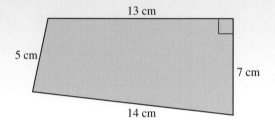

Symmetry

Learning outcomes

By the end of this unit you should be able to understand and use:

■ rotational and line symmetry (including order of rotational symmetry) in two dimensions

■ symmetry properties of triangles, quadrilaterals and circles

Symmetry means 'reflection', i.e. an image that is identical to the original object.

There are two main types of symmetry:

• line symmetry
• rotational symmetry.

20.01 Line symmetry

Line symmetry is also called reflection symmetry. Look at the equilateral triangle in Figure 20.01.

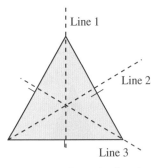

Fig. 20.01 Reflection symmetry in an equilateral triangle

This shape has three lines of symmetry, in lines 1, 2 and 3. Either side of each line, the reflection is identical, in this case a right-angled triangle.

Different shapes have different numbers of lines of symmetry. For example, a circle has an infinite number of lines of symmetry, while a square has four lines of symmetry.

20.02 Rotational symmetry

Many shapes can be rotated about their centre and still fit their original outline. The rectangle in Figure 20.02 illustrates this.

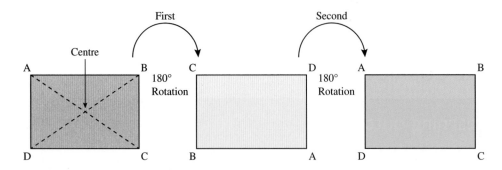

Fig. 20.02 Rotational symmetry of a rectangle

The first rotation is 180° clockwise and the image is identical although the corners have changed position. The second rotation is another 180° clockwise rotation, back to the original position. We can say that the rectangle has **rotational symmetry of order 2**.

Only shapes with **order 2 or greater** are classed as having rotational symmetry (a 360° turn only is not sufficient).

20.03 Triangles and quadrilaterals

We have already shown that an equilateral triangle has three lines of symmetry, and looking at Figure 20.01 we can see that it also has rotational symmetry of order 3. Any regular polygon has line symmetry equal to its rotational symmetry. For example, a regular pentagon has five lines of symmetry and also rotational symmetry of order 5.

Now we can consider the basic triangles and quadrilaterals and their respective symmetries.

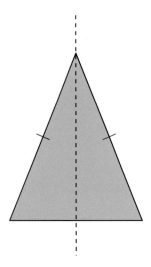

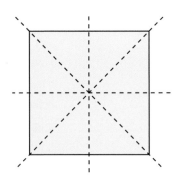

Fig. 20.03 Isosceles triangle: line symmetry = 1, no rotational symmetry

Fig. 20.04 Square: line symmetry = 4, rotational symmetry of order 4

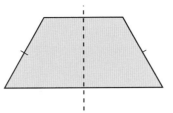

Fig. 20.05 Isosceles trapezium: line symmetry = 1, no rotational symmetry

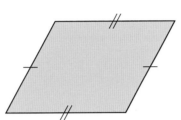

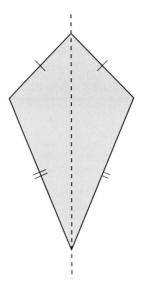

Fig. 20.06 Parallelogram: No line symmetry, rotational symmetry of order 2

Fig. 20.07 Kite: line symmetry = 1, no rotational symmetry

When you look at the shapes you can quickly see whether or not they are symmetrical. Sometimes, however, it is easier to trace the shape first and then practise folding it over to see if there are lines of symmetry. You can rotate it about its centre to check for rotational symmetry.

Remember the basic rules when describing a shape's symmetry:

- A **line of symmetry** is a mirror line that seems to cut the shape into identical halves when drawn.
- **Rotational symmetry** is the number of times a shape can be rotated about its centre and still look the same.
- All shapes have a rotational symmetry of at least 1, i.e. they can all make a full turn.
- For **regular shapes** (identical sides, identical angles), line symmetry = order of rotation symmetry.

Progress check

20.01 Describe fully the symmetry of the following shapes:

    a a circle   b a regular heptagon   c an isosceles trapezium

20.02 Draw a shape with no line symmetry but rotational symmetry of order 3.

20.03 Describe fully the symmetry of the following shapes:

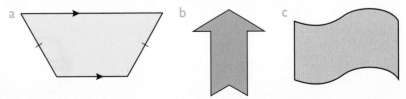

20.04 Draw a hexagon with just two lines of symmetry.

- **Line symmetry**
  A mirror line through the centre of the shape.

- **Rotation symmetry**
  Number of times a shape can be rotated about its centre and still look the same.

- **Regular shapes**
  Shapes with all sides equal and all angles equal.

Exam-style questions

20.01 Describe fully the symmetry of the following shapes:

   a a parallelogram   b a regular octagon   c a rhombus

20.02 Draw a shape with no line symmetry but rotation symmetry of order 4.

20.03 Describe fully the symmetry of the following shapes:

   a 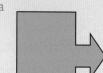   b 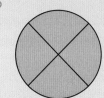   c

20.04 Write down the order of rotational symmetry of the diagram below.

Source: Cambridge IGCSE Mathematics 0580 Paper 1 Q2 November 2008.

20.05 a Draw the lines of symmetry on the two letters below.

   b Write down the order of rotational symmetry for each of the figures below.

Source: Cambridge IGCSE Mathematics 0580 Paper 1 Q20a, b November 2006.

EXTENDED CURRICULUM

20.04 Symmetry properties of prisms, cylinders, pyramids and cones

A solid has **plane symmetry** if it can be cut into two halves and each half is the mirror image of the other. The plane separating the two halves is called the plane of symmetry.

The following figures show the basic shapes with their **planes of symmetry**.

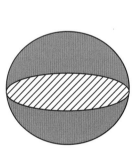

Figure 20.08 Sphere: infinite number of planes of symmetry

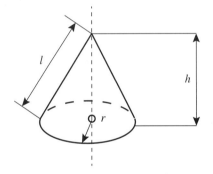

Fig. 20.09 Cone: infinite planes of symmetry through the centre

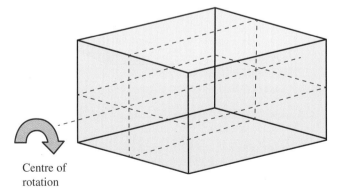

Centre of rotation

Fig. 20.10 Cuboid: three planes of symmetry

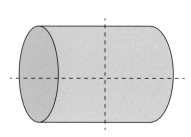

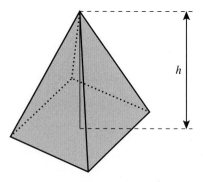

Fig. 20.11 Cylinder: infinite planes of symmetry

Fig. 20.12 Pyramid: four planes of symmetry through the centre

The shapes above also have rotational symmetry because when they are rotated about a central axis, they look the same. For example, the sphere has an infinite order of rotational symmetry, the cuboid has rotational symmetry of order 4 and the pyramid also has rotational symmetry of order 4 (because it has a square base). The cone and the cylinder have an infinite order of rotation symmetry.

Progress check

20.05 Draw and name a shape with:

    a two planes of symmetry   b four planes of symmetry.

20.06 Describe the symmetry of:

    a a cylinder   b a cone.

20.07 For each of the solid shapes below determine the order of rotation symmetry about the axis shown.

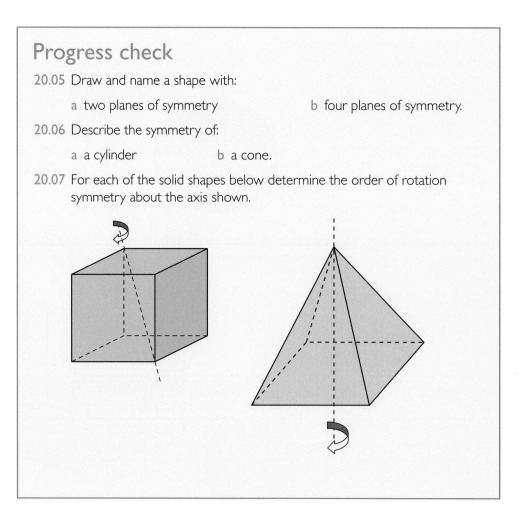

20.05 Equal chords and perpendicular bisectors

In the diagram of a circle in Figure 20.13, chords AB and XY are equal. Radii OA, OB, OX and OY are equal, so the triangles OAB and OXY are congruent isosceles triangles. Therefore,

line of symmetry OM = line of symmetry ON

So we can say that OM and ON are perpendicular bisectors of AB and XY, respectively.

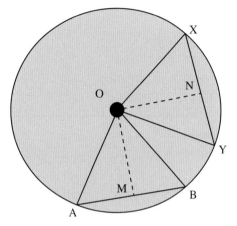

Fig. 20.13 Equal chords and perpendicular bisectors

20.06 Tangents from an external point

Triangles OAC and OBC are congruent because the angles at A and B are both right angles (OA = OB and OC is common to both triangles). Since OC is common to both triangles,

tangent AC = tangent BC

In other words, tangents drawn to the same circle from the same external point are equal in length.

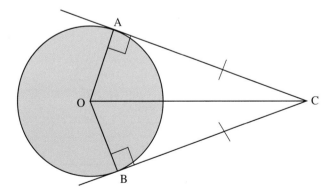

Fig. 20.14 Tangents to a circle from an external point

Progress check

20.08 In the diagram below O is the centre of the circle, WX and YZ are equal chords and the points A and B are their midpoints, respectively.

State whether the statements below are true or false, giving reasons for your answers.

a $\angle YOZ = 2 \times \angle WOA$

b $OA = OB$

c OA and OB are perpendicular bisectors of AB and CD, respectively.

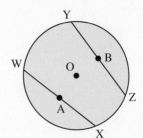

TERMS

• Plane of symmetry
A plane separating a solid shape into two halves.

• Chord
A line connecting two points on the circumference of a circle.

• Perpendicular (lines)
Lines which are at right angles to each other.

• Tangent
A line that touches an arc, or circumference, of a circle.

Exam-style questions

20.06 Draw and name a shape with:

a infinite planes of symmetry   b 9 planes of symmetry.

20.07 Describe the plane symmetry of:

a a cuboid (3 cm × 2 cm × 4 cm)   b a regular tetrahedron.

20.08 For each of the solid shapes below determine the order of rotational symmetry about the axis shown.

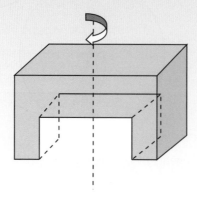
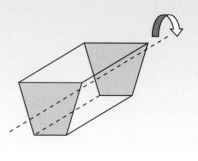

20.09 **a** On the diagram below, sketch one of the **planes** of symmetry of the cuboid.

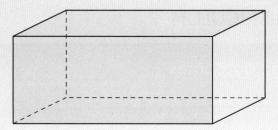

b Write down the order of rotational symmetry of the equilateral triangular prism about the axis shown.

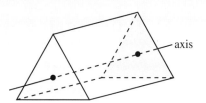

Source: *Cambridge IGCSE Mathematics 0580 Paper 2 Q21b, c June 2006.*

Angle properties

CORE CURRICULUM

Learning outcomes

At the end of this unit you should be able to

- ☐ calculate unknown angles at a point and in parallel lines

- ☐ calculate unknown angles in shapes and circles

21.01 Angles at a point

Angles at a point add up to 360°. Using this rule we can calculate a missing angle by subtracting the remaining angles from 360°.

21.01 Worked example

Find the angle x in Figure 21.01.

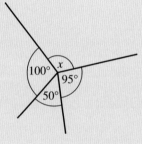

Fig. 21.01 Find x

The angles at a point add up to 360°, so

$x = 360 - 100 - 95 - 50$

$x = 115°$

21.02 Angles within parallel lines

Angles within parallel lines (see Figure 21.02) follow certain rules.

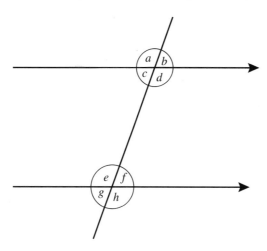

$a + b = 180°$ adjacent angles

Fig. 21.02 Angles within parallel lines

$\left.\begin{array}{l} a = d \\ b = c \\ e = h \\ g = f \end{array}\right\}$ vertically opposite angles

$\left.\begin{array}{l} c = f \\ d = e \end{array}\right\}$ alternate angles

$\left.\begin{array}{l} c + e = 180° \\ d + f = 180° \end{array}\right\}$ supplementary angles

$\left.\begin{array}{l} a = e \\ b = f \end{array}\right\}$ corresponding angles

21.02 Worked example

Find the unknown angles in Figure 21.03.

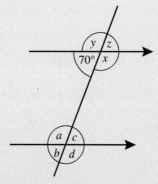

Fig. 21.03 Find the unknown angles

$x = 180° - 70° = 110°$
(angles on a straight line)

$y = 110°$
(y is vertically opposite x)

$z = 70°$
(z is vertically opposite 70°)

$a = 180° - 70° = 110°$
(a is supplementary to 70°)

$b = 70°$
(a and b are angles on a straight line)

$c = 70°$ and $d = 110°$
(similar reasons to above)

21.03 Angle properties of triangles

A triangle has three sides and the sum of its angles is 180° (see Figure 21.04).

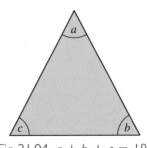

Fig. 21.04 $a + b + c = 180°$

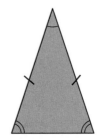

Fig. 21.05 Isosceles triangle: two equal base angles, two equal sides

The different types of triangle are shown in the following figures.

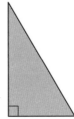

Fig. 21.06 Right-angled triangle: contains a right angle

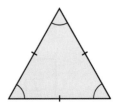

Fig. 21.07 Equilateral triangle: all angles equal, all sides equal

21.04 Angle properties of quadrilaterals

A quadrilateral has four sides and its angles add up to 360° (see Figure 21.08).

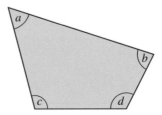

Fig. 21.08 $a + b + c + d = 360°$

The following figures show some special quadrilaterals, together with their properties.

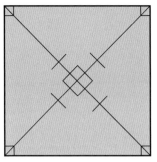

Fig. 21.09 Square

Properties of a square

1 All angles equal 90°.
2 Opposite sides are parallel.
3 All sides are equal.
4 Diagonals are equal in length and bisect each other at right angles.

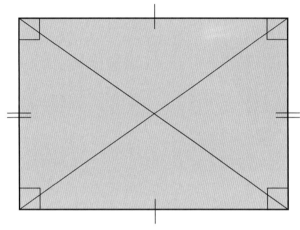

Fig. 21.10 Rectangle

Properties of a rectangle

1 All angles equal 90°.
2 Opposite sides are parallel.
3 Opposite sides are equal.
4 Diagonals are equal in length and bisect each other.

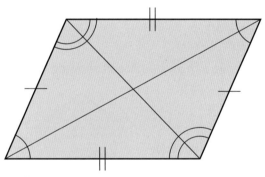

Fig. 21.11 Parallelogram

Properties of a parallelogram

1 Opposite sides are parallel.
2 Opposite sides are equal.
3 Opposite angles are equal.
4 Diagonals bisect each other.

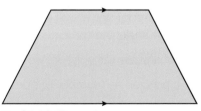

Fig. 21.12 Trapezium

Properties of a trapezium

1 One pair of opposite parallel sides.

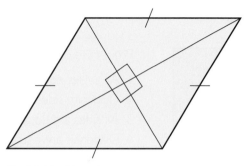

Fig. 21.13 Rhombus

Properties of a rhombus

1 Opposite sides are equal.
2 Opposite sides are parallel.
3 Opposite angles are equal.
4 Diagonals cross at right angles.
5 Diagonals bisect each other.

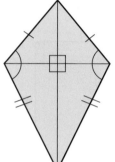

Fig. 21.14 Kite

Properties of a kite

1 Adjacent sides are equal.
2 One pair of opposite angles is equal.
3 Diagonals cross at right angles.
4 One diagonal is bisected.

21.05 Angle properties of regular polygons

A polygon is a closed shape with straight sides. There are two types:

- A regular polygon has all sides equal and all angles equal.
- An irregular polygon has at least one side a different size from the others and at least one angle unequal.

Figure 21.15 shows a regular pentagon, showing its interior and exterior angles.

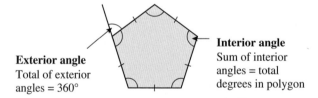

Exterior angle
Total of exterior angles = 360°

Interior angle
Sum of interior angles = total degrees in polygon

Fig. 21.15 A regular pentagon: interior angle + exterior angle = 180°

For any regular polygon, the interior angles will be equal and the exterior angles will be equal. The sum of the interior angle and the exterior angle is 180°.

To find the total degrees of any regular polygon, we can use the formula:

total degrees in a polygon = (number of sides − 2) × 180°

i.e. $t = (n − 2) \times 180°$

The common polygons have special names and angle properties. We have to know their names but we can use the rules above to find their angle properties.

21.03 Worked example

Find the total degrees, the interior angle and the exterior angle of a regular eight-sided polygon.

Using the formula for total degrees,
$t = (n - 2) \times 180°$
$t = (8 - 2) \times 180°$
$t = 1080°$

Interior angle = total degrees ÷ number of sides
$= 1080° ÷ 8$
$= 135°$

Exterior angle = $180°$ − interior angle
$= 180° - 135°$
$= 45°$

Alternatively, the exterior angle can be found by using the following formula:

$$\text{exterior angle} = \frac{360}{\text{number of sides}}$$

If we apply these steps to the most common polygons we obtain the numbers given in Table 21.01.

Table 21.01 Angle properties of regular polygons

Number of sides	Name	Total degrees	Interior angle
3	Triangle	180	60
4	Quadrilateral	360	90
5	Pentagon	540	108
6	Hexagon	720	120
7	Heptagon	900	128.57…
8	Octagon	1080	135
9	Nonagon	1260	140
10	Decagon	1440	144
11	Hendecagon	1620	147.27…
12	Dodecagon	1800	150

Remember that a regular triangle is an equilateral triangle and a regular quadrilateral is a square.

21.06 Angle in a semicircle

Any triangle using the diameter of a circle as its longest side is a right-angled triangle (see Figure 21.16).

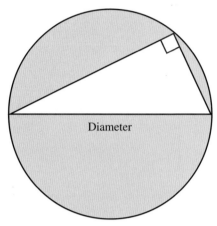

Fig. 21.16 Angle in a semicircle

21.07 Angle between tangent and radius of a circle

A tangent is a straight line that just touches the circumference of a circle. The circle in Figure 21.17 has two tangents at its circumference.

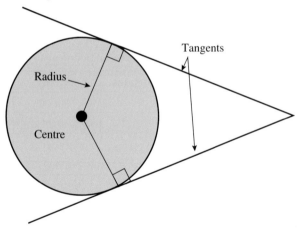

Fig. 21.17 Tangents to a circle

The angle formed between the tangent and the radius of a circle is 90°.

Progress check

21.01 For the following diagrams, calculate the value of the missing letters:

a

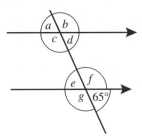

b

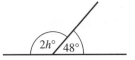

c

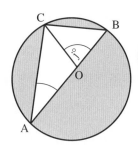

AOB is the diameter of the circle, OC and OB are radii.

21.02 Find the size of each exterior angle of the following regular polygons:

a a pentagon   b a decagon   c a heptagon

21.03 Calculate the number of sides a regular polygon has if an interior angle is five times the size of an exterior angle.

21.04 The interior angles of a quadrilateral are x, $2x$, $2x + 40$ and $3x + 80$ degrees. Find the value of x.

Exam-style questions

21.01 The interior angles of a pentagon increase by 10° as you progress anticlockwise.

    a Write an expression for the sum of the interior angles.
    b Find the value of each interior angle.
    c Calculate the largest exterior angle.
    d Show that the sum of the exterior angles is 360°.

21.02 The three angles in a triangle are in the ratio $1 : 3 : 5$. Find them.

21.03 The interior angles in a quadrilateral are $4x + 30, 3x + 10, 3x$ and $2x + 20$ degrees. Find the value of each angle.

21.04 a A triangle using the diameter AB as its longest side meets the circumference of the circle at C. Find angle B and the length of BC.

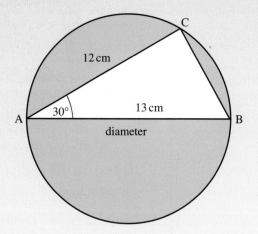

    b Two tangents meet a circle at A and B. Find the values of angles x, y, z.

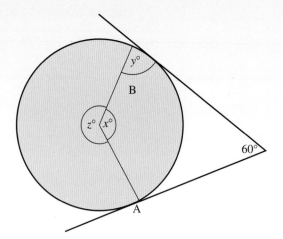

21.08 Angle properties of irregular polygons

Although irregular polygons do not have all equal angles or all equal sides, the interior and exterior angles still sum to 180°.

21.04 Worked example

For the polygon in Figure 21.18, find the sum of the interior angles and the size of angle x.

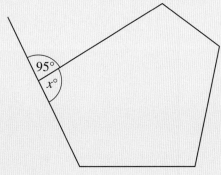

Fig. 21.18 Irregular polygon

The polygon in the diagram has five sides, so it is an irregular pentagon.
Using the formula to find the angle sum:

$t = (n - 2) \times 180°$

$t = (5 - 2) \times 180°$

$t = 540°$

To find x, we know that interior angle + exterior angle = 180°, so:

$x = 180 - 95$

$x = 85°$

Note that we are not able to calculate the other four angles without more information, but we know that the sum of the remaining four angles is $540 - 85 = 455°$.

The permutations for this type of question are endless; just remember the three basic formulae:

- $t = (n - 2) \times 180°$
- Interior angle + exterior angle = 180°
- Sum of exterior angles = 360°

21.09 Angle at the centre of a circle is twice the angle at the circumference

If the angle on the circumference is *x* degrees then the angle at the centre will be 2*x* degrees – see Figure 21.19 for examples.

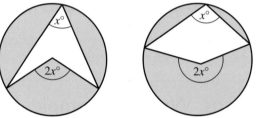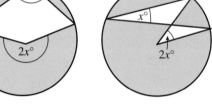

Fig. 21.19 Angles at the centre and circumference

21.05 Worked example

Find the values of *x* and *y* in Figure 21.20.

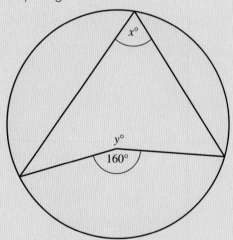

Fig. 21.20 Find *x* and *y*

The angle at the centre is twice the value of the angle at the circumference.

So *x* = 160° ÷ 2 = 80°

y = 360° − 160° = 200° (angles at a point)

21.10 Angles in the same segment are equal

A segment is a part of a circle. The large part is called the **major segment** and the smaller part the **minor segment** (see Figure 21.21).

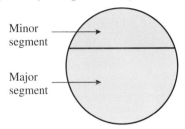

Fig. 21.21 Major and minor segments

Angles in the same segment are equal (see Figure 21.22).

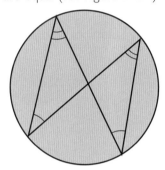

Fig. 21.22 Angles in the same segment

Note that two triangles are formed and that they are similar to each other – all the angles in one triangle are equal to the angles in the other triangle.

21.11 Angles in opposite segments are supplementary

Remember that supplementary angles add up to 180°. Looking at Figure 21.23, angles x and y are opposite to each other and are supplementary:

$x + y = 180°$

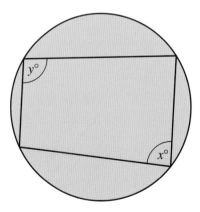

Fig. 21.23 Angles in opposite segments

The same will be true for the other two opposite angles. Note that we can also say that the opposite angles of a cyclic quadrilateral are supplementary.

Progress check

21.05 Find the values of the letters in each of the diagrams below. (Assume the point marked O is the centre of the circle.)

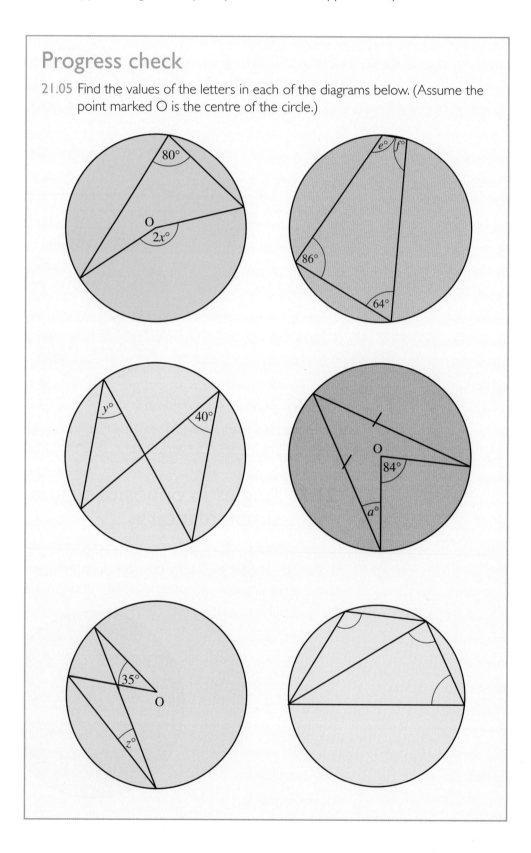

• Supplementary
  Angles that add up to 180°.

• Chord
  A line joining one point of a circle's
  circumference to another point.

• Segment
  A part of a circle separated by a chord.

• Irregular (polygon)
  At least one angle or side is different from the
  others.

Exam-style questions

21.05 *AD* is a diameter of the circle *ABCDE*. Angle *BAC* = 22° and angle *ADC* = 60°.
AB and *ED* are parallel lines. Find the values of *w, x, y* and *z*.

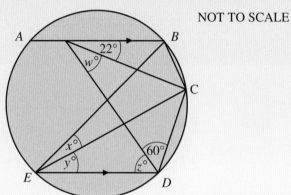

NOT TO SCALE

Source: Cambridge IGCSE Mathematics 0580 Paper 2 Q18 June 2006.

21.06 *A, B, C* and *D* lie on a circle, centre *O*. *SCT* is the tangent at *C* and is parallel
to *OB*. Angle *AOB* = 130°, and angle *BCT* = 40°. Angle *OBC* = *x*°, angle
OBA = *y*° and angle *ADC* = *z*°.

i   Write down the geometrical word which completes the following
statement.
    '*ABCD* is a _____ quadrilateral'.
ii Find the value of *x, y* and *z*.
iii Write down the value of angle *OCT*.
iv Find the value of **reflex** angle *AOC*.

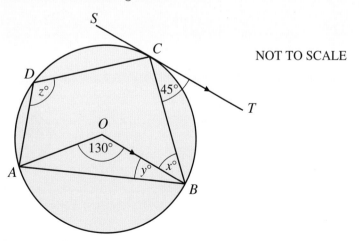

NOT TO SCALE

Source: Cambridge IGCSE Mathematics 0580 Paper 4 Q7a (i) to (iv) June 2008.

Locus

CORE CURRICULUM

Learning outcomes

By the end of this unit you should be able to construct, using compasses and rulers:

- loci which are a given distance from a fixed point
- loci which are a given distance from a straight line
- loci which are equidistant from two fixed points
- loci which are equidistant from two intersecting straight lines

A **locus** is the path traced by a moving object. The plural of locus is **loci**.

There are four types we need to examine.

22.01 Loci which are at a given distance from a fixed point

An object moving at a fixed distance from a fixed point will always follow a **circular** path.

22.01 Worked example

Draw the locus of a point P which is always 3 cm from a fixed point X.

First mark point X on the paper, allowing at least 3 cm space around it.

Make a string of length 3 cm. Holding one end in place at point X, place a pencil at the other end and draw all the points around X which are 3 cm away.

Label the locus of points P (see Figure 22.01).

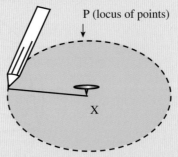

Fig. 22.01 Locus at a given distance from a fixed point

Alternatively, we could have used compasses set to 3 cm and drawn a circle around X.

22.02 Loci which are at a given distance from a straight line

The locus of points at a fixed distance from a line is two parallel lines, one on either side of the line.

22.02 Worked example

Draw the locus of points P which are 2 cm from a straight line XY.

First we draw two parallel lines 2 cm either side of the fixed straight line XY.

Then, using compasses set to 2 cm, at each end of the line draw a 2 cm semicircle.

Join the parallel lines to the compass-drawn loci to give the final locus as in Figure 22.02.

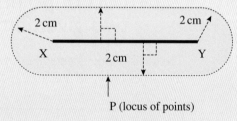

Fig. 22.02 Locus at a fixed distance from a line

22.03 Loci which are equidistant from two fixed points

The easiest way to draw the locus of points which are an equal distance from two fixed points is to use a set of compasses. Draw a line connecting the two fixed points, then construct the perpendicular bisector of the line.

22.03 Worked example

Draw the locus of points P which are equidistant from two fixed points X and Y.

First join points X and Y.

Construct the perpendicular bisector of this line.

This perpendicular bisector is now the locus of points which are equidistant from points X and Y (see Figure 22.03).

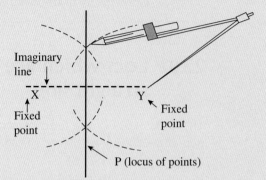

Fig. 22.03 Locus at a fixed distance from two points

Progress check

22.02 Draw a line XY of length 10 cm. Construct the locus of a point which is equidistant from X and Y.

22.04 Loci of points which are equidistant from two given intersecting straight lines

The locus of points equidistant from two intersecting straight lines is the bisector of the angles between the lines.

22.04 Worked example

Draw the locus of points P which are equidistant from two intersecting straight lines AB and XY.

First bisect the angle between the two lines AB and XY (see Unit 19).

The angle bisector is the locus of points which are equidistant from the two intersecting lines (see Figure 22.04).

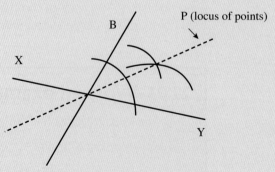

Fig. 22.04 Locus equidistant from two intersecting lines

22.05 Summary

- For loci of points from a fixed point X, use compasses at the required setting and draw a circle around X.
- For loci of points from a straight line XY, draw parallel lines either side of XY and use compasses for arcs around X and Y.
- For loci of points from two fixed points X and Y, draw the perpendicular bisector of X and Y.
- For loci of points from two intersecting straight lines AB and XY, draw the bisector of the angles between AB and XY.

Progress check

22.03 Lines AB and CD are both 8 cm in length and intersect at a right angle. Draw the locus of points which are equidistant from lines AB and CD.

22.04 Treasure is buried in a rectangular garden measuring 5 m by 8 m. The treasure is within 1 m of each corner and nearer to the longer side than the shorter side. Using construction techniques, shade the locus of points which may contain the treasure.

22.05 Describe in words the locus of W, the tip of the minute hand of a clock as the time changes from 5 p.m. to 6 p.m.

TERMS

- **Locus**
  The path traced by a moving object.

- **Equidistant**
  A point or points that are equal distance from either side.

- **Intersector**
  A line that cuts across another line.

- **Bisector**
  A line that cuts an angle or another line in half.

Exam-style questions

22.01 Tarek and Miriam were visiting Cairo for the day. While trying to find the museum of Antiques, Miriam found herself lost and couldn't find Tarek. Using a GPS tracking app on her phone, Miriam located Tarek's mobile. From the strength of the signal received at points A and B, Miriam knows that Tarek is:

a   not more than 50 m from A

b   no more than 30 m for B

Make a scale drawing and show the possible positions of Tarek.

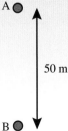

22.02 A rectangular garden measures 8 m by 5 m. Draw a scale diagram of the garden and identify the locus of the points which are:

a   at least 1 m from the edge of the garden

b   more than 3 m from the centre of the garden.

22.03 The quadrilateral *ABCD* is a scale drawing of a park. Angle *ABC* = 90° and 1 centimetre represents 10 metres.

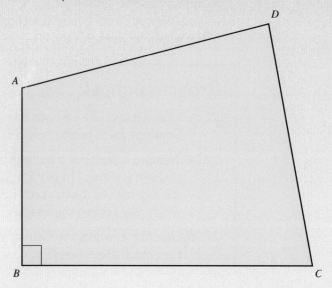

Write down:

a   Write down
  i   the actual length, in metres, of the side *CD*,
  ii   the size of angle *BAD*.
b   Two straight paths cross the park. One path is the same distance from *AB* as from *BC*. The other path is the same distance from *A* as from *D*.
  i   Using a straight edge and compasses only, construct the lines which show each path.
  ii   Tennis courts in the park are situated in a region closer to *AB* than to *BC* and closer to *A* than to *D*. Label this region *T*.

Source: Cambridge IGCSE Mathematics 0580 Paper 3 Q9 a (I, ii), b (I, ii) June 2008.

22.04 Sitora has two plants in her school classroom. Plant A needs a lot of light and must not be more than 2.5 metres from the window. Plant B needs very little light and must be further from the window than from the door. For each plant, draw accurately the boundary of the region in which it can be placed. In the diagram, 1 centimetre represents 1 metre.

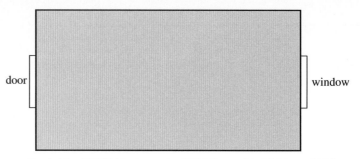

Source: Cambridge IGCSE Mathematics 0580 Paper 21 Q14 June 2008.

Mensuration

CORE CURRICULUM

Learning outcomes

By the end of this unit you should be able to understand and calculate:

- the perimeter and area of a rectangle, triangle, parallelogram and trapezium
- the circumference and area of a circle
- the volume of a cuboid, prism and cylinder
- the surface area of a cuboid and a cylinder

23.01 Perimeter and area of a rectangle and a triangle

The formulae for the area and perimeter are shown below.

Fig. 23.01 Rectangle

From Figure 23.01:

$$\text{Area} = \text{length} \times \text{width} = l \times w$$
$$\text{Perimeter} = 2l + 2w$$

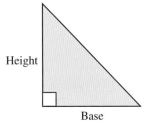

Fig. 23.02 Triangle

From Figure 23.02:

$$\text{Area} = \frac{\text{base} \times \text{height}}{2} = \frac{b \times h}{2}$$
$$\text{Perimeter} = \text{sum of lengths of the three sides}$$

23.01 Worked example

Find the area and perimeter of the following shapes:

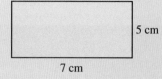

a

5 cm

7 cm

b

6 cm

10.8 cm

9 cm

a	Area	$= \text{length} \times \text{width} = 7\,\text{cm} \times 5\,\text{cm} = 35\,\text{cm}^2$
	Perimeter	$= 2l + 2w = 2(7) + 2(5) = 24\,\text{cm}$
b	Area	$= \dfrac{\text{base} \times \text{height}}{2} = \dfrac{9\,\text{cm} \times 6\,\text{cm}}{2} = 27\,\text{cm}^2$
	Perimeter	$= \text{sum of three sides} = 6\,\text{cm} + 9\,\text{cm} + 10.8\,\text{cm} = 25.8\,\text{cm}$

23.02 Circumference and area of a circle

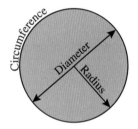

Circumference

Diameter

Radius

Fig. 23.03 Circle

From Figure 23.03:

Circumference = distance around the circle
Diameter = distance across the centre
Radius = distance from centre to any point on the circumference
Area of circle $= \pi r^2$, where $\pi = 3.1415\ldots$, r = radius
Circumference of circle $= 2\pi r$ or πd, where d = diameter

23.02 Worked example

Find the area and circumference of a circle with a diameter of 8 cm.

Substituting into the above formulae (note that we need to halve the diameter to get the radius):

Area $= \pi r^2 = 3.142 \times 4^2 = 3.142 \times 16 = 50.28\,\text{cm}^2$

Circumference $= 2\pi r = 2 \times 3.142 \times 4 = 25.14\,\text{cm}$

Note that to find the area of a semicircle with a diameter of 8 cm, halve the answer above.

23.03 Area of a parallelogram and a trapezium

The formulae for the areas of these shapes are shown below.

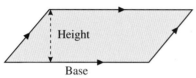

Fig. 23.04 Parallelogram

From Figure 23.04:

Area = base × height

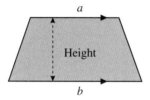

Fig. 23.05 Trapezium

From Figure 23.05:

$$\text{Area} = \frac{a+b}{2} \times \text{height} = \frac{\text{sum of parallel sides}}{2} \times \text{height}$$

23.03 Worked example

Find the area of the two shapes below:

a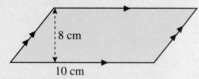

b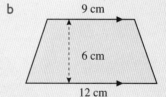

a Area = base × height = 10 cm × 8 cm = 80 cm²

b Area = $\frac{a+b}{2}$ × height = $\frac{9+12}{2}$ × 6 = 10.5 × 6 = 63 cm²

203

Progress check

23.03 The semi-circle has a diameter of 8 cm, the trapezium has parallel sides of 8 cm and 12 cm, and the parallelogram has a perpendicular height of 7 cm. Find the total area of the combined shapes.

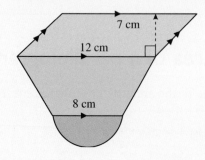

23.04 Volume and surface area of a cuboid, prism and cylinder

A prism is a solid with a constant cross-section. The following are the important prisms.

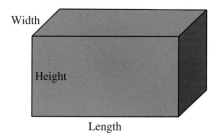

Fig. 23.06 Cuboid

A **cuboid** is a prism with a rectangular base. An example would be a block of wood. From Figure 23.06:

Volume = length × width × height
Surface area = total area of all six faces

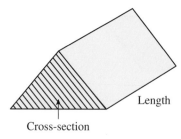

Fig. 23.07 Triangular prism

The solid in Figure 23.07 has a triangular cross-section, so it is a **triangular prism**.

Volume = area of cross-section × length
Surface area = 2(area of cross-section) + area of other faces

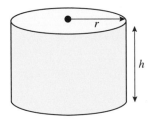

Fig. 23.08 Cylinder

A **cylinder** is a prism with a circular cross-section. An example would be a drinks can. From Figure 23.08:

$$\text{Volume} = \pi r^2 h$$
$$\text{Surface area} = 2\pi r(h + r)$$

We will now look at a few examples using the shapes mentioned.

23.04 Worked example

Figure 23.09 shows the cross-section of a metal bar. If it is 12 cm long, find its volume.

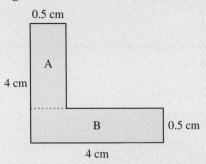

Fig. 23.09 Cross-section of a metal bar

First, split the shape into two rectangles (see dotted line), then calculate the areas of each and add them to get the area of the cross-section.

Area A = 3.5 cm × 0.5 cm = 1.75 cm²
Area B = 4 cm × 0.5 cm = 2 cm²
Total area = 3.75 cm²

Volume = area of cross-section × length = 3.75 cm² × 12 = 45 cm³

23.05 Worked example

Find the total surface area of the cuboid in Figure 23.10.

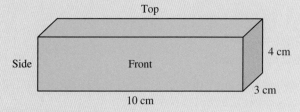

Fig. 23.10 Cuboid

The cuboid has six faces, so we need to find the area of each and add them.

The front face and the hidden opposite face are each 10 cm by 4 cm rectangles.
The top and bottom faces are each 10 cm by 3 cm rectangles.
The side faces are each 4 cm by 3 cm rectangles.

Area of front face = 10 cm × 4 cm = 40 cm²
Area of top face = 10 cm × 3 cm = 30 cm²
Area of side face = 4 cm × 3 cm = 12 cm²

So total surface area = 40 × 2 + 30 × 2 + 12 × 2 = 80 + 60 + 24 = 164 cm²

Progress check

23.04 Find the surface area and volume of the following shapes:

a

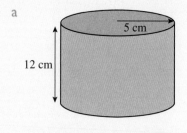

b

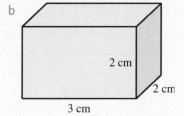

c

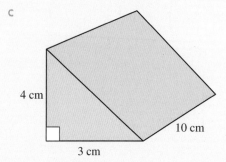

- Perimeter
  Distance around the outside of a shape.

- Area
  Surface covered by a shape.

- Volume
  Total amount of space inside a shape (also known as capacity).

- Prism
  A three-dimensional shape with a constant cross-section, e.g. a cuboid.

- Surface area
  Total area of all surfaces added together.

Exam-style questions

23.01 Find the area and circumference of a circle with radius 5 cm.

23.02 Find the surface area and volume of the following shapes:

a

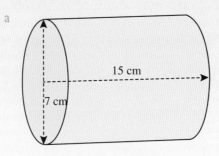

15 cm

7 cm

b

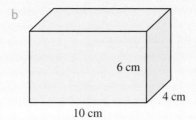

6 cm

4 cm

10 cm

c

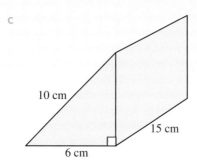

10 cm

15 cm

6 cm

23.03 The area of a square is 55.25 cm². Work out the length of one side of the square.

23.04 a Calculate the volume of a cylinder of radius 50 cm and height 138 cm.
      b Write your answer to **part (a)** in cubic metres.
      Source: Cambridge IGCSE Mathematics 0580 Paper 1 Q18a, b November 2008.

23.05

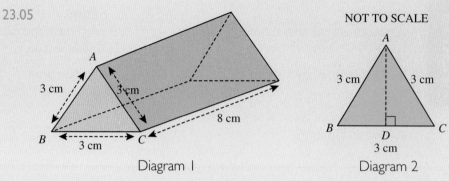

NOT TO SCALE

Diagram 1   Diagram 2

A physics teacher uses a set of identical triangular glass prisms in a lesson. Diagram 1 shows one of the prisms. Diagram 2 shows the cross-section of one prism. The triangle ABC is equilateral, with sides of length 3 cm and height AD.

a **Calculate** the length AD.
b **Calculate** the area of triangle ABC.
c The length of the prism is 8 cm. Calculate the volume of the prism.
d After the lesson, the glass prisms are put into a box, which is also a triangular prism. The cross-section is an equilateral triangle, with sides of length 9 cm. The length of the box is 16 cm.

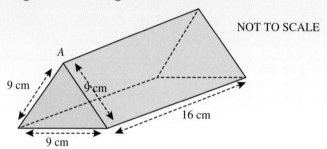

NOT TO SCALE

i Work out the largest number of glass prisms that can fit into the box.
ii Calculate the surface area of the box.

Source: Cambridge IGCSE Mathematics 0580 Paper 3 Q7 a (i), (ii), (iii), b (i), (iii) November 2007.

Learning outcomes

By the end of this unit you should be able to understand and use:

■ problems involving the arc length and sector area of a circle

■ the surface area and volume of a sphere, pyramid and cone (given formulae for the sphere, pyramid and cone)

23.05 Finding the arc length and sector area of a circle

Figure 23.11 illustrates arc length and sector area.

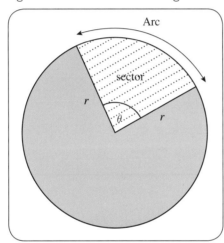

Fig. 23.11 Arc and sector of a circle

As the arc length is a fraction of the circumference of a circle, the formula is:

$$\text{Arc length} = \frac{\theta}{360} \times 2\pi r$$

The sector area is a fraction of the total area of the circle, so the formula is:

$$\text{Sector area} = \frac{\theta}{360} \times \pi r^2$$

Here is an example on finding the arc length and sector area.

23.06 Worked example

Find the arc length and sector area of a circle with radius 8 cm and $\theta = 40°$.

$$\text{Arc length} = \frac{\theta}{360} \times 2\pi r = \frac{40}{360} \times 3.142 \times 8 = 59 \text{ cm}$$

$$\text{Sector area} = \frac{\theta}{360} \times \pi r^2 = \frac{40}{360} \times 3.142 \times 8^2 = 22.34 \text{ cm}^2$$

23.07 Worked example

Figure 23.12 shows a laboratory flask which may be considered to be a sphere with a cylindrical neck. Calculate the volume of the flask (volume of a sphere $= \frac{4}{3}\pi r^3$).

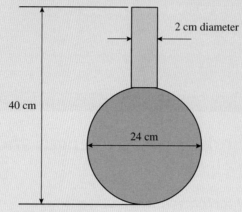

Fig. 23.12 Flask

We have two basic shapes: a sphere of 24 cm diameter and a cylinder of 2 cm diameter. We need to calculate the volume of each and add them.

Cylinder length $= 40\,\text{cm} - 24\,\text{cm} = 16\,\text{cm}$

Sphere volume $= \frac{4}{3}\pi r^3 = \frac{4}{3} \times 3.142 \times 12^3 = 7238.2\,\text{cm}^3$

Cylinder volume $= \pi r^2 h = 3.142 \times 1^2 \times 16 = 50.272\,\text{cm}^3$

Total volume $= 7239.2 + 50.272 = 7289.472\,\text{cm}^3$

If you are given the diameter instead of the radius, you need to halve the diameter. In other questions you will be given the arc length or sector area and asked to find the radius or the angle θ. In such cases you have to transpose the formula (see Unit 12).

Progress check

23.05 Calculate the arc length of each of the following sectors. The angle θ and radius r are given in each case.

    a $\theta = 45°, r = 15\,\text{cm}$ b $\theta = 150°, r = 13.5\,\text{cm}$

23.06 Surface area and volume of a sphere, pyramid and cone

The formulae will be given for these in the exam, but it is useful to look at some problems on this topic. The formulae are given below.

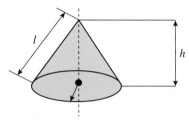

Fig. 23.13 Cone: volume $= \frac{1}{3}\pi r^2 h$

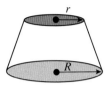

Fig. 23.14 Frustum of a cone:

volume $= \frac{1}{3}\pi h(R^2 + Rr + r^2)$

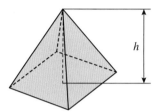

Fig. 23.15 Pyramid:

volume $= \frac{1}{3}Ah$ (A = area of base)

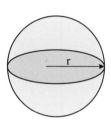

Fig. 23.16 Sphere: volume $= \frac{4}{3}\pi r^3$

23.08 Worked example

A sphere has a diameter of 8 cm. Calculate its volume and surface area, given the formulae:

Volume $= \frac{4}{3}\pi r^3$ Surface area $= 4\pi r^2$ (where r is the radius).

Substitute the given values into the formulae:

Volume $= \frac{4}{3} \times 3.142 \times 4^3 = 268.2\,\text{cm}^3$

Surface area $= 4 \times 3.142 \times 4^2 = 201.09\,\text{cm}^2$

23.09 Worked example

A pyramid has a square base of side 4 cm and a volume of 16 cm³. Calculate its height. (The volume of a pyramid $= \frac{1}{3}Ah$, where A is the area of the base and h is the height.)

We have the volume and the area, so we need to rearrange the formula to find h.

$$V = \frac{1}{3}Ah \text{ so } h = \frac{3V}{A}$$

$$\text{So } h = \frac{3 \times 16}{16} = 3 \text{ cm} \qquad (A = \text{area of the base, which is } 4 \text{ cm} \times 4 \text{ cm} = 16 \text{ cm}^2)$$

23.10 Worked example

A cone has a diameter of 7 cm and a volume of 308 cm³. Taking $\pi = 3.142$, calculate the vertical height of the cone. (Volume of cone $= \frac{1}{3}\pi r^2 h$, where r is the radius of the base and h is the height.)

We have the diameter and the volume, so we need to rearrange the formula to find h:

$$V = \frac{1}{3}\pi r^2 h, \text{ so } h = \frac{3V}{\pi r^2}$$

$$\text{So } h = \frac{3 \times 308}{3.142 \times 3.5^2} = 24 \text{ cm}$$

Progress check

23.06 A sphere has a radius of 4.5 cm. Calculate to 1 d.p.:

    a its total surface area   b its volume.

23.07 A pyramid has a square base of side 6 cm and a volume of 28 cm³. Calculate its height. (Volume of pyramid $= \frac{1}{3}Ah$, where A is the area of the base and h is the height.)

23.08 A wooden object is made from a hemisphere and a cone, both of base radius 12 cm. The height of the object is 36 cm. Calculate:

    a The volume of the hemisphere.
    b The volume of the cone.
    c The total surface area of the object.

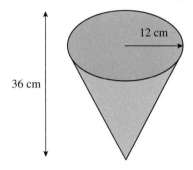

23.09 Calculate the area of the sector shown.

Exam-style questions

23.06 Calculate the arc length of each of the following sectors. The angle θ and radius r are given in each case.

    a $\theta = 70°, r = 10$ cm   b $\theta = 225°, r = 12$ cm

23.07 A sphere has a radius of 15 cm. Calculate to 1 d.p.:

    a its total surface area   b its volume.

23.08 A regular tetrahedron has edges of length of 10 cm. Calculate:

    a The surface area of the tetrahedron.
    b The radius of a sphere with the same surface area as the tetrahedron.

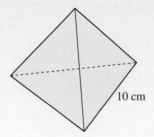

23.09 The diagram shows part of a fan. *OFG* and *OAD* are sectors, centre *O*, with radius 18 cm and sector angle 40°. *B, C, H* and *E* lie on a circle, centre *O* and radius 6 cm. Calculate the shaded area.

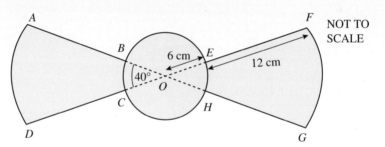

Source: *Cambridge IGCSE Mathematics 0580 Paper 21 Q19 June 2009.*

Trigonometry

CORE CURRICULUM

Learning outcomes

By the end of this unit you should be able to understand and use:

- bearings
- trigonometric ratios to find missing sides and angles
- Pythagoras' theorem

24.01 Revision on bearings

Bearings are angular directions. They are measured from due north in a clockwise direction and are written in three figures.

24.01 Worked example

Point B lies on a bearing of 095° from point A. Construct the bearing diagram.

The starting point is A, since the question gives the bearing of B from A. The angle of 95° is drawn using a protractor, from due north, in a clockwise direction (see Figure 24.01). Note how we have written the angle as three figures and shown the direction arrows.

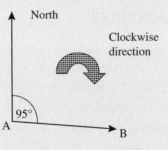

Fig. 24.01 Bearing of 095°

When we have bearings of 100° or more, these are already in three figures, so there is no need to add a zero.

24.02 Worked example

A ship sails from port (P) on a bearing of 120° for 10 km to a point X and then changes direction to bearing 070° to a point Y which is 8 km away. Construct an accurate scale diagram to show the ship's journey and hence find the shortest distance from the port to point Y.

Starting at P, we construct a north, then measure 120° with a protractor and draw a line of length 10 cm in this direction towards X.

At point X, we construct another north and measure 70° and draw a line of length 8 cm towards Y.

Figure 24.02 is a representation of the journey drawn to scale.

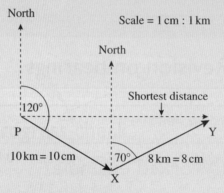

Fig. 24.02 Scale diagram of ship's journey

Measure the distance PY with a ruler. It is 16 cm.

Therefore, distance PY = 16 km

24.02 Back bearings

Although not specifically mentioned in the syllabus statement, it is important to know what these are and how to calculate them. A back bearing is the reverse of a bearing, so if A is on a bearing from B, then the bearing of B from A is the back bearing.

Use the rule below to calculate a back bearing from a given bearing:
    If the original bearing is less than 180°, add 180° to get the back bearing.
    If the original bearing is greater than 180°, subtract 180° to get the back bearing.

24.03 Worked example

If A is on a bearing of 055° from B, what is the back bearing of B from A?

As 055° is less than 180° we simply add 180° to it:

$$055° + 180° = 235°$$

We show this diagrammatically in Figure 24.03.

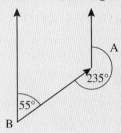

Fig. 24.03 Bearing of A from B = 055°; bearing of B from A = 235°

Back bearings are used extensively in geography, to calculate the compass headings when returning from a journey, and in the shipping and aeronautical industries.

24.03 Trigonometric ratios

We can use the trigonometric ratios to find the missing side(s) or angle(s) of any right-angled triangle, provided we have sufficient information.

The sides of a right-angled triangle are shown in Figure 24.04. The **hypotenuse** is the longest side (always opposite the right angle), the **opposite** is the side opposite the angle *x* and the **adjacent** is the side next to the angle *x*. Remember their names and the corresponding ratios.

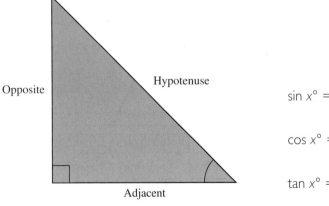

$$\sin x° = \frac{\text{opposite}}{\text{hypotenuse}}$$

$$\cos x° = \frac{\text{adjacent}}{\text{hypotenuse}}$$

$$\tan x° = \frac{\text{opposite}}{\text{adjacent}}$$

Fig. 24.04 Right-angled triangle

We often use the word SOHCAHTOA to remember the ratios:

s	o	h	c	a	h	t	o	a
i	p	y	o	d	y	a	p	d
n	p	p	s	j	p	n	p	j

24.04 Using the trigonometric ratios to find missing angles and sides

First familiarise yourself with the following keys on your scientific calculator:

These are the trigonometric functions. The inverse functions, $\sin^{-1}$, $\cos^{-1}$ and $\tan^{-1}$, are usually obtained by pressing the inv or second function key on your calculator.

Finding a missing angle

In order to calculate a missing angle, we need to know the lengths of at least two sides. We can then name the sides accordingly and choose the appropriate ratio.

24.04 Worked example

Find angle x in the triangle in Figure 24.05.

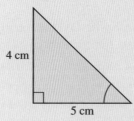

Fig. 24.05 Find x

We can see from the triangle that the two given sides are the opposite and the adjacent, so we have to use the tan ratio.

$$\tan x = \frac{\text{opposite}}{\text{adjacent}} = \frac{4}{5} = 0.8$$

$$\tan^{-1} 0.8 = 38.7° \text{ (to 1 d.p.)}$$

To find the angle from the ratio, press the tan⁻¹ key.

24.05 Worked example

Find angle y in the triangle shown in Figure 24.06.

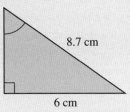

Fig. 24.06 Find y

This time the two given sides are the hypotenuse and the opposite, so we have to use the sin ratio. (Note how the triangle has turned round but this does not affect the naming of the sides.)

$$\sin y = \frac{\text{opposite}}{\text{hypotenuse}} = \frac{6}{8.7} = 0.6897$$

$\sin^{-1} 0.6897 = 43.6°$ (to 1 d.p.)

If we were asked to find the remaining angle in the triangle, we would subtract the right-angle and the calculated angle from 180°. So in this case the remaining angle is $180 - 90 - 43.6 = 46.4°$.

Finding a missing side

In order to calculate a missing side we need the angle x and one other side.

(If we had two of the sides then there would be no need to use trigonometry, we could use Pythagoras' theorem instead to calculate the remaining side.)

24.06 Worked example

Find the length of sides y and z in the triangle in Figure 24.07.

Since we have the hypotenuse and the angle, we could use either the sine or cosine ratio. Using the sine ratio:

$$\sin 62° = \frac{\text{opposite}}{\text{hypotenuse}} = \frac{z}{20}$$

Rearranging for z:

$z = \sin 62° \times 20\,\text{cm} = 17.7\,\text{cm}$

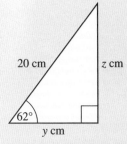

Fig. 24.07 Find y and z

To find y we can use Pythagoras' theorem as we now have two of the sides:

$$z = \sqrt{20^2 - 17.7^2} = 9.3\,\text{cm}$$

24.07 Worked example

Find angle x in the triangle in Figure 24.08.

In this question, the unknown is the hypotenuse while the known side (4 cm) is adjacent to the known angle. Therefore we have to use the cosine ratio:

$$\cos 42° = \frac{\text{adjacent}}{\text{hypotenuse}} = \frac{4\,\text{cm}}{x}$$

Rearranging for x:

$$x = \frac{4\,\text{cm}}{\cos 42} = 5.4\,\text{cm}$$

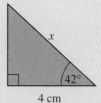

Fig. 24.08 Find x

24.08 Worked example

Two boats X and Y, sailing in a race, are shown in Figure 24.09. Boat X is 145 metres due north of a buoy B. Boat Y is due east of buoy B. Boats X and Y are 320 metres apart. Calculate:

a the distance BY
b the bearing of Y from X
c the bearing of X from Y.

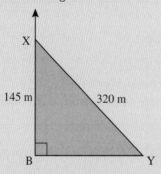

Fig. 24.09 Boat race

a Distance BY can be found using Pythagoras' theorem:

$$BY = \sqrt{320^2 - 145^2} = 285.3 \text{ metres}$$

b First find angle X and then subtract it from 180° to get the bearing of Y from X:

$$\cos X = \frac{\text{adjacent}}{\text{hypotenuse}} = \frac{145}{320} = 0.4531$$

$\cos^{-1} 0.4531 = 63°$, so the bearing $= 180 - 63 = 117°$

c The bearing of X from Y is the back bearing of Y from X:

bearing of X from Y $= 117° + 180° = 297°$

Progress check

24.01 Using Pythagoras' theorem, trigonometry or both, calculate the marked value in each of the following diagrams:

a

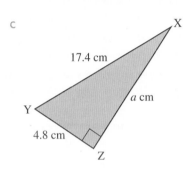

b

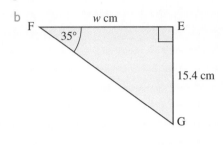

c

24.02 A sailing boat sets off from a point A and heads towards B, a point 16 km due north. At point B it changes direction and heads towards point C, a point 12 km away on a bearing of 090°. Once at C the crew want to sail back to A. Calculate:

  a the distance CA   b the bearing of A from C.

24.03 A rectangular swimming pool measures 45 m long by 15 m wide. Calculate the length of the diagonal of the pool. Give your answer correct to 1 d.p.

TERMS

• **Bearing**
A three-figure angular direction, measured clockwise from due north.

• **Back bearing**
The bearing in the reverse direction.

• **Opposite**
The side facing the angle we are given or need to find (x).

• **Adjacent**
The side next to the angle (x).

• **Hypotenuse**
The longest side, directly facing the right angle.

Exam-style questions

24.01 ABC is a right-angled triangle.
AB = 3.6 m and BC = 2.3 m.
Calculate the length of AC.

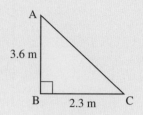

24.02 In the diagram *AB* is the diameter of a circle, centre *O*. The length of *AB* is 12 cm.

a Write down the size of angle *APB*.
b Angle *PAB* = 40°. Calculate the length of *PB*.
c Calculate the area of the circle.

Source: Cambridge IGCSE Mathematics 0580 Paper 1 Q16 June 2003.

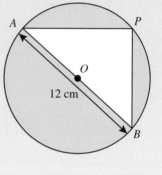

24.03 A straight road between *P* and *Q* is shown in the diagram. *R* is the point south of *P* and east of *Q*.
PR = 8.3 km and *QR* = 4.8 km. Calculate

a the length of the road *PQ*
b the bearing of *Q* from *P*.

Source: Cambridge IGCSE Mathematics 0580 Paper 1 Q17 June 2003.

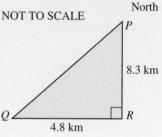

24.04 On the diagram, *AB* = 2 cm, *BD* = 6 cm, *AE* = 10 cm, angle *BCD* = 40° and angle *BDE* = 90°.

a Write down the length of *AD*.
b Calculate the length of *DE*.
c Calculate the size of angle *AED*.
d Calculate the length of *CD*.
e Find the length of *CE*.

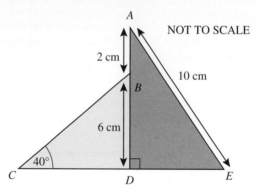

Source: Cambridge IGCSE Mathematics 0580 Paper 3 Q3a-e October/November 2004.

EXTENDED CURRICULUM

24.05 Angles of elevation and depression

The angle of elevation is the angle above the horizontal through which a line of sight is raised.

24.09 Worked example

Figure 24.10 shows a tower 70 metres away from a point X on the ground. If the angle of elevation of the top of the tower from X is 40°, calculate the height of the tower.

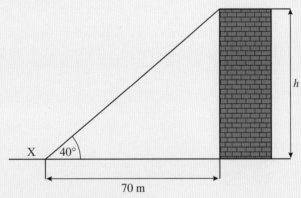

Fig. 24.10 Angle of elevation

$$\tan 40° = \frac{h}{70}, \text{ so } h = \tan 40° \times 70 = 58.7 \text{ metres (to 1 d.p.)}$$

The angle of depression is the angle below the horizontal through which a line of sight is lowered.

24.10 Worked example

The diagram shows an aeroplane receiving a signal from point X on the ground. If the angle of depression of point X from the aeroplane is 30°, calculate the height at which the plane is flying.

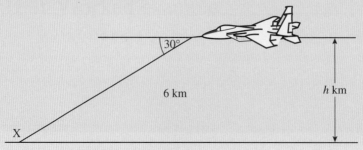

Fig. 24.11 Angle of depression

$$\sin 30° = \frac{h}{6}, \text{ so } h = \sin 30° \times 6 = 3.0 \,\text{km}$$

Progress check

24.04 A girl standing on a cliff top at Y can see a boat sailing on the lake at X. The vertical height of the girl above sea level is 126 metres, and the horizontal distance between the boat and the girl is 2 kilometres. Calculate:

a The distance XY to the nearest metre.
b The angle of depression of the boat from the girl.

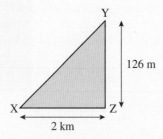

24.06 Angles between 0° and 360°

When calculating the sizes of angles using trigonometry, there are often two solutions between 0° and 360°. Most calculators, however, will only give the first solution. In order to calculate the value of the second possible solution, an understanding of the shape of the sine and cosine curves is required. See the curves in Figures 24.12 and 24.13 and follow the examples.

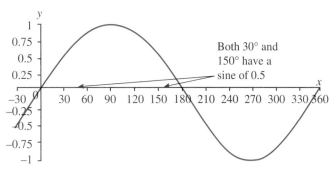

Fig. 24.12 The sine curve

Figure 24.12 is the graph of $y = \sin x$, where x is the size of the angle in degrees. We can see from the graph that:

- It has a period of 360° (repeats itself every 360°).
- It has a maximum value of 1.
- It has a minimum value of -1.

If we take, for example, sin 30° = 0.5, we notice that the sine of 150° is also 0.5, although this second value would not be shown on our calculators.

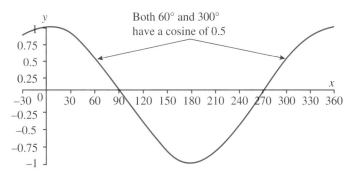

Fig. 24.13 The cosine curve

Figure 24.13 is the graph of $y = \cos x$, where x is the size of the angle in degrees. We can see from the graph that:

- It has a period of 360°.
- It has a maximum value of 1.
- It has a minimum value of -1.

If we take, for example, cos 60° = 0.5, we notice that the cosine of 300° is also 0.5. Again, this second value would not be shown on our calculators.

Progress check

24.05 Draw the graph of $y = \sin x°$ for 0° ⩽ $x°$ ⩽ 360°. Mark on the graph the angles 0°, 90°, 270° and 360° and also the minimum and maximum values of y.

24.07 The sine and cosine rules

These are extremely powerful since they can be used for any type of triangle, not just a right-angled triangle. The basic notation used for the triangle is shown in Figure 24.14, where angle *A* is opposite side *a*, angle *B* is opposite side *b* and angle *C* is opposite side *c*.

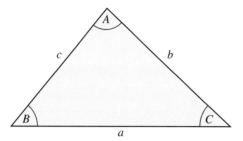

Fig. 24.14 The sine and cosine rules

The sine rule

The sine rule is used when we are given:

i) one side and any two angles, or

ii) two sides and an angle opposite to one of the sides.

$$\frac{a}{\sin A} = \frac{b}{\sin B} = \frac{c}{\sin C}$$

This can be transposed so that the angles are on top.

24.11 Worked example

Calculate the length of side BC in Figure 24.15.

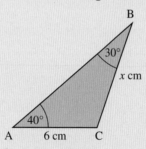

Fig. 24.15 Find *x*

The sine rule has to be used because it is not a right-angled triangle. Side BC is *a*:

Using $\dfrac{a}{\sin A} = \dfrac{b}{\sin B}$,

$$a = \frac{\sin 40° \times 6\,\text{cm}}{\sin 30°} = 7.7 \text{ cm (to 1 d.p.)}$$

Note that we did not need to use sin *C*, because angle *B* and side *b* were available.

24.12 Worked example

Calculate the size of angle C in Figure 24.16.

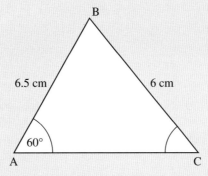

Fig. 24.16 Find C

Now that we are looking for an angle we need to invert the formula:

$$\frac{\sin C}{c} = \frac{\sin A}{a}$$

$$\sin C = \frac{6.5\,\text{cm} \times \sin 60°}{6\,\text{cm}} = 0.94$$

$$\sin^{-1} C = 69.8° \ (1 \text{ d.p.})$$

Note that we didn't have angle B or indeed side b to use, but angle C and side c were sufficient.

The cosine rule

The cosine rule is used when we are given:

i) two sides of a triangle and the angle between them, or

ii) three sides of a triangle.

$$a^2 = b^2 + c^2 - 2bc \cos A, \text{ or } \cos A = \frac{b^2 + c^2 - a^2}{2bc}$$

24.13 Worked example

Calculate the size of angle A in Figure 24.17.

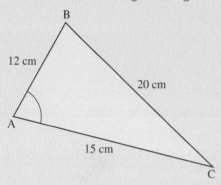

Fig. 24.17 Find A

Using the formula to find angle A:

$$\cos A = \frac{15^2 + 12^2 - 20^2}{2 \times 15 \times 12} = -0.086$$

$$\cos^{-1} A = 94.9° \text{ (to 1 d.p.)}$$

Note that we can find any angle using the formula, we just have to rearrange for the required angle.

24.14 Worked example

Calculate the length of side AB in Figure 24.18.

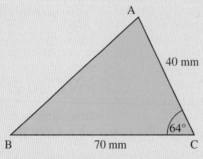

Fig. 24.18 Find AB

Side AB is side c of the triangle, so we have to rearrange the formula for c:

$$c = \sqrt{a^2 + b^2 - 2ab \cos C} = \sqrt{70^2 + 40^2 - 2 \times 70 \times 40 \times \cos 64°}$$
$$= 63.60 \text{ mm}$$

You only need the minimum amount of information to be able to calculate all of the sides and all of the angles of a triangle. It is always worth doing a check. **Remember** that the longest side is always directly opposite the largest angle, and the shortest side is opposite the smallest angle.

24.08 Area of a triangle

The formula for the area of a triangle is $\frac{1}{2}ab\sin C$, where a and b are two sides and angle C is the angle between them. This formula can be rearranged for any angle.

24.15 Worked example

Find the area of the triangle shown in Figure 24.19.

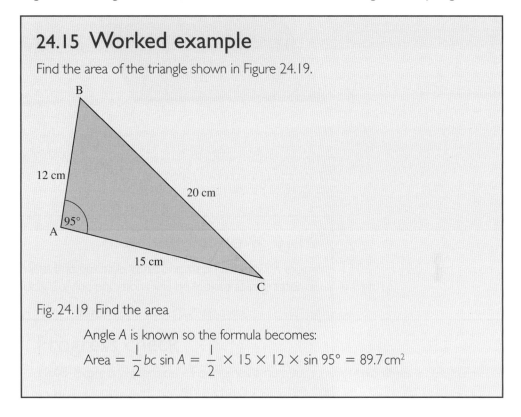

Fig. 24.19 Find the area

Angle A is known so the formula becomes:

$$\text{Area} = \frac{1}{2}bc\sin A = \frac{1}{2} \times 15 \times 12 \times \sin 95° = 89.7\,\text{cm}^2$$

In some questions we are given the area of the triangle and some other information and asked to find either a missing side or the missing angle between the sides. This is straightforward provided we can rearrange formulae (see Unit 12).

24.09 Trigonometry in three dimensions

Three-dimensional shapes are **solid** shapes. In order to calculate angles and sides in solid shapes we need to understand the terms **plane** and **angle between a line and a plane**.

The plane
A plane is a surface such as the top of a table or the cover of a book. A plane has two dimensions.

The angle between a line and a plane

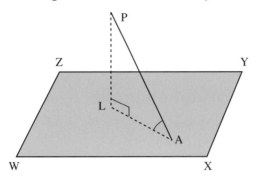

Fig. 24.20 Angle between a line and a plane

In Figure 24.20, the line *PA* intersects the plane *WXYZ* at *A*. To find the angle between *PA* and the plane, draw *PL* perpendicular to the plane and join *AL*. The angle *PAL* is now the angle between the line and the plane.

24.16 Worked example

Figure 24.21 shows a square-based pyramid of side 8 cm. The height of the pyramid is 12 cm. Calculate:

a EF   **b** angle VEF   **c** VE (slant height)   **d** area of $\triangle$VAD.

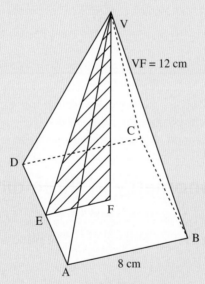

Fig. 24.21 Square-based pyramid

a   EF = base of triangle VEF = 4 cm   (this is half way across the square of side 8 cm)

b   Angle VEF = $\tan^{-1} \dfrac{12}{4}$ = 71.6°   (angle formed between line and plane)

c   VE = $\sqrt{12^2 + 4^2}$ = 12.6 cm   (using Pythagoras)

d   Area $\triangle$VAD = $\dfrac{1}{2} \times$ base $\times$ height = $\dfrac{1}{2} \times 8 \times 12.6$ = 50.4 cm²

24.17 Worked example

Figure 24.22 shows a pyramid on a rectangular base. Calculate the length VA and the angle VAE .

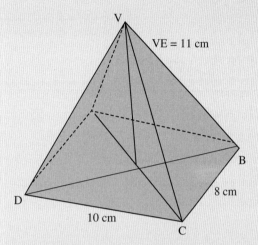

Fig. 24.22 Rectangular-based pyramid

To calculate VA we can use Pythagoras:

$$VA = \sqrt{VE^2 + AE^2}$$

First we need to calculate AE. AE is half the distance of AC, so we can say:

$$AE = \frac{1}{2}\sqrt{10^2 + 8^2} = 6.4\,cm$$

So $$VA = \sqrt{11^2 + 6.4^2} = 12.7\,cm$$

Angle $$VAE = \tan^{-1}\frac{11}{6.4} = 59.8°$$

Progress check

24.06 For the quadrilateral (left), calculate:

- a The length WY.
- b Angle XWY.
- c The length WZ.
- d The area of WXYZ.

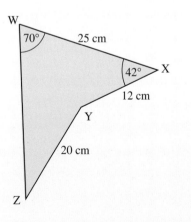

- **Elevation**
  Raising the line of sight above the horizontal.

- **Depression**
  Lowering the line of sight below the horizontal.

- **Sine rule**
  Used for any triangle where we have two sides and an angle opposite one of the sides.

- **Cosine rule**
  Used where we only have the three sides or when we cannot use the sine rule.

- **Plane**
  A surface such as the top of a table or the surface of a book.

Exam-style questions

24.05 In triangle ABC, $AB = 2x$ cm, $AC = x$ cm, $BC = 21$ cm and angle $BAC = 120°$. Calculate the value of x.

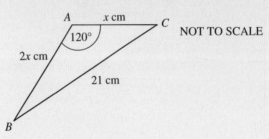

NOT TO SCALE

Source: *Cambridge IGCSE Mathematics 0580 Paper 21 Q11 June 2008.*

24.06 Find the missing letters in the following diagrams:

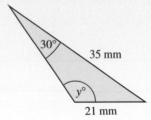

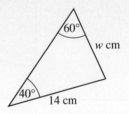

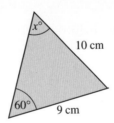

24.07 a Calculate the area of the triangle.

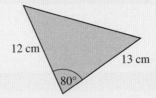

12 cm

13 cm

80°

b Calculate the value of x.

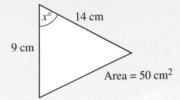

$x°$ 14 cm

9 cm

Area = 50 cm^2

24.08 The diagram shows a pyramid on a horizontal rectangular base ABCD.
The diagonals of *ABCD* meet at *E*. *P* is vertically above *E*. *AB* = 8 cm,
BC = 6 cm and *PC* = 13 cm.

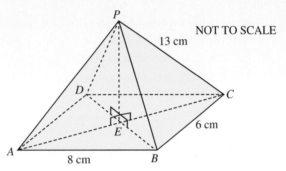

P

NOT TO SCALE

13 cm

D

C

6 cm

E

A

8 cm

B

a Calculate *PE*, the height of the pyramid.

b Calculate the volume of the pyramid. [The volume of a pyramid is given
by $\frac{1}{3}$ × area of base × height.]

c Calculate angle *PCA*.

d *M* is the mid-point of *AD* and *N* is the mid-point of *BC*. Calculate
angle *MPN*.

e Calculate angle *PBC*.

Source: Cambridge IGCSE Mathematics 0580 Paper 4 Q6a - e(i) June 2006.

Statistics

Learning outcomes

By the end of this chapter you should be able to:

- interpret, tabulate and draw bar charts, pictograms, pie charts and histograms from data
- calculate the mean, median and mode and distinguish between their uses
- construct scatter diagrams (including line of best fit by eye)
- understand positive, negative and zero correlation

The word **statistics** means 'gathering and displaying of information (data)'. We have all seen the use of statistics in our world, e.g. population growth, temperature or rainfall charts, and we should be able to draw simple conclusions from them. When we conduct our own statistical survey we need to follow some simple procedures so that the information is first collected, then ordered and finally displayed in a suitable fashion.

25.01 Collect, classify and tabulate statistical data

This refers to the actual collection and ordering of the data we require. To collect the data we could write a questionnaire and ask people to answer the relevant questions, or we could ask people directly and complete the results ourselves, provided that the sample size is small.

25.01 Worked example

In a recent mathematics test involving 50 students, the following results were obtained:

40	30	50	50	60	50	80	70	60	70	80	30
90	50	40	10	80	70	50	60	60	70	50	20
50	20	60	90	50	70	60	50	60	20	80	60
70	30	30	80	70	60	50	50	60	40	30	40
50	70										

Classify and tabulate the data.

We can order the data by using a **frequency distribution** as shown in Table 25.01.

Table 25.01 Frequency distribution of test results

Score	Tally	Frequency
10	I	1
20	III	3
30	IIII	5
40	IIII	4
50	IIII IIII II	12
60	IIII IIII	10
70	IIII III	8
80	IIII	5
90	II	2
		Total = 50

Note how the data was placed in numerical order and the total then checked to ensure that we had accounted for all 50 students.

We can also see from the table that most students' scores are in the 50 to 70 range, which is what you'd expect from a well-constructed test.

25.02 Bar charts, pie charts and pictograms

It is easier to draw conclusions if data is displayed in some form. The example that follows shows the different ways we can do this.

25.02 Worked example

Ninety people were asked for their favourite flavour of crisps. The results were as follows.

Plain	Cheese and Onion	Salt and Vinegar	Chicken	Tomato
20	25	18	15	12

Show the information as   **a** a bar chart   **b** a pie chart   **c** a pictogram.

a With a bar chart, the number of crisps or **frequency** goes on the vertical axis while the **category** or data goes on the horizontal axis – see Figure 25.01.

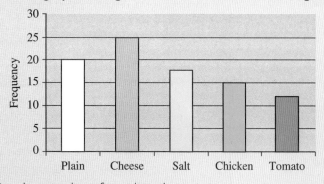

Fig. 25.01 Bar chart to show favourite crisps

b This time the data is shown as sectors of a circle (see Figure 25.02). The larger the circle sector, the greater the number of students who prefer that flavour.

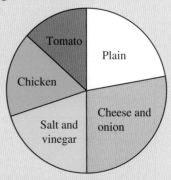

Fig. 25.02 Pie chart to show favourite crisps

We can use the following formula to calculate the sector angle:

$$\text{angle} = \frac{\text{number} \times 360}{\text{total}}$$

$$\text{Plain} = \frac{20 \times 360}{90} = 80°$$

$$\text{Cheese} = \frac{25 \times 360}{90} = 100°$$

$$\text{Salt\&Vin} = \frac{18 \times 360}{90} = 72°$$

$$\text{Chicken} = \frac{15 \times 360}{90} = 60°$$

$$\text{Tomato} = \frac{12 \times 360}{90} = 48°$$

When you have the sector angles, use your protractor to draw the angles, using the top as the starting point.

c A pictogram to show favourite crisps, key: ⚲ = 2 students:

Plain	⚲⚲⚲⚲⚲⚲⚲⚲⚲⚲	(10 × 2 = 20)
Cheese and Onion	⚲⚲⚲⚲⚲⚲⚲⚲⚲⚲⚲⚲⚲	(12.5 × 2 = 25)
Salt and Vinegar	⚲⚲⚲⚲⚲⚲⚲⚲⚲	(9 × 2 = 18)
Chicken	⚲⚲⚲⚲⚲⚲⚲⚲	(7.5 × 2 = 15)
Tomato	⚲⚲⚲⚲⚲⚲	(6 × 2 = 12)

With a pictogram, the number in each category is shown as a symbol or picture. In this case we are showing students, so we can use one matchstick person to represent every 2 students.

For the Cheese and Onion and Chicken flavours we have shown half a picture to represent one person. Every pictogram must have a suitable key, so we can read the data correctly.

25.03 Histograms

Histograms with equal intervals

A **histogram** shows the frequency of the data in the form of bars; the area of the bars gives the number of items in the class interval. If all the class intervals are the same, then the bars will be the same width and frequencies can be represented by the heights of the bars.

So if we now show the data from Worked example 25.01 as a histogram it would look like Figure 25.03.

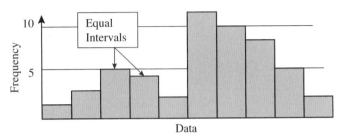

Fig. 25.03 Histogram of test results

As the intervals are the same size, i.e. every 10 marks, then the change in height will represent the actual change in area.

Note that histograms with equal intervals are virtually identical to bar charts except that the bars are always joined.

Grouped class intervals

This time the data will lie in ranges of values.

25.03 Worked example

Draw a histogram from the table which shows the distribution of heights of 21 students in a mathematics class. The measurements were made to the nearest centimetre.

Class interval	120–129	130–139	140–149	150–159	160–169
Frequency	2	4	7	5	3

The class boundaries are 119.5, 129.5, 139.5, 149.5, 159.5, 169.5. The class width is 10 cm for each class (e.g. 120–129).

Area of rectangle = class width × height of rectangle

Frequencies will be on the vertical axis and class intervals on the horizontal axis — see Figure 25.04.

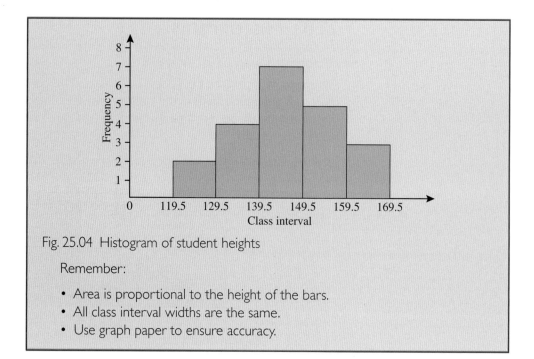

Fig. 25.04 Histogram of student heights

Remember:

- Area is proportional to the height of the bars.
- All class interval widths are the same.
- Use graph paper to ensure accuracy.

25.04 Mean, median and mode

These are all types of averages. The word 'average' usually means 'somewhere in the middle', but there are three types of statistical averages in common use today. Depending on the circumstances where they are used, each one has an advantage over the others.

Mean

This is the most commonly used type of average. It is used to give an accurate arithmetic middle value for a group of figures, e.g. finding the average height of a population.

$$\text{Mean} = \frac{\text{Total of all values}}{\text{Number of values}}$$

Median

This is a lesser used type of average. It is useful when you want to find the middle value of a set of numbers which contains extreme values.

Median = Middle value when numbers are in ascending order

Mode

This is useful when you need to know which value occurs most often.

Mode = Value which occurs most frequently

The following example shows how we calculate each type of average and their relative advantages.

25.04 Worked example

A survey was done on the shoe sizes of 25 pupils. The results were as follows:

39, 40, 40, 44, 44, 40, 40, 41, 41, 44, 42, 42, 45,45, 41, 41, 41, 42, 42, 43, 38, 39, 39, 43, 45.

Find the mean, median and mode of the results.

$$\text{Mean} = \frac{\text{total of values}}{\text{number of values}} = \frac{39 + 40 + 40 + \cdots + 43 + 45}{25} = 41.64$$

For the median, first we place the numbers in ascending order, from the 1st to the 25th:
38, 39, 39, 39, 40, 40, 40, 40, 41, 41, 41, 41, 41, 42, 42, 42, 42, 43, 43, 44, 44, 44, 45, 45, 45

Then we count along to the value which is in the middle, in this case the 13th value.

Median = 41

Mode = most frequent value = 41

The mean would be the most useful if you wanted to find an accurate middle value and then conclude who has bigger or smaller feet than average.

If a shoe shop wanted to keep adequate stocks of shoes relating to the most commonly requested size, it would want to know the median and the mode.

25.05 Worked example

The heights, in centimetres, of 10 students are: 152, 155, 153, 162, 148, 149, 152, 154, 155, 152. Find the mean, median and mode.

$$\text{Mean} = \frac{\text{total of values}}{\text{number of values}}$$

$$= \frac{152 + 155 + 153 + 162 + 148 + 149 + 152 + 154 + 155 + 152}{10} = 153.2\,\text{cm}$$

For the median, again place the numbers in ascending order:
148, 149, 152, 152, 152, 153, 154, 155, 155, 162
The middle number is between the fifth and sixth numbers (152 and 153), so we take the average of these two values.
Median = 152.5 cm

Mode = most frequent value = 152 cm

Progress check

25.01 Find the mean, median and mode of the following sets of numbers:

a 3, 3, 4, 5, 6, 5, 5, 4, 6

b 8, 0 −1, 3, 1, −2, −3, −2, 0, −2

c $1, \frac{1}{2}, \frac{1}{4}, \frac{3}{4}, \frac{1}{2}, \frac{1}{8}, \frac{3}{4}, 2$

25.02 The mean of 3, 7, 8, 10 and x is 6. Find x.

25.03 A number of people were asked how many coins they had in their pockets; the results are shown below. Calculate the mean, median and mode of coins per person.

Number of coins	0	1	2	3	4	5	6	7
Frequency	2	6	4	7	6	8	5	2

25.05 Scatter diagrams

Scatter diagrams (or scatter graphs) are used to see if there are any relationships between two sets of data. The data are plotted as points on a graph and if these points tend to lie in a straight line, we can say that there is a relationship or **correlation** between them.

Types of correlation

There are three types of correlation:

1 Positive correlation (Figure 25.05)
2 Negative correlation (Figure 25.06)
3 No correlation (Figure 25.07)

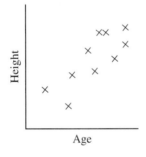

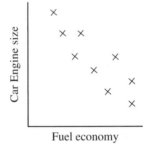

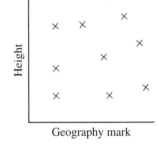

Fig. 25.05 Positive correlation: as age increases, so does height

Fig. 25.06 Negative correlation: as engine size increases, fuel economy decreases

Fig. 25.07 No correlation: there is no link between geography mark and height

25.06 Worked example

The table below shows the percentage marks gained in recent physics and English tests by the same 14 students.

Physics	47	57	64	50	70	80	67	62	76	90	83	93	90	76
English	43	46	51	55	55	65	65	67	69	72	74	78	79	79

We will now plot a graph of the data and construct a line of best fit, which should go through the middle of all the points – see Figure 25.08.

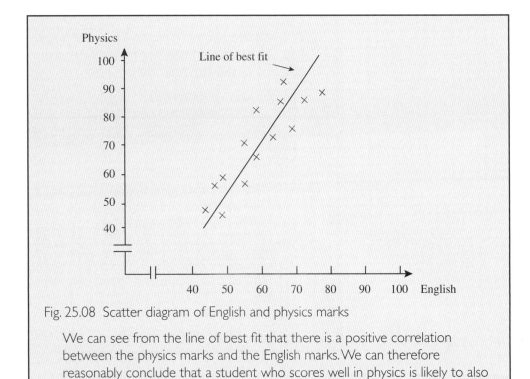

Fig. 25.08 Scatter diagram of English and physics marks

We can see from the line of best fit that there is a positive correlation between the physics marks and the English marks. We can therefore reasonably conclude that a student who scores well in physics is likely to also score well in English.

Apart from using lines of best fit to give a clearer indication as to what type of correlation exists (if any), we can also use them for estimating a value not given in the table.

25.07 Worked example

If a fifteenth student took the physics test from Worked example 25.06, scoring 61%, but missed the English test, write down a reasonable estimate of the score he or she would have obtained for English.

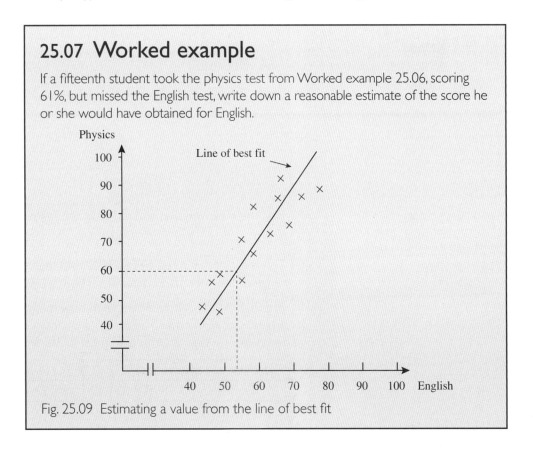

Fig. 25.09 Estimating a value from the line of best fit

By constructing a line from the 61% value for physics to meet the line of best fit, we can then make a reasonable estimate of the likely English mark obtained by the same student.

The estimated value is 60%.

Progress check

25.04 The following data gives the marks of 9 students in a science test and in a mathematics test.

Science	15	35	34	22	23	27	43	40	26
Mathematics	7	28	34	19	27	28	37	46	18

a Plot this data on a scatter graph, with science marks on the horizontal axis.
b Draw the line of best fit.
c Estimate the mathematics mark of a student who got 30 in science.

TERMS

• Correlation
A link or connection between two sets of variables.

• Mean
Arithmetic middle of a group of numbers. Total of numbers divided by number of numbers.

• Mode
The data value that occurs most often (most frequent).

• Median
The middle value of numerically ordered data.

• Histogram
Similar to a bar chart but used for continuous data; the area of the bar represents frequency.

Exam-style questions

25.01 Find the mean, median and mode of the following sets of numbers:

    a 7, 3, 4, 10, 11, 7, 4, 7   b −3, −4, −5, −5, −4, 0, 2, 3, 2, 1

25.02 The mean age of three people is 22 and their median age is 20. If the range of their ages is 26, how old is each person?

25.03 A group of 100 people were asked how many books they had read over a period of six months. The results are shown in the table below. Calculate the mean, median and mode number of books per person.

Number of books	0	1	2	3	4	5	6	7	8
Frequency	10	10	12	18	22	14	10	3	1

25.04 Marie counts the number of people in each of 60 cars one morning.

a She records the first 40 results as shown below.

Number of people in a car	Tally	Number of cars
1	ⅢⅡ	
2	ⅢⅡ ⅢⅡ	
3	ⅢⅡ Ⅰ	
4	ⅢⅡ Ⅰ	
5	ⅢⅡ ⅠⅠ	
6	ⅢⅡ Ⅰ	

The remaining 20 results are

2, 2, 5, 2, 2,   4, 2, 6, 5, 3,   4, 5, 4, 6, 2,   5, 3, 2, 1, 6.

 i Use these results to complete the frequency table above.
 ii On the grid below, draw a bar chart to show the information for the 60 cars.
 iii Write down the mode.
 iv Find the median.
 v Work out the mean.

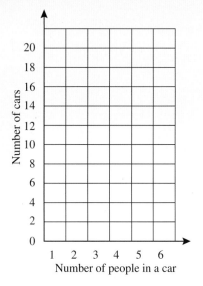

b Manuel uses Marie's results to draw a pie chart. Work out the sector angle for the number of cars with 5 people.

Source: Cambridge IGCSE Mathematics 0580 Paper 3 Q3 a(i, ii,iii,iv,v), b June 2008.

Learning outcomes

By the end of this unit you should be able to understand and use:

■ histograms with unequal intervals

■ cumulative frequency diagrams, including the estimate of the median and upper and lower quartiles and the interquartile range

■ estimate of the mean for grouped data

■ finding the modal class and median from a grouped frequency distribution

25.06 Histograms with unequal intervals

We know that a histogram shows the frequency in terms of the bar areas. When we have equal intervals each bar width will be equal and hence the area is proportional to the height of the bar. However, when the intervals are unequal, we have to find the height of the bar in another way so that it is the area of bar that shows the frequency.

A histogram with unequal intervals is shown in Figure 25.10.

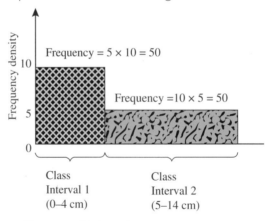

Fig. 25.10 Histogram with unequal intervals

The height of the bar is now called the frequency density and it is found by the following formula:

$$\text{frequency density} = \frac{\text{frequency}}{\text{class interval}}$$

From Figure 25.10 we can see that, although the frequency densities are different, the actual areas (frequencies) are the same. Although the first bar is twice the height of the second, the width of the second bar is twice the width of the first.

Ideally, histograms should be drawn on graph paper with each axis to a specified scale so that we can compare the areas accurately. Worked example 25.08 shows a practical example of a histogram.

25.08 Worked example

The heights of 21 seedlings were measured and the results recorded in the table below. Draw a histogram to display this data and comment on which class interval had the greatest number of seedlings.

Height (cm)	Frequency
$0 \leqslant h < 1.0$	6
$1.0 \leqslant h < 1.5$	3
$1.5 \leqslant h < 2.0$	4
$2.0 \leqslant h < 2.25$	3
$2.25 \leqslant h < 2.5$	5

We know the frequency and the class interval but we need to calculate the height of the bars (frequency density), so we'll use the formula:

$$\text{frequency density} = \frac{\text{frequency}}{\text{class interval}}$$

By adding another column to the table to include frequency density, we can then plot the histogram shown in Figure 25.11.

Height (cm)	Frequency	Frequency density
$0 \leqslant h < 1.0$	6	$6 \div 1 = 6$
$1.0 \leqslant h < 1.5$	3	$3 \div 0.5 = 6$
$1.5 \leqslant h < 2.0$	4	$4 \div 0.5 = 8$
$2.0 \leqslant h < 2.25$	3	$3 \div 0.25 = 12$
$2.25 \leqslant h < 2.5$	5	$5 \div 0.25 = 20$

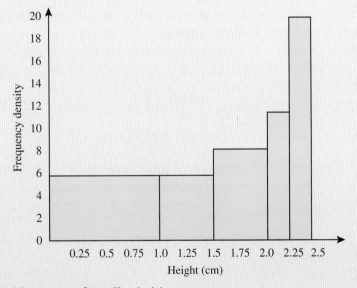

Fig. 25.11 Histogram of seedling heights

In Figure 25.11 the frequencies are now represented by the areas of the bars, e.g. there are 3 seedlings with a height of 1.0–1.5 cm because the area of the bar is $0.5 \times 6 = 3$.

The class interval with the greatest number of seedlings is 0–1.0 cm as this has the greatest area.

Note that both axes should be drawn to scale.

25.07 Cumulative frequency diagrams

A cumulative frequency diagram is an alternative to a histogram for presenting a frequency distribution. It is a useful way to find the median and quartiles (upper and lower quarters) of a distribution, and also for determining if the data is fair. A fair distribution will always take the typical shape shown in Figure 25.12.

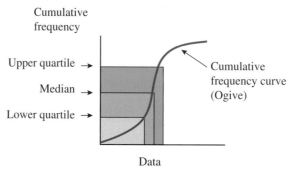

Fig. 25.12 Cumulative frequency diagram for a fair distribution

When plotting a cumulative frequency curve we must follow certain steps:

1 In the table add another column (or row) for cumulative frequency next to the frequency figures.
2 Plot the graph of cumulative frequency figures against the upper boundary of each class interval.
3 Use the cumulative frequency curve to find the median and percentiles.

From Figure 25.12:

- The **median** is the 50% value of cumulative frequency (using the graph, read off the value).
- The **upper quartile** is the 75% value of cumulative frequency (as above, construct the line from the graph). The upper quartile is the value of data corresponding to 75% of the total frequency.
- The **lower quartile** is the 25% value of cumulative frequency (construct line again). The lower quartile is the value of the data corresponding to 25% of the total frequency.
- **Interquartile range** = upper quartile − lower quartile (the middle 50% of the data).

25.09 Worked example

The table below shows the distribution of the scores obtained by 200 pupils in a maths test. Draw a cumulative frequency curve and hence find the:

a median   **b** upper and lower quartiles   **c** interquartile range.

Score	26–30	31–35	36–40	41–45	46–50	51–55	56–60	61–65	66–70	71–75	76–80
Pupils (freq.)	3	6	10	21	38	55	32	19	9	5	2
Cum. Freq.	3 (0+3)	9 (3+6)	19 (9+10)	40 (19+21)	78 (40+38)	133 ...	165	184	193	198	200

The first step is to include an extra row for cumulative frequency, which is a running total of frequencies. Note how the final figure is 200, which corresponds to the 200 people in the question.

Plot the graph of cumulative frequency against the upper boundary of each class interval (see Figure 25.13). The axes should be drawn to scale so that the answers obtained are as accurate as possible.

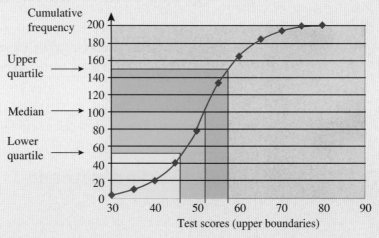

Fig. 25.13 Cumulative frequency curve of pupils' test results

From Figure 25.13 we find:

a Median (50% of 200 = 100) = 53 (approx.)

b Upper quartile = 75% value = 58 (approx.)
Lower quartile = 25% value = 46 (approx.)

c Interquartile range = 58 − 46 = 12

Progress check

25.05 The mean mass of five women is 67 kg. The masses of four of the women are 62 kg, 64 kg, 65 kg and 71 kg. What is the mass of the fifth woman?

25.06 The ages of 110 people passing through a train station turnstile were recorded, and are shown in the frequency table.

Age (years)	Frequency
$0 < \text{age} \leqslant 10$	17
$10 < \text{age} \leqslant 15$	46
$15 < \text{age} \leqslant 20$	36
$20 < \text{age} \leqslant 30$	13
$30 < \text{age} \leqslant 40$	8

a Find an estimate of the mean.
b Construct a histogram and a cumulative frequency diagram of the data.
c Use your cumulative frequency diagram to estimate the median and the interquartile range.

25.08 Calculating an estimate of the mean for grouped and continuous data

We have looked at calculating the mean for individual and discrete data. When we have grouped data the method is slightly different:

$$\text{Mean (estimate)} = \frac{\text{mid-value of class intervals} \times \text{frequencies}}{\text{total frequency}}$$

For each class interval we have to find the mid-value and multiply by its frequency. We then find the sum of these products and finally divide by the total frequency.

25.10 Worked example

In a chemistry experiment, the mass (in grams) of 100 grains of salt were found. The distribution of mass is given in the following table. Calculate an estimate of the mean.

Mass (g)	0–4	5–9	10–14	15–19	20–24	25–29	30–34	35–39	40–44
Frequency	1	2	15	21	26	28	4	2	1

The mid-value of the 0–4 range is 2, the mid-value of the 5–9 range is 7, and so on. So:

Mean (estimate) =

$$\frac{(2 \times 1) + (7 \times 2) + (12 \times 15) + (17 \times 21) + (22 \times 26) + (27 \times 28) + (32 \times 4) + (37 \times 2) + (42 \times 1)}{100}$$

$$= \frac{2 + 14 + 180 + 357 + 572 + 756 + 128 + 74 + 42}{100} = 21.25$$

This is only an estimate because we don't know exactly how the numbers were arranged in each class interval. For example, in the 10–14 gram interval we know there were 15 salt grains but they could have been anywhere in that range (near the lower boundary or higher boundary).

25.09 Finding the modal class of a grouped distribution

As mentioned in Section 25.04, the mode is the number which occurs most frequently, so if we have a grouped distribution, the interval with the highest frequency is the modal class.

Look at the table of results from Worked example 25.10:

Mass	0–4	5–9	10–14	15–19	20–24	**25–29**	30–34	35–39	40–44
Frequency	1	2	15	21	26	**28**	4	2	1

The modal class is 25–29 since this has the highest frequency.

25.10 Finding the median from a grouped frequency distribution

This question is usually asked in relation to individual data, so we use the table of results in Table 25.02 as an example.

Table 25.02 A survey of the number of children in 17 families

Children	0	1	2	3	4	5
Frequency	2	3	5	4	2	1
Running total	2	5	10	14	16	17

We know that the median is the middle value when the data is in ascending order, but in a frequency diagram the data is already in the correct order, so we just need to find the middle value.

A quick method of finding the middle value is to use the formula

$$\text{middle value} = \frac{\text{frequency} + 1}{2}$$

So median $= \dfrac{17 + 1}{2} = 9$th value $= 2$ children

Progress check

25.07 The results of 25 students in a test are given in the table.

Mark	Frequency
85–99	4
70–84	7
55–69	8
40–54	6

a Find the midpoint of each group of marks and calculate an estimate of the mean.

b Explain why your answer is an estimate.

• Lower quartile
Value of data corresponding to 25% of the total frequency.

• Upper quartile
Value of data corresponding to 75% of the total frequency.

• Interquartile range
The middle 50% of the data.

• Ogive
The cumulative frequency curve (an elongated S).

Exam-style questions

25.05 The mean height of 15 men is 1.70 m, and the mean height of 9 women is 1.60 m. Find:

a   The total height of the 15 men.
b   The total height of the 9 women.
c   The mean height of the 24 men and women.

25.06 The table below shows the distribution of ages of passengers travelling on a flight to London.

a   Calculate an estimate of the mean age.
b   Find the modal class.
c   Draw i) a histogram and ii) a cumulative frequency diagram of the data.
d   Using your cumulative frequency diagram, estimate the median and the interquartile range.

Ages	Frequency
$0 \leqslant x < 20$	27
$20 \leqslant x < 40$	36
$40 \leqslant x < 50$	19
$50 \leqslant x < 70$	30
$70 \leqslant x < 100$	18

Probability

CORE CURRICULUM

Learning outcomes

By the end of this unit you should be able to understand and know how to:

■ calculate the probability of a single event as either a fraction or a decimal (not a ratio)

■ use the probability scale from 0 to 1

Probability is the study of chance or the likelihood of an event happening. We can find the probability of an event as a numerical value by using the formula:

$$\text{Probability} = \frac{\text{number of favourable outcomes}}{\text{total number of possible outcomes}}$$

For example, consider a dice numbered 1, 2, 3, 4, 5, 6. We want to find the probability of throwing a number 6 with one throw. Using the formula:

$$P(6) = \frac{\text{number of times a 6 is thrown once}}{\text{total number of possible outcomes}} = \frac{1}{6}$$

The answer $\frac{1}{6}$ could also be shown as a decimal: $1 \div 6 = 0.166666\ldots$

We can show this as a percentage by multiplying the decimal by 100. The probability now becomes $16.666\ldots\%$.

Simplify your answers, if possible, and give the final answer as required, as either a fraction or a decimal.

26.01 Worked example

From one throw of a dice find the probability of getting:

a an even number **b** a multiple of 3 **c** a number 7

a There are 3 even numbers (2, 4 and 6) out of 6 possible outcomes.
So $P(\text{even}) = \frac{3}{6} = \frac{1}{2}$

b There are 2 multiples of 3 (3 and 6) out of 6 possible outcomes.
So $P(\text{multiple of 3}) = \frac{2}{6} = \frac{1}{3}$

c Number 7 is not possible, so $P(7) = 0$

Progress check

26.01 From one throw of a dice find the probability of getting:

a a number 4   b either a 3 or a 4   c a prime number.

26.01 The probability scale

Probabilities can be expressed on a scale as shown in Figure 26.01.

Impossible	Evens	Certain
0	0.5/½	1

Fig. 26.01 The probability scale

If an event is more likely to happen than another event, then it will be further to the right on the scale. An unlikely event will be somewhere between 0 and 0.5, while a likely event will be between 0.5 and 1. Sometimes a probability scale will have percentages instead of decimals. In this case the 0 will be 0%, 0.5 will be 50% and 1 will be 100%.

26.02 Probability of an event not occurring

Knowing that the probability of a certain event is 1 and that the probability of an impossible event is 0, we can calculate the probability of an event happening if we already know the probability of its not happening. We can show this as a simple formula:

Probability of event occurring $= 1 -$ probability of event not occurring

26.02 Worked example

From a bag of 8 coloured counters, the probability of *not* selecting a green counter is 0.25. Calculate the probability of selecting a green counter.

Probability of green $= 1 - 0.25 = 0.75$

Progress check

26.02 From a bag of 10 coloured counters, the probability of *not* selecting a red counter is 0.3. Calculate the probability of selecting a red counter.

26.03 Relative frequency

If we know the theoretical probability of an event happening, then we can make a reasonable estimation of what to expect in practice.

For example, if we have a dice numbered 1 to 6, then from 120 throws of that dice we would expect each number to occur 20 times (one sixth of 120).

26.03 Worked example

A car manufacturer estimates that the probability of their car developing a fault in the first year is 0.05. If the manufacturer produces 200 000 cars, how many would it expect to develop a fault after one year?

Expected number of faulty cars = $0.05 \times 200\,000 = 10\,000$

The next example shows how experimental results can be used to estimate relative frequency. The best estimate for relative frequency is obtained from the highest number of trials as any inconsistencies will have been minimised.

26.04 Worked example

Kiera throws a drawing pin in the air and records the number of times that it lands with its point up. The table below shows her results.

a What is the relative frequency of the drawing pin landing point up after 100 throws?

b Write down the best estimate for the relative frequency of the drawing pin landing point up from the table. Explain your answer.

Number of trials	10	20	100	200	1000
Point up	8	13	38	70	355

a Relative frequency after 100 throws = $\dfrac{38}{100} = 0.38$

b Best estimate for the relative frequency = $\dfrac{355}{1000} = 0.355$

The answer to (b) is obtained from the most trials. This is the most reliable estimate because inconsistent or lucky results will be less likely to affect the total.

Progress check

26.03 A television manufacturer estimates that the probability of its television developing a fault in the first three years of its life is 0.1. If the manufacturer produces 280 000 televisions in a three-year period, how many televisions would it expect to develop a fault after three years?

26.04 Callum drops a coin on the floor and records the number of times it lands on heads. The table shows his results.

a What is the relative frequency of the coin landing on heads after 100 throws?

b Write down the best estimate for the relative frequency of the coin landing on heads from the table. Explain your answer.

Number of trials	10	20	50	100	500
Heads	3	9	24	51	258

- **Evens**
  An event which has an equal chance of either happening or not happening.

- **Relative frequency**
  An estimate of what is likely to happen based on theory or actual trials.

- **Complementary probability**
  The probability of an event not occurring.

Exam-style questions

26.01 A bag contains 6 red balls and 4 green balls. Find the probability of selecting at random:

    a a red ball   b a white ball

    c a green ball if a red ball has already been selected and not replaced.

26.02 One letter is selected from the word PROBABILITY. Find the probability of selecting:

    a the letter B   b a vowel   c **not** a letter Y.

26.03 Cards with the number 2 to 102 are placed in a hat. Find the probability of selecting at random:

    a an even number   b a number less than 15   c a square number.

26.04 A shopkeeper estimates that the probability that he sells a liquorice sweet is 0.2. If he sells 240 sweets in total, how many liquorice sweets would he expect to sell?

26.05 Tia kicks a football at a target and records the number of times she hits it. The table shows her results.

    a What is the relative frequency of hitting the target after 50 throws?

    b Write down the best estimate for the relative frequency of hitting the target from the table?

Number of trials	10	20	30	50	100	200
Hits target	3	8	16	22	51	110

26.04 Combined events

There are two types of combined event:

- **Independent event**, where the first event has no effect on the second event.
- **Dependent event**, where the first event has an effect on the second event.

When dealing with combined probabilities we can use the **and/or** rule:

P(1st event and 2nd event) = P(1st event) × P(2nd event)
P(1st event or 2nd event) = P(1st event) + P(2nd event)

where P(1st event) is the probability of the first event happening and P(2nd event) is the probability of the second event happening.

If we have to find the probability of the first event happening **and** also the second event happening, we can see from the rule that we **multiply** the probabilities together.

If we have to find the probability of **either** the first event happening **or** the second event happening, we can see from the rule that we **add** the probabilities together. So remember, in probability:

and = multiply (×)   or = add (+)

In the following example the first event has no effect on the second event, so the events are **independent**.

26.05 Worked example

From two throws of a dice, find the probability of getting:

a two sixes   **b** one six followed by an even number (in order)
c a six from either dice.

a $P(6 \text{ and } 6) = \dfrac{1}{6} \times \dfrac{1}{6} = \dfrac{1}{36}$

b $P(6 \text{ and even}) = \dfrac{1}{6} \times \dfrac{3}{6} = \dfrac{1}{12}$

c $P(6 \text{ or } 6) = \dfrac{1}{6} + \dfrac{1}{6} = \dfrac{1}{3}$

For the *and* probabilities we have multiplied and for the *or* probabilities we have added. We have also simplified each of the answers, where possible.

In the next example the or/and rules still apply but the first event has an effect on the second event – it is **dependent**.

26.06 Worked example

Three red, 10 white, 5 blue and 2 green counters are put into a bag. Out of two selections, without replacing the first selection, find the probability of getting:

a two red counters
b a red and a blue counter in that order
c a red and blue counter in any order
d two counters of the same colour.

a $P(\text{red and red}) = \dfrac{3}{20} \times \dfrac{2}{19} = \dfrac{3}{190}$

b $P(\text{red and blue}) = \dfrac{3}{20} \times \dfrac{5}{19} = \dfrac{3}{76}$

c Note that the order could be red/blue or blue/red, so we have to calculate the probabilities of each and add them:

$$P[(\text{red and blue}) \text{ or } (\text{blue and red})] = \left(\dfrac{3}{20} \times \dfrac{5}{19} \right) + \left(\dfrac{5}{20} \times \dfrac{3}{19} \right)$$

$$= \dfrac{3}{76} + \dfrac{3}{76} = \dfrac{3}{38}$$

d If we let red = r, blue = b, green = g, w = white,
$P[(\text{r and r}) \text{ or } (\text{b and b}) \text{ or } (\text{g and g}) \text{ or } (\text{w and w})]$

$$= \left(\dfrac{3}{20} \times \dfrac{2}{19} \right) + \left(\dfrac{5}{20} \times \dfrac{4}{19} \right) + \left(\dfrac{2}{20} \times \dfrac{1}{19} \right) + \left(\dfrac{10}{20} \times \dfrac{9}{19} \right)$$

$$= \dfrac{3}{190} + \dfrac{1}{19} + \dfrac{1}{190} + \dfrac{9}{38} = \dfrac{59}{190}$$

Note how in each part of the question, the first event had an effect on the second event because there was no replacement of the first selection. For example, when calculating the probabilities of two reds, there was one less red and one less counter altogether available for the second selection.
Note also that the answers were presented in their simplest forms.

Progress check

26.05 From two throws of a dice, find the probability of getting:

    a two threes   b a four followed by an odd number
    c a two from either dice.

26.06 Four blue, 6 white, 3 green and 1 yellow marbles are put into a bag. Out of two selections, without replacing the first selection, find the probability of getting:

    a two blue counters   b a white and green counter in that order
    c two counters of the same colour.

26.05 Possibility diagrams

Possibility diagrams are used to show all possible results of two combined events. For example, if we throw two dice together and add up the scores each time, we could get the following results:

$$1 + 1 = 2$$
$$1 + 2 = 3$$
$$2 + 1 = 3$$
$$2 + 2 = 4$$
$$\ldots = \ldots$$

This would obviously take a long time since we have to account for all possibilities. We will set up a possibility diagram instead, where the first event is shown horizontally and the second event is shown vertically.

Table 26.01 shows all the possible results from adding the two dice. We can see that there are 36 different possibilities from the two events.

Table 26.01 Adding the results of two dice throws

		First dice score					
		1	**2**	**3**	**4**	**5**	**6**
Second	**1**	2	3	4	5	6	7
dice	**2**	3	4	5	6	7	8
score	**3**	4	5	6	7	8	9
	4	5	6	7	8	9	10
	5	6	7	8	9	10	11
	6	7	8	9	10	11	12

26.07 Worked example

Find the probability of getting a total of 7 from a throw of the two dice.

If we look at Table 26.01, we can see that the score of 7 occurs 6 times out of a total of 36 possible outcomes, therefore:

$$P(7) = \frac{6}{36} = \frac{1}{6} \qquad \text{(simplified answer)}$$

We could have worked this out without using a possibility diagram:

$$\left. \begin{array}{l} 1 + 6 = 7 \\ 6 + 1 = 7 \\ 2 + 5 = 7 \\ 5 + 2 = 7 \\ 3 + 4 = 7 \\ 4 + 3 = 7 \end{array} \right\} \; 6 \text{ ways}$$

Progress check

26.07 Draw a possibility diagram showing the results from two dice thrown together, with the numbers added together. Find the probability of getting a total score of 11.

26.06 Tree diagrams

When two or more combined events are being considered, a **tree diagram** could be used instead.

A tree diagram displays all the possible outcomes of an event as branches or paths and each branch is labelled as a probability.

For example, if a coin is tossed twice and the results recorded, there are four possibilities: heads and heads, heads and tails, tails and heads or tails and tails. We can show this as a tree diagram, with the combined probabilities – see Figure 26.02.

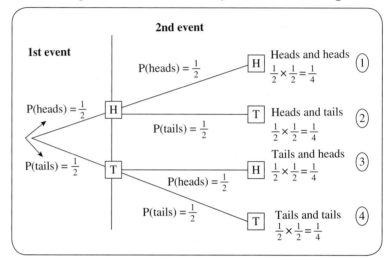

Fig. 26.02 Tree diagram for two coin tosses

Figure 26.02 shows a tree diagram for a combined independent event as the first coin throw will have no effect on the second event. Note that the branches in each selection add up to 1 because it is absolutely certain that you will get either heads or tails.

If we want to know the probability of, for example, getting either two heads or two tails, we add the appropriate branches (1 and 4): $\frac{1}{4} + \frac{1}{4} = \frac{1}{2}$.

We can say that when you go *along* the branches you *multiply* the probabilities, and when you have *alternative* branches you *add* the total probabilities.

The next example shows a dependent event.

26.08 Worked example

A box contains 4 black balls and 6 red balls. A ball is drawn from the box and is not replaced. A second ball is then drawn. Find the probabilities of:

a red then black being drawn
b red then black in any order
c two of the same colour being drawn.

As we only have two different colours, we will have two branches for each selection – see Figure 26.03.

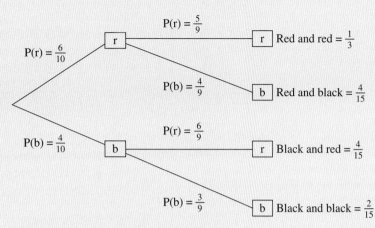

$P(r) = \frac{6}{10}$ $P(r) = \frac{5}{9}$ r   Red and red $= \frac{1}{3}$

$P(b) = \frac{4}{9}$ b   Red and black $= \frac{4}{15}$

$P(b) = \frac{4}{10}$ $P(r) = \frac{6}{9}$ r   Black and red $= \frac{4}{15}$

$P(b) = \frac{3}{9}$ b   Black and black $= \frac{2}{15}$

Fig. 26.03 Tree diagram of possibilities

a $P(\text{red and black}) = \dfrac{6}{10} \times \dfrac{4}{9} = \dfrac{4}{15}$

b $P[(\text{red and black}) \text{ or } (\text{black and red})] = \dfrac{4}{15} + \dfrac{4}{15} = \dfrac{8}{15}$

c $P[(\text{red and red}) \text{ or } (\text{black and black})] = \dfrac{1}{3} + \dfrac{2}{15} = \dfrac{7}{15}$

Progress check

26.08 The probability that a golfer hits the ball straight is 0.1. If three separate attempts are made, find the probability (using a tree diagram) that the ball will be hit straight:

    a   three times   b   at least once   c   not at all.

26.09 A bag contains 3 red, 4 blue and 2 green balls. Two balls are selected *without* replacement. Using a tree diagram find the probability that the three balls chosen are:

    a   2 blue   b   a green and then a red   c   2 balls of the same colour.

TERMS

- **Combined (events)**
  More than one event is taken into account when calculating the probability.

- **Independent (event)**
  This event's probability is not affected by another event happening.

- **Dependent (event)**
  This event's probability has been affected by another event happening.

Exam-style questions

26.06 The letters of the word MATHEMATICS are written on individual cards and the cards are put into a box. A card is selected and then replaced and then a second card is selected. Find the probability of obtaining:

    a the letter C twice   b a letter E or a letter A

    c the letter M and then the letter S.

26.07 Santy buys five raffle tickets out of 1000 sold. She does not win first prize. What is the probability that she wins second prize?

26.08 A coin is biased so that it shows 'heads' with a probability of 0.7. The same coin is tossed three times. Find the probability of obtaining:

    a two tails on the first two tosses

    b a head, a tail and a head in that order.

26.09 Shona places 3 red balls, 4 black balls and 5 green balls in a box. A ball is selected and then replaced, and then a second ball is selected. Find the probability of obtaining:

    a two black balls   b a red and a green ball in any order.

26.10 There are 400 sweets in a box, of which 100 are known to be red. Two sweets are selected at random, without replacement. Using a tree diagram, find the probability of selecting:

    a 2 red sweets   b no red sweets   c a red sweet *and then* any other colour.

Vectors

CORE CURRICULUM

A vector is a two-dimensional movement given in the form $\begin{pmatrix} x \\ y \end{pmatrix}$, where x is the horizontal movement and y is the vertical movement.

Consider the vector $\overrightarrow{AB} = \begin{pmatrix} 2 \\ 3 \end{pmatrix}$.

This vector starts at point A and moves 2 units across and 3 units vertically. This can be shown in a diagram, as in Figure 27.01.

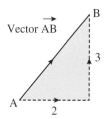

Fig. 27.01 Vector $\overrightarrow{AB}$

Note that the vector moves to the right which is the positive x-direction and then moves vertically up which is the positive y-direction.

Now consider a vector with negative x and y values, for example $\overrightarrow{CD} = \begin{pmatrix} -2 \\ -3 \end{pmatrix}$.

This vector starts at point C, moves 2 units across in the other direction and then 3 units down (see Figure 27.02).

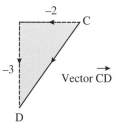

Fig. 27.02 Vector $\overrightarrow{CD}$

Remember the co-ordinate directions when drawing these vectors:

If x is positive, the vector moves to the right.
If x is negative, the vector moves to the left.
If y is positive, the vector moves up.
If y is negative, the vector moves down.

The vector could also be given a letter value. For example, $\mathbf{a} = \begin{pmatrix} 4 \\ -2 \end{pmatrix}$ means that the

vector $\mathbf{a}$ moves 4 units across and 2 units down (see Figure 27.03).

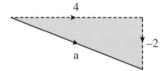

Fig. 27.03 Vector $\mathbf{a}$

27.01 Adding vectors

When adding vectors we simply add the x values together and then the y values together.

For example, if we have two vectors $\overrightarrow{AB}$ and $\overrightarrow{BC}$, where $\overrightarrow{AB} = \begin{pmatrix} 2 \\ -3 \end{pmatrix}$ and $\overrightarrow{BC} = \begin{pmatrix} 3 \\ 1 \end{pmatrix}$,
then

$$\overrightarrow{AB} + \overrightarrow{BC} = \begin{pmatrix} 2+3 \\ -3+1 \end{pmatrix} = \begin{pmatrix} 5 \\ -2 \end{pmatrix}.$$

The final vector, $\overrightarrow{AC}$, is 5 units across and 2 units down, as Figure 27.04 shows. $\overrightarrow{AC}$ is called the resultant vector.

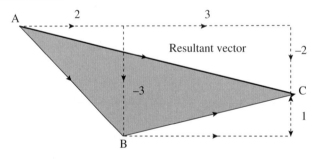

Fig. 27.04 $\overrightarrow{AC} = \overrightarrow{AB} + \overrightarrow{BC}$

27.02 Multiplying vectors by scalars

A scalar is a numerical value, e.g. 1, 2, 3, -1, -0.5, which, when multiplied by a vector, will change its size.

For example, if we have a vector $\overrightarrow{AB} = \begin{pmatrix} 3 \\ -2 \end{pmatrix}$ and we multiply it by the scalar quantity 3, it becomes

$$3\overrightarrow{AB} = 3 \times \begin{pmatrix} 3 \\ -2 \end{pmatrix} = \begin{pmatrix} 9 \\ -6 \end{pmatrix}$$ (we multiply both the x and the y values by 3). This is shown

in the diagram below.

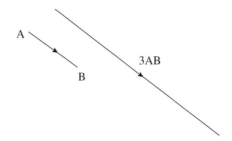

The vector $3\overrightarrow{AB}$ is 3 times the size of the vector $\overrightarrow{AB}$. Note that the vectors are still in the same direction but the first vector has been increased by a factor of 3 (enlarged by 3).

Progress check

27.01

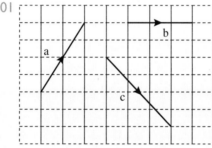

a Describe each of the translations **a**, **b**, **c** shown in the diagram, using column vectors.

b Calculate:

i   **a** + **b**
ii **b** − **c**
iii 2**a** + 3**c**
iv 3**a** + 2**b** − 4**c**

27.02 In the following questions, $\mathbf{e} = \begin{pmatrix} 3 \\ 4 \end{pmatrix}$, $\mathbf{f} = \begin{pmatrix} -2 \\ 1 \end{pmatrix}$, $\mathbf{g} = \begin{pmatrix} -4 \\ -3 \end{pmatrix}$ and $\mathbf{h} = \begin{pmatrix} 3 \\ -2 \end{pmatrix}$.

Draw vector diagrams to represent the following:

a **e** + **f**   b **f** + **e**   c **e** + **h**   d **f** + **g**   e 2**f** + 3**g**

TERMS

- **Vector**
  A two-dimensional movement in the x, y direction.

- **Scalar**
  A numerical value which, when multiplied by a vector, changes the vector's size accordingly.

For example, $2\mathbf{a}$ is twice the length of $\mathbf{a}$, and in the same direction; $-3\mathbf{b}$ is three times the length of $\mathbf{b}$, but in the opposite direction.

Exam-style questions

27.01 $\mathbf{a} = \begin{pmatrix} 3 \\ -2 \end{pmatrix}, \mathbf{b} = \begin{pmatrix} -1 \\ -2 \end{pmatrix}$.

a Work out: i $\mathbf{a} + 4\mathbf{b}$ ii $\mathbf{b} - \mathbf{a}$

b $\overrightarrow{CD} = 2\mathbf{b}$. The point C is marked on the grid below. Draw the vector $\overrightarrow{CD}$ on the grid.

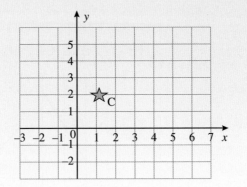

27.02 $\mathbf{a} = \begin{pmatrix} 2 \\ -3 \end{pmatrix}, \mathbf{b} = \begin{pmatrix} 0 \\ -3 \end{pmatrix}, \mathbf{c} = \begin{pmatrix} 4 \\ -1 \end{pmatrix}$. Express each of the following vectors in terms of $\mathbf{a}, \mathbf{b}$ and $\mathbf{c}$:

a $\begin{pmatrix} -4 \\ 6 \end{pmatrix}$ b $\begin{pmatrix} 0 \\ 3 \end{pmatrix}$ c $\begin{pmatrix} 4 \\ -4 \end{pmatrix}$ d $\begin{pmatrix} 8 \\ -2 \end{pmatrix}$

27.03 The magnitude of a vector |a|

The magnitude or modulus of a vector is its length.

27.01 Worked example

$\overrightarrow{AB} = \begin{pmatrix} 3 \\ 4 \end{pmatrix}$. Find the magnitude of vector $\overrightarrow{AB}$, i.e. $|AB|$.

We first sketch the vector – see Figure 27.05.

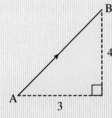

Fig. 27.05 Vector $\overrightarrow{AB}$

We can see from Figure 27.05 that the x and y dimensions form the two shorter sides of a right-angled triangle, and AB forms the longer side.

We can then use Pythagoras' theorem to find the longer side of a right-angled triangle:

$$|AB| = \sqrt{x^2 + y^2} = \sqrt{3^2 + 4^2} = 5 \text{ units}$$

The same method can be used for negative vectors. Try the above example using negative values of x and y. You should get the answer 5 units again.

27.04 Representing vectors by line segments

We know that vectors can be shown as letters. We can also show the addition of vectors in terms of letters – see Figure 27.06.

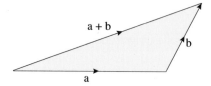

Fig. 27.06 Resultant vector = vector **a** plus vector **b** = **a** + **b**

The resultant vector follows the same general direction, i.e. it starts at the same point as vector **a** and finishes at the end point of vector **b**.

A negative vector can be called an inverse vector. Figure 27.07 shows the inverse vector of **b**, which is −**b**. We can see that the vectors are equal in size but opposite in direction.

Fig. 27.07 Inverse vector

We can show the subtraction of vectors using letter notation. Figure 27.08 shows the resultant vector of **a** − **b**.

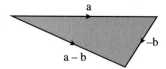

Fig. 27.08 Resultant vector of **a** − **b** = **a** + (−**b**)

The vector −**b** is in the opposite direction to the vector **b** in Figure 27.06.

The following example involves several vectors.

27.02 Worked example

In Figure 27.09, ABCDEF is a regular hexagon. If $\overrightarrow{AB} = \mathbf{a}$, $\overrightarrow{AF} = \mathbf{b}$ and $\overrightarrow{BC} = \mathbf{c}$, express each of the following in terms of $\mathbf{a}$, $\mathbf{b}$ and $\mathbf{c}$:

a $\overrightarrow{DC}$ b $\overrightarrow{DE}$ c $\overrightarrow{FE}$ d $\overrightarrow{FC}$ e $\overrightarrow{AE}$

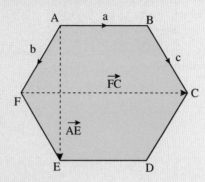

Fig. 27.09 Hexagon ABCDEF

a $\overrightarrow{DC} = -\overrightarrow{AF} = -\mathbf{b}$ (it is equal in length but in the opposite direction to $\overrightarrow{AF}$)

b $\overrightarrow{DE} = -\overrightarrow{AB} = -\mathbf{a}$ (it is equal in length but in the opposite direction to $\overrightarrow{AB}$)

c $\overrightarrow{FE} = \overrightarrow{BC} = \mathbf{c}$ (it is equal in length and in the same direction as $\overrightarrow{BC}$)

d $\overrightarrow{FC} = \overrightarrow{FA} + \overrightarrow{AB} + \overrightarrow{BC}$ (see the path of the resultant vector from F to C)

    $= -\mathbf{b} + \mathbf{a} + \mathbf{c} = \mathbf{a} - \mathbf{b} + \mathbf{c}$

e $\overrightarrow{AE} = \overrightarrow{AF} + \overrightarrow{FE} = \mathbf{b} + \mathbf{c}$ (again, see the path of the resultant vector from A to E)

There are alternative paths that the resultant vectors could take. For example, $\overrightarrow{FC}$ could also take the path $\overrightarrow{FE} + \overrightarrow{ED} + \overrightarrow{DC}$, which still gives the same answer as before: $\mathbf{a} - \mathbf{b} + \mathbf{c}$.

27.05 Position vectors

These are vectors which start at the origin O, co-ordinates (0, 0). The method of finding the vectors is the same as before.

27.03 Worked example

In Figure 27.10, P is the point $(1, 1)$. The vector $\mathbf{a} = \begin{pmatrix} 1 \\ 2 \end{pmatrix}$ and $\mathbf{b} = \begin{pmatrix} 2 \\ -1 \end{pmatrix}$.

a   Find the vector $\mathbf{a} + 2\mathbf{b}$.

b $\overrightarrow{PQ} = \mathbf{a} + 2\mathbf{b}$. Find the position vector of Q.

c   Calculate $|\mathbf{a}|$, the magnitude of $\mathbf{a}$.

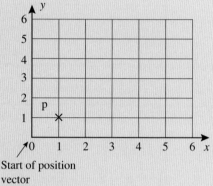

Start of position vector

Fig. 27.10 Position vector example

a $\mathbf{a} + 2\mathbf{b} = \begin{pmatrix} 1 \\ 2 \end{pmatrix} + 2 \times \begin{pmatrix} 2 \\ -1 \end{pmatrix} = \begin{pmatrix} 5 \\ 0 \end{pmatrix}$

b $\overrightarrow{PQ} = \mathbf{a} + 2\mathbf{b}$. The position vector of Q is its vector from the origin $(0, 0)$, $\overrightarrow{OQ}$.

$\overrightarrow{OQ} = \overrightarrow{OP} + \overrightarrow{PQ} = \begin{pmatrix} 1 \\ 1 \end{pmatrix} + \begin{pmatrix} 5 \\ 0 \end{pmatrix} = \begin{pmatrix} 6 \\ 1 \end{pmatrix}$

c $|\mathbf{a}| = \sqrt{1^2 + 2^2} = 2.2$ units

Note how the method is almost exactly the same as before, the only difference being that the vector started from the origin and went to another stated point.

Progress check

27.04 In the diagram, $\overrightarrow{OC} = 2\overrightarrow{OB}$, $\overrightarrow{OD} = 4\overrightarrow{OE}$, $\overrightarrow{OB} = \mathbf{x}$ and $\overrightarrow{OE} = \mathbf{y}$.

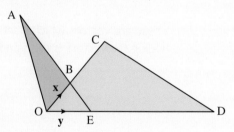

a   Express the following in terms of $\mathbf{x}$ and $\mathbf{y}$:

   i $\overrightarrow{OC}$ and $\overrightarrow{OD}$ ii $\overrightarrow{EB}$ iii $\overrightarrow{DC}$

b   Given that $\overrightarrow{EA} = 3\overrightarrow{EB}$, express $\overrightarrow{OA}$ in terms of $\mathbf{x}$ and $\mathbf{y}$.

• Magnitude/modulus
  The actual length or size of a vector.

• Position vector
  A vector that starts from the origin $(0, 0)$.

• Inverse vector
  A vector equal in size but in the opposite direction.

Exam-style questions

27.03 OPQR is a parallelogram. O is the origin. $\overrightarrow{OP} = \mathbf{p}$ and $\overrightarrow{OR} = \mathbf{r}$. M is the mid-point of PQ and L is on OR such that $OL : LR = 2:1$. The line PL is extended to the point S.

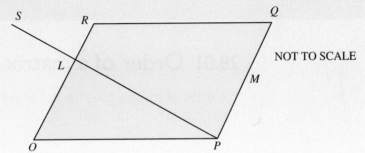

NOT TO SCALE

a Find, in terms of $\mathbf{p}$ and $\mathbf{r}$, in their simplest forms,

  i $\overrightarrow{OQ}$,   ii $\overrightarrow{PR}$,   iii $\overrightarrow{PL}$,   iv the position vector of M.

b PLS is a straight line and $PS = \frac{3}{2} PL$. Find, in terms of $\mathbf{p}$ and/or $\mathbf{r}$, in their simplest forms,

  i $\overrightarrow{PS}$,   ii $\overrightarrow{QS}$.

c What can you say about the points Q, R and S?

Source: *Cambridge IGCSE Mathematics 0580 Paper 4 Q9a, b, c June 2008.*

27.04 E is the mid-point of the line AD and C divides the line BD in the ratio $1 : 3$. $\overrightarrow{AE} = \mathbf{c}$ and $\overrightarrow{AB} = \mathbf{d}$.

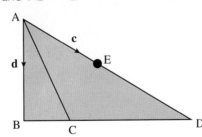

a Express each of the following in terms of $\mathbf{c}$ and $\mathbf{d}$:

  i $\overrightarrow{AD}$ ii $\overrightarrow{BD}$ iii $\overrightarrow{AC}$

b Show that $\overrightarrow{CE} = \frac{1}{4}(2\mathbf{c} - 3\mathbf{d})$.

Matrices

EXTENDED CURRICULUM

Learning outcomes

By the end of this unit you should be able to understand and use:

- matrix notation, addition, subtraction and multiplication

- equations involving matrices

- determinants and inverses of 2×2 matrices

28.01 Order of a matrix

The **order** of a matrix gives the number of rows followed by the number of columns in the matrix.

Matrix order = number of rows $\times$ number of columns

$$\begin{array}{cc} \text{Column 1} & \text{Column 2} \\ \text{Row 1} \quad \begin{pmatrix} a & b \\ c & d \end{pmatrix} & \\ \text{Row 2} & \end{array}$$

Fig. 28.01 2×2 matrix

The order of the matrix in Figure 28.01 is therefore 2×2, and we say it is 'of order 2 by 2'.

These are matrices of different orders:

$1 \times 2 \quad \begin{pmatrix} a & b \end{pmatrix}$

$2 \times 3 \quad \begin{pmatrix} a & b & c \\ d & e & f \end{pmatrix}$

$3 \times 3 \quad \begin{pmatrix} a & b & c \\ d & e & f \\ g & h & i \end{pmatrix}$

$1 \times 3 \quad \begin{pmatrix} a & b & c \end{pmatrix}$

28.02 Addition and subtraction of two or more matrices

The general rule is that only matrices of the same order can be added or subtracted.

For example, a 2 × 2 matrix can be added to another 2 × 2 matrix and a 1 × 3 matrix can be added to another 1 × 3 matrix.

28.01 Worked example

If $A = \begin{pmatrix} 3 & -2 \\ 4 & -3 \end{pmatrix}$ and $B = \begin{pmatrix} -3 & 6 \\ -4 & 2 \end{pmatrix}$, find   **a** A + B   **b** A − B.

a $\begin{pmatrix} 3 & -2 \\ 4 & -3 \end{pmatrix} + \begin{pmatrix} -3 & 6 \\ -4 & 2 \end{pmatrix} = \begin{pmatrix} 3+(-3) & (-2)+6 \\ 4+(-4) & (-3)+2 \end{pmatrix} = \begin{pmatrix} 0 & 4 \\ 0 & -1 \end{pmatrix}$

Each element in the first matrix is added to the element in the corresponding position in the second matrix, e.g. the number at (row 1, column 1) in matrix **A** is added to the number at (row 1, column 1) in matrix **B**.

b $\begin{pmatrix} 3 & -2 \\ 4 & -3 \end{pmatrix} - \begin{pmatrix} -3 & 6 \\ -4 & 2 \end{pmatrix} = \begin{pmatrix} 3-(-3) & (-2)-6 \\ 4-(-4) & (-3)-2 \end{pmatrix} = \begin{pmatrix} 6 & 8 \\ 8 & -5 \end{pmatrix}$ (taking care with double negatives)

The same rules apply for all types of matrices, whatever the size.

28.03 The product of two matrices

These are the rules we need to follow to find the product of two matrices:

- The number of rows in the first matrix must equal the number of columns in the second matrix.
- The order of the resulting matrix is the number of rows in the first matrix multiplied by the number of columns in the second matrix.
- When multiplying, multiply the elements in a row of the first matrix by the elements in a column of the second matrix and add the products. For example, the sum of the products of the elements in the first row of the first matrix and the elements in the second column of the second matrix gives the element in the first row and second column of the product matrix.

When you multiply two matrices together, the final matrix will take the form:

$$\begin{pmatrix} \text{row 1} \times \text{column 1} & \text{row 1} \times \text{column 2} \\ \text{row 2} \times \text{column 2} & \text{row 2} \times \text{column 2} \end{pmatrix}$$

28.02 Worked example

If $A = \begin{pmatrix} 3 & -2 \\ 4 & -3 \end{pmatrix}$ and $B = \begin{pmatrix} -3 & 6 \\ -4 & 2 \end{pmatrix}$, find $A \times B$.

$$A \times B = \begin{pmatrix} 3 & -2 \\ 4 & -3 \end{pmatrix} \times \begin{pmatrix} -3 & 6 \\ -4 & 2 \end{pmatrix} = \begin{pmatrix} 3\times(-3)+(-2)\times(-4) & 3\times6+(-2)\times2 \\ 4\times(-3)+(-3)\times(-4) & 4\times6+(-3)\times2 \end{pmatrix}$$

$$= \begin{pmatrix} -9+8 & 18+(-4) \\ -12+12 & 24+(-6) \end{pmatrix} = \begin{pmatrix} -1 & 14 \\ 0 & 18 \end{pmatrix}$$

Note that matrix multiplication is **not** commutative, so $B \times A$ would give $\begin{pmatrix} 15 & -12 \\ -4 & 2 \end{pmatrix}$.

28.04 Scalar multiplication of a matrix

When you multiply a matrix by a scalar quantity, every element of the matrix is multiplied by that number. For example, if the scalar quantity is 2 then all elements in the matrix are multiplied by 2.

28.03 Worked example

If $C = \begin{pmatrix} 2 & -1 \\ 4 & -3 \end{pmatrix}$ and $D = \begin{pmatrix} 4 & -3 \\ -1 & 2 \end{pmatrix}$, find: **a** $2C$ **b** $-3D$ **c** $2C - 3D$.

a $2C = 2 \times \begin{pmatrix} 2 & -1 \\ 4 & -3 \end{pmatrix} = \begin{pmatrix} 4 & -2 \\ 8 & -6 \end{pmatrix}$

(every term inside C has been multiplied by the scalar quantity 2)

b $-3D = -3 \times \begin{pmatrix} 4 & -3 \\ -1 & 2 \end{pmatrix} = \begin{pmatrix} -12 & 9 \\ 3 & -6 \end{pmatrix}$

(every term inside the matrix has been multiplied by the scalar quantity of -3)

c $2C - 3D = \begin{pmatrix} 4 & -2 \\ 8 & -6 \end{pmatrix} + \begin{pmatrix} -12 & 9 \\ 3 & -6 \end{pmatrix} = \begin{pmatrix} -8 & 7 \\ 11 & -12 \end{pmatrix}$

The scalar quantity can be positive, negative or a fraction; every element inside the matrix is multiplied by the scalar quantity.

We have only looked at 2×2 matrices so far with scalar quantities, but the method is essentially the same for matrices of other orders.

28.05 Using algebra within matrices

28.04 Worked example

If $\begin{pmatrix} 2 & x \\ 4 & y \end{pmatrix}\begin{pmatrix} 5 \\ 2 \end{pmatrix} = \begin{pmatrix} 14 \\ 30 \end{pmatrix}$, find x and y.

First we'll find the left-hand side of the problem by multiplying the matrices together:

$$\begin{pmatrix} 2 & x \\ 4 & y \end{pmatrix}\begin{pmatrix} 5 \\ 2 \end{pmatrix} = \begin{pmatrix} 2\times5+(x)\times2 \\ 4\times5+(y)\times2 \end{pmatrix} = \begin{pmatrix} 10+2x \\ 20+2y \end{pmatrix}$$

Now we can rewrite the problem:

$$\begin{pmatrix} 10+2x \\ 20+2y \end{pmatrix} = \begin{pmatrix} 14 \\ 30 \end{pmatrix}$$

As the left-hand side equals the right-hand side, we can remove the matrices and now treat the problem as two linear equations:

$10 + 2x = 14$	and	$20 + 2y = 30$
$2x = 14 - 10$		$2y = 30 - 20$
$2x = 4$		$2y = 10$
$x = 2$		$y = 5$

Note that we can use this method on other orders of matrices, provided that it is *possible* to multiply the matrices together.

28.06 Zero matrix

The **zero matrix** is one in which all the elements are zero. It is sometimes called a **null** matrix.

This is a 2 × 2 null matrix: $\begin{pmatrix} 0 & 0 \\ 0 & 0 \end{pmatrix}$.

28.07 The identity matrix (I)

A **diagonal matrix** has all its elements zero except for those in the leading diagonal (from top left to bottom right).

The **identity matrix**, I, is a diagonal matrix with the elements equal to 1.

This is the 2 × 2 identity matrix: $\begin{pmatrix} 1 & 0 \\ 0 & 1 \end{pmatrix}$.

If you multiply a matrix by the identity matrix the result is the original matrix.

So, if $\mathbf{A} = \begin{pmatrix} 2 & 3 \\ 1 & 4 \end{pmatrix}$ then $\mathbf{A} \times \mathbf{I} = \begin{pmatrix} 2 & 3 \\ 1 & 4 \end{pmatrix}$.

28.08 Calculating the determinant of a matrix |A|

If $\mathbf{A} = \begin{pmatrix} a & b \\ c & d \end{pmatrix}$, then the determinant of $\mathbf{A}$, given the symbol $|\mathbf{A}|$, is found using the following formula:

$$|\mathbf{A}| = ad - bc$$

28.05 Worked example

Find the determinant of the matrix $\mathbf{X} = \begin{pmatrix} 3 & 5 \\ 2 & 4 \end{pmatrix}$.

Using the formula above, $|\mathbf{X}| = 3 \times 4 - 5 \times 2 = 2$

Note that the determinant can also be a negative value, depending on the values of the elements inside the matrix.

28.09 Inverse of a matrix ($\mathbf{A}^{-1}$)

As its name suggests, this is simply the inverse or reciprocal of a matrix. If we multiply any matrix by its inverse we will obtain the identity matrix:

$$\mathbf{AA}^{-1} = \mathbf{I}$$

To find the inverse of the 2 × 2 matrix $\mathbf{A} = \begin{pmatrix} a & b \\ c & d \end{pmatrix}$, use the formula:

$$\mathbf{A}^{-1} = \frac{1}{|\mathbf{A}|}\begin{pmatrix} d & -b \\ -c & a \end{pmatrix}$$

Note how we have interchanged the a and d values and changed the signs on the b and c values.

28.06 Worked example

Find the inverse of the following matrix and perform the appropriate check to ensure that is correct:

$$\mathbf{A} = \begin{pmatrix} 4 & 1 \\ 2 & 3 \end{pmatrix}.$$

Using the formula for the inverse:

$$\mathbf{A}^{-1} = \frac{1}{4 \times 3 - 2 \times 1}\begin{pmatrix} 3 & -1 \\ -2 & 4 \end{pmatrix} = \frac{1}{10}\begin{pmatrix} 3 & -1 \\ -2 & 4 \end{pmatrix} = \begin{pmatrix} 0.3 & -0.1 \\ -0.2 & 0.4 \end{pmatrix}$$

To check, we need to show that $\mathbf{AA}^{-1} = \mathbf{I}$:

$$\begin{pmatrix} 4 & 1 \\ 2 & 3 \end{pmatrix}\begin{pmatrix} 0.3 & -0.1 \\ -0.2 & 0.4 \end{pmatrix} = \begin{pmatrix} 4 \times 0.3 + 1 \times (-0.2) & 4 \times (-0.1) + 1 \times 0.4 \\ 2 \times 0.3 + 3 \times (-0.2) & 2 \times (-0.1) + 3 \times 0.4 \end{pmatrix} = \begin{pmatrix} 1 & 0 \\ 0 & 1 \end{pmatrix}$$

Progress check

28.01 $X = \begin{pmatrix} 4 & 2 \\ 3 & 8 \end{pmatrix}$, $Y = \begin{pmatrix} -3 & 2 \\ -4 & 4 \end{pmatrix}$, $Z = \begin{pmatrix} -5 & 3 \\ -2 & -6 \end{pmatrix}$. Calculate:

    a $X + Y$ b $2X + 3Y$ c XY d X^{-1} e $|Z|$ f $(X + Y)^{-1}$

28.02 $A = \begin{pmatrix} 2 & 3 & 6 \\ -1 & 5 & 8 \end{pmatrix}$, $B = \begin{pmatrix} -3 & 4 & -2 \\ 2 & 8 & 3 \\ 1 & -3 & -5 \end{pmatrix}$, $C = (4\ 5\ -3)$ Find, if possible:

    a AB b BA c CA d BC

TERMS

- **Order of a matrix**
  The row number multiplied by the column number.

- **Identity matrix**
  A diagonal matrix with the elements equal to 1.

- **Determinant**
  Given by the formula $ad - bc$; if the determinant is zero there is no inverse.

- **Inverse**
  Any matrix multiplied by its inverse gives the identity matrix.

- **Not commutative**
  Product is different if matrix position is changed.

Exam-style questions

28.01 a **A** is a (2×4) matrix, **B** is a (3×2) matrix and **C** is a (1×3) matrix. Which two of the following matrix products is it possible to work out?

    A^2 B^2 C^2 AB AC BA BC CA CB

  b Find the inverse of $\begin{pmatrix} \frac{1}{2} & \frac{3}{4} \\ \frac{1}{8} & \frac{1}{4} \end{pmatrix}$. Simplify your answer as far as possible.

  c Explain why the matrix $\begin{pmatrix} 4 & 2 \\ 6 & 3 \end{pmatrix}$ does not have an inverse.

28.02 $A = \begin{pmatrix} x & 6 \\ 4 & 3 \end{pmatrix}$, $B = \begin{pmatrix} 2 & 3 \\ 2 & 1 \end{pmatrix}$

  a Find **AB**.   b When **AB** = **BA**, find the value of x.

Source: *Cambridge IGCSE Mathematics 0580 Paper 21 Q21a, b June 2009.*

28.03 Work out $\begin{pmatrix} 2 & 4 & 7 \\ 1 & -3 & 4 \\ 3 & -3 & 2 \end{pmatrix}\begin{pmatrix} 3 \\ -2 \\ -8 \end{pmatrix}$

Transformations

CORE CURRICULUM

Learning outcomes

By the end of this unit you should be able to:

- reflect an object in a mirror line and in the x- or y-axis
- rotate an object from a fixed point in multiples of 90° in either a clockwise or anticlockwise direction
- translate an object according to a given vector
- enlarge an object from a given fixed point according to a given scale factor

29.01 Reflecting an object in a mirror line

When an object is reflected it undergoes a 'flip' movement about a mirror line. The size of the object remains unchanged.

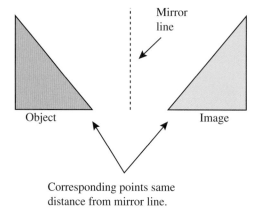

Fig. 29.01 Reflection in a mirror line

The triangle in Figure 29.01 'flips' over the mirror line to become its image.

Each corresponding point on the object and the image should be exactly the same distance from the mirror line. Use a ruler or tracing paper to check that the image has been drawn in the correct position.

29.02 Reflection in the *x*- or *y*-axis

This time the *x*-axis or *y*-axis is the mirror line – see Figure 29.02.

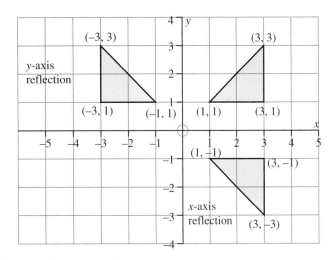

Fig. 29.02 Reflections in the *x* and *y* axes

When the *x*-axis is the mirror line notice how the *y* co-ordinates change sign. When the *y*-axis becomes the mirror line, only the *x* co-ordinates change sign. Note how a reflection does not change the shape or size of the object.

29.03 Rotation

When an object is **rotated**, it undergoes a turning movement about a specific point called the **centre of rotation**. When we describe a rotation we need to state:

- the position of the centre of rotation
- the direction of rotation
- the angle of rotation.

Figures 29.03 and 29.04 show some examples of rotation.

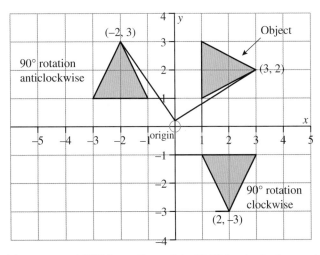

Fig. 29.03 An object rotated 90° from the origin (0, 0) in clockwise and anticlockwise directions

When the object is rotated 90° from the origin each point will turn the same angle and remain the same distance from the origin. Note how a rotation does not change the shape or size of the object.

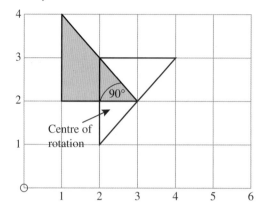

Fig. 29.04 A 90° clockwise rotation using the mid-point of an edge as the centre of rotation

The object has remained the same shape and size and each rotated point is the same distance from the centre of rotation.

When performing rotations, use a protractor to give accurate angles of rotation or use grid lines to help you. Use compasses to ensure the rotated points are equal distances from the centre of rotation.

29.04 Translation

When an object is translated, it undergoes a vector type movement, i.e. the whole shape moves to another location on a grid without changing size or rotating. You might find it helpful to revise directed numbers in Unit 2 and vectors in Unit 27.

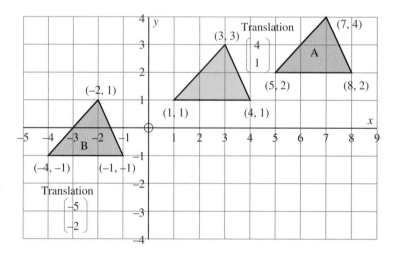

Fig. 29.05 Translation examples

In Figure 29.05, Shape A has translated 4 units to the right and 1 unit up. Shape B has translated 5 units to the left and 2 units down.

When performing a translation, remember that the x movement is always above the y movement. A positive translation moves either right or up and a negative translation moves either left or down.

29.05 Enlargement

When an object undergoes an enlargement, the resulting image is of a similar shape but a different size. When we perform an enlargement, we need to state:

• the position of the centre of enlargement
• the scale factor of enlargement.

If we use a scale factor of 2, then the image will be twice the size of the original object (Figure 29.06); however, if the scale factor of enlargement is less than 1, then the object actually reduces in size (Figure 29.07). The scale factor can also be negative (Figure 29.08).

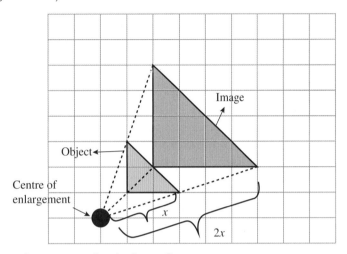

Fig. 29.06 An enlargement of scale factor 2

The distance from the centre of enlargement to each corner is measured with a ruler. This distance is multiplied by the scale factor to give the position of the same corner on the image.

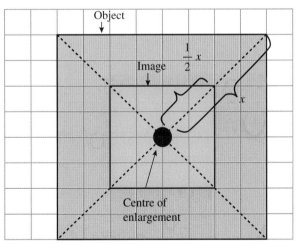

Fig. 29.07 An enlargement of scale factor $\dfrac{1}{2}$

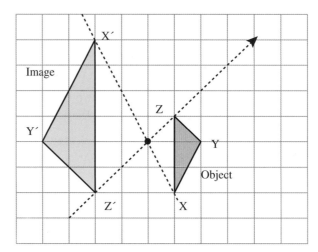

Fig. 29.08 A negative enlargement of scale factor −2

To perform the negative enlargement shown in Figure 29.08, the distance from the centre of enlargement to each corner is measured with a ruler. This distance is multiplied by the negative scale factor to give the position of the same corner on the image but in the **opposite** direction. Note how this gives a similar result to a 180° rotation; indeed, a scale factor of −1 enlargement is exactly the same as a 180° rotation.

Progress check

29.01 Which type of transformation results in the object changing size?

29.02 When performing a translation, name two key things to remember.

29.03 A rotation involves only multiples of how many degrees?

29.04 What is the effect of a negative scale factor enlargement?

29.05 How can you ensure the image is in the correct position?

TERMS

- **Transformation**
  A two-dimensional movement of an object to its new position (its image).

- **Reflection**
  The shape reflects about a mirror line (or the x- or y-axis) to become its image; it remains the same size.

- **Rotation**
  The shape rotates in multiples of 90° about a centre of rotation, either clockwise or anticlockwise; it remain the same size.

- **Translation**
  The shape performs a vector or 'sliding' movement on a grid without rotating or changing size.

- **Enlargement**
  The whole shape changes in size according to a given scale factor (>1 means larger, <1 means smaller), from a centre of enlargement.

Exam-style questions

29.01 Copy the grid below and perform the following transformations on A:

   a Reflection in the x-axis; label the image B.

   b Rotation of 180°, using the origin as centre of rotation. Label the image C.

   c Enlargement of scale factor 2 from co-ordinate (3, 1). Label the image D.

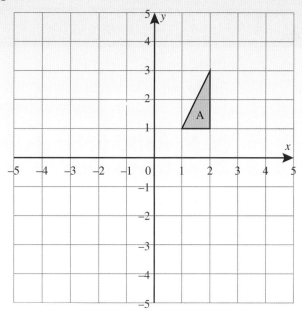

Learning outcomes

By the end of this unit you should be able to understand and use:

■ reflections, rotations, translations, enlargements, and their combinations

■ precise descriptions of transformations connecting given figures

■ transformations using co-ordinates and matrices

The fundamentals of reflection, rotation, translation and enlargement have already been covered, but now we need to extend these basic principles.

29.06 Reflections: stating the equation of the mirror line

We now need to state the exact position of the mirror line on the grid. Consider the reflection shown in Figure 29.09.

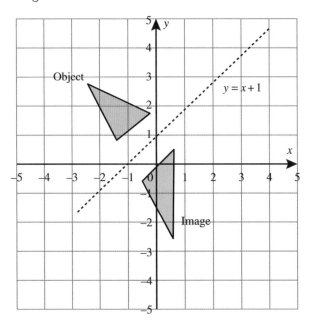

Fig. 29.09 Finding the equation of the mirror line

The image in Figure 29.09 has been reflected in the mirror line shown. We can work out the equation of the mirror line by using the $y = mx + c$ rule covered in Unit 11.

The line intercepts the y-axis at 1 (therefore $c = 1$) and the gradient is also 1 (therefore $m = 1$).

The object has undergone a reflection in the line $y = x + 1$.

29.07 Rotations: finding the centre and angle of rotation

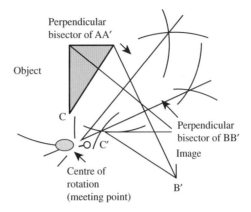

Fig. 29.10 Finding the centre of rotation

To find the centre of rotation (see Figure 29.10):

1. Join a point on the object to its corresponding point on the image, e.g. join A to A′.
2. Construct the perpendicular bisector of this line.
3. Repeat this process for another point, e.g. B to B′.
4. The two perpendicular bisectors meet at the centre of rotation.

To find the angle, simply measure with a protractor the angle turned from any point to its corresponding point on the image.

29.08 Enlargement: finding the centre and scale factor of enlargement

To find the centre of enlargement (see Figure 29.11):

1. Join up any point on the image to its corresponding point on the object. Continue this line back for a few centimetres.
2. Repeat this process for another point.
3. The two lines meet at the centre of enlargement.

To find the scale factor, divide the length of any side of the image by the length of the corresponding side on the object, e.g. in Figure 29.11, the scale factor is 4 ÷ 2 = 2.

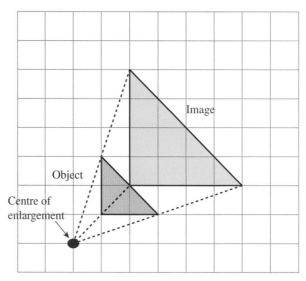

Fig. 29.11 Finding the centre of enlargement

29.09 Combinations of transformations

Sometimes we have more than one transformation of a shape on the same grid. Figure 29.14 shows three transformations:

- Object to image 1 is a rotation of 90° clockwise using the origin as the centre of rotation.
- Image 1 to image 2 is a reflection in the y-axis.
- Image 2 to image 3 is an enlargement of scale factor 2, centre of enlargement $(-1, -4)$.

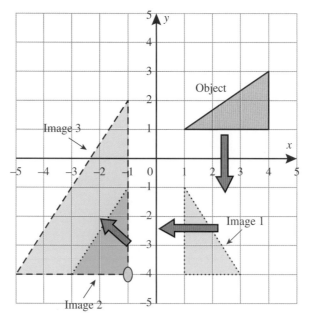

Fig. 29.14 Multiple transformations

29.10 Transformations and matrices

Any shape on a grid can be shown as a matrix by using the co-ordinate positions of each of its corners (vertices).

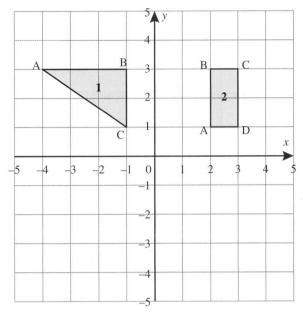

Fig. 29.15 Co-ordinate matrices

In Figure 29.15, shape 1 has the matrix $\begin{matrix} A & B & C \end{matrix}$ $\begin{pmatrix} -4 & -1 & -1 \\ 3 & 3 & 1 \end{pmatrix}$, while shape 2 $= \begin{matrix} A & B & C & D \end{matrix}$ $\begin{pmatrix} 2 & 2 & 3 & 3 \\ 1 & 3 & 3 & 1 \end{pmatrix}$,

where the first row shows the x co-ordinate and the second row the y co-ordinate.

Performing a matrix transformation on a shape

When we multiply the matrix of vertices of a shape by another matrix, we perform a transformation on that shape. We have already studied multiplication of matrices in Unit 28, so we know the method involved.

29.01 Worked example

Triangle XYZ has co-ordinates X $(-4, 4)$, Y $(-4, 1)$ and Z $(-1, 1)$. Draw the image of triangle XYZ under the transformation matrix $\begin{pmatrix} 0 & 1 \\ -1 & 0 \end{pmatrix}$.

Plot the triangle XYZ using the co-ordinates given and then calculate the new position of each vertex after the matrix multiplication:

$$\begin{matrix} & X & Y & Z & X' & Y' & Z' \end{matrix}$$
$$\begin{pmatrix} 0 & 1 \\ -1 & 0 \end{pmatrix} \times \begin{pmatrix} -4 & -4 & -1 \\ 4 & 1 & 1 \end{pmatrix} = \begin{pmatrix} 4 & 1 & 1 \\ 4 & 4 & 1 \end{pmatrix}$$

We then plot these new co-ordinates on the grid, as in Figure 29.16.

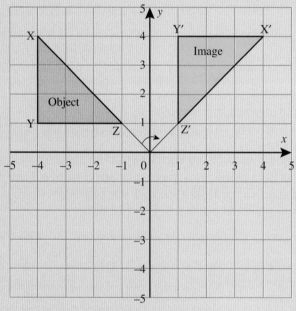

Fig. 29.16 Transformation of triangle XYZ

We can see that the object has undergone a rotation of 90° clockwise with the origin as the centre of rotation.

Transformations involving more than one matrix: A′ = MR(A)

In this case the object or point (**A**) is first multiplied by the matrix **R** and then the result is multiplied by matrix **M** to give its final position (**A′**).

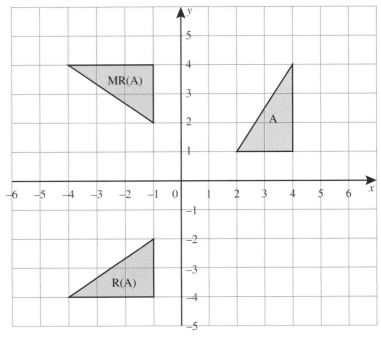

Fig. 29.17 Multiple matrix transformations

In Figure 29.17, shape $\mathbf{A} = \begin{pmatrix} 2 & 4 & 4 \\ 1 & 1 & 4 \end{pmatrix}$, matrix $\mathbf{R} = \begin{pmatrix} 0 & -1 \\ -1 & 0 \end{pmatrix}$ and matrix $\mathbf{M} = \begin{pmatrix} 1 & 0 \\ 0 & -1 \end{pmatrix}$.

Matrix **R** performs a reflection of **A** in the line $y = -x$ to become **R(A)** and then matrix **M** performs a reflection in the x-axis to give **MR(A)**.

The combined transformation is therefore a 90° anticlockwise rotation from the origin.

Note that a quicker method would be to multiply **M** by **R** to find the resultant matrix, and then multiply this by **A** to get **A′**. Check for yourself.

Inverse transformations

We may we need to find the **inverse** of a transformation, i.e. the operation which reverses the image back to its original position.

- The inverse of an **image reflection** is simply the object itself (a mirror image is the inverse of a shape).
- The inverse operation of a **translation** is the inverse of the x and y movements, e.g. the inverse of the translation $\begin{pmatrix} 2 \\ -3 \end{pmatrix}$ is $\begin{pmatrix} -2 \\ 3 \end{pmatrix}$.
- The inverse operation of an **enlargement** is to divide the image by the scale factor instead of multiplying.
- The inverse operation of a **rotation** is to rotate the image in the opposite direction using the same angle.

Transformations and inverse matrices

To find the inverse of a matrix transformation, multiply the transformation matrix **A** by the inverse matrix $\mathbf{A}^{-1}$ (see Unit 28 for revision on inverse matrices).

So, using triangle XYZ from Worked example 29.01, if **A** is the transformation matrix $\begin{pmatrix} 0 & 1 \\ -1 & 0 \end{pmatrix}$, then $\mathbf{A}^{-1} = \begin{pmatrix} 0 & -1 \\ 1 & 0 \end{pmatrix}$.

Now, if we multiply the inverse matrix by the image, we should get back to the original object:

$$\begin{pmatrix} 0 & -1 \\ 1 & 0 \end{pmatrix} \times \begin{pmatrix} 4 & 1 & 1 \\ 4 & 4 & 1 \end{pmatrix} = \begin{pmatrix} -4 & -4 & -1 \\ 4 & 1 & 1 \end{pmatrix}$$

These are the co-ordinates of the original triangle XYZ given by a 90° rotation of triangle X'Y'Z' anticlockwise, using the origin as the centre of rotation.

Progress check

29.06 On a grid, draw a quadrilateral of your choice and label its vertices A, B, C and D. Draw its image under the transformation of the matrix $\begin{pmatrix} 0 & -1 \\ -1 & 0 \end{pmatrix}$.

Describe the transformation, using appropriate terminology.

29.07 Find the centre and angle of rotation for the following diagram:

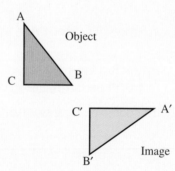

29.08 Rectangle ABCD lies on the invariant line XY. Perform the following transformations on the shape:

a A rotation 90° clockwise using the origin as the centre of rotation.
b A reflection in the line $y = x$.

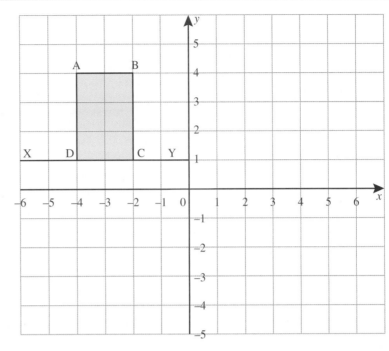

29.09 a Draw axes so that both x and y can take values from -2 to $+8$.

b Draw triangle PQR at P(2, 1), Q(7, 1) and R(2, 4).

c Find the image of PQR under the transformation represented by the matrix $\begin{pmatrix} 1 & -1 \\ 1 & 1 \end{pmatrix}$ and plot the image on the graph.

d The transformation is a rotation followed by an enlargement. Calculate the angle of the rotation and the scale factor of the enlargement.

Exam-style questions

29.02 Draw a quadrilateral at P(3, 4), Q(4, 0), R(3, 1), S(0, 0). Find the image of PQRS under the transformation represented by the matrix $\begin{pmatrix} -2 & 0 \\ 0 & -2 \end{pmatrix}$.

    a Describe the transformation, using appropriate terminology.

    b Find the ratio $\dfrac{\text{area of image}}{\text{area of object}}$.

29.03 Triangle ABC has co-ordinates A(2, 1), B(4, 1), C(4, 2). Draw the triangle on a grid with *x*- and *y*-values from −5 to 5.

    a Perform the matrix transformation $\begin{pmatrix} -1 & 0 \\ 0 & 1 \end{pmatrix}$ and describe it geometrically.

    b Perform the matrix transformation $\begin{pmatrix} 1 & 0 \\ 0 & -1 \end{pmatrix}$ and describe it geometrically.

    c Perform the matrix transformation $\begin{pmatrix} 0 & -1 \\ -1 & 0 \end{pmatrix}$ and describe it geometrically.

29.04 The vertices of a triangle DEF are given by the co-ordinates D(−3, 2), E(1, 1) and F(−3, −1).
Triangle DEF is mapped onto triangle D′E′F′, the co-ordinates of its vertices being D′(−3, −5), E′(1, 0) and F′(−3, −2).

    a Find the matrix which maps triangle DEF onto triangle D′E′F′.
    b Find the matrix which maps triangle D′E′F′ onto triangle DEF.

29.05 Answer the whole of this question on a sheet of graph paper.

    a Draw and label *x* and *y* axes from −6 to 6, using a scale of 1 cm to 1 unit.
    b Draw triangle ABC with A(2, 1), B(3, 3), C(5, 1).
    c Draw the reflection of triangle ABC in the line *y* = *x*. Label this $A_1B_1C_1$.
    d Rotate triangle $A_1B_1C_1$ about (0, 0) through 90° anticlockwise. Label this $A_2B_2C_2$.

    e Describe fully the single transformation which maps triangle ABC onto triangle $A_2B_2C_2$.
    f A transformation is represented by the matrix $\begin{pmatrix} 1 & 0 \\ -1 & 1 \end{pmatrix}$.

        i Draw the image of triangle ABC under this transformation. Label this $A_3B_3C_3$.
        ii Describe fully the single transformation represented by the matrix $\begin{pmatrix} 1 & 0 \\ -1 & 1 \end{pmatrix}$.

        iii Find the matrix which represents the transformation that maps triangle $A_3B_3C_3$ onto triangle ABC.

Source: Cambridge IGCSE Mathematics 0580 Paper 4 Q2 a–f (i), (ii), (iii) June 2007.

Core exam-style practice questions

These practice papers contain short-answer questions and structured type questions. The marks for each part of the question are given on the right-hand side.

Core practice set 1

1.01 Given that y is a positive integer, if $y \leqslant 7$ and $y \neq 4$, list the possible values of y. (2)

1.02 A building labourer is paid $480 each week.

    a One week, the ratio of the money he spends to the money he saves is $7 : 5$.

      Calculate how much money he saves in that week. (2)

    b He spends 20% of the $480 on clothes. Calculate how much he spends on clothes. (2)

1.03 A bank charges $42 simple interest when $700 is borrowed for 6 months.

    Calculate the annual percentage interest rate. (3)

1.04 An international athlete starts a marathon at 9.45 a.m. and finishes at 12.03 p.m.

    How long does he take? Give your answer in hours and minutes. (2)

1.05

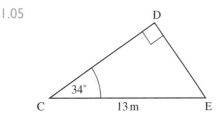

    The diagram shows the cross-section of the roof of a garden shed.

    It is 13 metres long, angle DCE = 34° and angle CDE = 90°.

    Calculate the lengths of the two sides of the roof, CD and DE. (4)

1.06 The width of a bridge is estimated as 1000 metres. The estimate is correct to the nearest hundred metres. Between what limits does the actual width of the bridge lie? (2)

1.07 Three adults and one child have a meal at a restaurant. The adults' meals all cost the same, the child's meal is half the price. The total bill is $49.70.

    What is the cost of one adult's meal? (2)

1.08 a Complete the statement below by putting the correct symbol, $>$ or $<$, between the two numbers.

        $24.8 \times 10^3 \qquad 2.5 \times 10^5$ (1)

    b Which one of the above two numbers is written in standard form? (1)

    c Rewrite the other number in standard form. (1)

1.09

a   What is the order of rotational symmetry of a regular pentagon,
     as shown in the diagram?   (1)

b   How many lines of symmetry does a regular octagon have?   (1)

1.10   Théo has two coins. One has a radius of 1 cm while the other has a radius of
       0.7 cm. Calculate the total area of the coins.   (3)

1.11

a   Describe **fully** the single transformation which maps

     i   triangle A onto B   (2)

     ii   triangle A onto C   (2)

     iii triangle A onto D.   (2)

b   On the grid, draw the image of an enlargement of scale factor 2 on
     triangle **B**, from centre of enlargement (4, 1). Label your new image E.   (3)

1.12 Five hundred schoolchildren were asked for their favourite flavour crisps and the results are displayed on the pie chart shown.

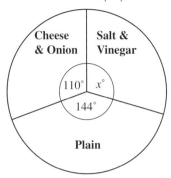

a   What angle should represent Salt & Vinegar? (1)

b   How many schoolchildren said Plain? (2)

1.13 A football shirt costs $x and a rugby shirt costs $y.

a i   Find an expression, in terms of x and y, for the total cost of 4 football shirts and 3 rugby shirts. (1)

   ii   The total cost of 4 football shirts and 3 rugby shirts is $80. Write down an equation, in terms of x and y, to show this information. (1)

b   The total cost of 6 football shirts and 9 rugby shirts is $174. Write down an equation, in terms of x and y, to show this information. (1)

c   Solve the simultaneous equations from part (a) (ii) and part (b) to find the cost of:

   i   one football shirt

   ii   one rugby shirt. (4)

Core practice set 2

2.01 Subtract 8.25 from 9. Give your answer:

a   as a decimal. (1)

b   as a fraction in its lowest terms. (1)

2.02 Find $\sqrt{6.25}$. (1)

2.03 Solve the equation $3y - 4 = y + 6$. (2)

2.04 How many integers between 1 and 75 contain the digit 7? (2)

2.05 In triangle XYZ, angle Y = 90°, side XY = 7 cm and side XZ = 8 cm. Calculate:

a   side YZ (2)

b   angle Z. (2)

2.06 Santy bought a stereo player for £76.

After six months she sold it to her friend Yolander making a 20% loss.

  a How much did Yolander pay for it? (2)

  b If Yolander later sold it to her sister Raffa, making a 20% profit, how much did Raffa pay for it? (2)

2.07 Lucas and Amelie share $350 in the ratio 3 : 4. How much does each receive? (2)

2.08   a Write $4^0 + 4^2$ as a single number without indices. (1)

  b Write 4^{-1} as a decimal. (1)

2.09 Make x the subject of the formula $y = ax + c$. (2)

2.10 Factorise:

  a $5xy + 10x$ (1)

  b $x^2 - 4x$ (1)

2.11 A piece of cork is suspended by a length of string from a fixed point above it.

In the wind, it swings from side to side but the length of the string remains constant.

Describe or draw the locus of the cork. (2)

2.12   a Complete the table for the function $y = x^2 - 4x + 2$ for $-2 \leqslant x \leqslant 5$: (2)

x	-2	-1	0	1	2	3	4	5
y	14		2	-1	-2	-1		7

  b On a sheet of graph paper, draw the graph of $y = x^2 - 4x + 2$. (5)

  c Use your graph to estimate

    i the solutions of the equation $x^2 - 4x + 2 = 0$ (2)

    ii the minimum value of $x^2 - 4x + 2$. (1)

  d Complete the table for the function $y = 5 - x$. (2)

x	-2	0	5
y		5	

  e On the same grid, draw the graph of $y = 5 - x$ for $-2 \leqslant x \leqslant 5$. (2)

  f The two graphs intersect at two points A and B. Write down the co-ordinates of both points of intersection. (2)

2.13 In a recent mathematics test involving 50 students, scored out of a maximum of 10, the following results were obtained:

1	9	2	5	6	5	8	7	6	7	8	3
9	5	4	10	8	7	5	6	6	7	5	2
5	2	6	9	5	7	6	5	6	2	8	6
7	3	3	8	7	6	5	5	6	4	3	4
5	10										

a Use the scores to complete the tally chart below.   (3)

Score	Tally	Frequency
I	I	I
2		4
3		
4		
5		
6		
7		
8		
9		
10		
		Total = 50

b Calculate the mean score.   (2)

c Find the median score.   (2)

d Write down the mode and the range of the scores.   (2)

e On a piece of graph paper, draw a bar chart to show
   the information clearly.   (4)

Core practice set 3

3.01 Calculate   a $8 + 7 \times 3$ b $\frac{1}{4}(9 \times 6 - 6 \div 3)$ (1) (2)

3.02 Last year, Ahmed's wages were \$80 per week. His wages are now \$92 per week.
      Calculate the percentage increase.   (2)

3.03 Write 0.455, $\sqrt{0.25}$, 46%, $\frac{9}{20}$ in order of size, using the appropriate
      inequality signs.   (2)

3.04 Gina has three counters, two of them red and one black. She places them
      side by side, in random order, on a table. One possible arrangement is:

      black   red   red

      a Write down the other possible arrangements.   (1)

      b What is the probability that the two red counters are next to each other? (1)

3.05 The daily maximum temperatures in Kuwait City for a week in July were:
      48 °C, 51 °C, 49 °C, 50 °C, 51 °C, 50 °C, 49 °C

      a Find the median temperature.   (2)

      b Calculate the mean (average) temperature.   (2)

3.06 Give an example of:

      a a prime number between 80 and 90   (1)

      b an irrational number   (1)

      c a negative number which is not an integer.   (1)

3.07 The vector $\mathbf{a} = \begin{pmatrix} 3 \\ 1 \end{pmatrix}$ and $\mathbf{b} = \begin{pmatrix} -2 \\ -3 \end{pmatrix}$. Find:

a) $\mathbf{a} + \mathbf{b}$ (1)

b) $3\mathbf{a} - \mathbf{b}$ (2)

3.08 Solve the simultaneous equations

$3a - b = 11$

$4a + b = 10$ (3)

3.09

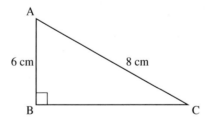

a Write down the correct mathematical name for the shape in the diagram. (1)

b Calculate its total surface area. (2)

c Find its volume, giving your answer in mm³. (2)

3.10 £1 (pound) = 1.53€ (euros)

a Francois changed 10 000 euros into pounds sterling.

How many pounds did he receive? (2)

b Francois took his pounds to London and spent £4000 over a period of two months.

He then converted his remaining pounds back into euros, at the same exchange rate.

How many euros did he have left? (2)

3.11

Triangle ABC is right angled with side AB = 6 cm and side AC = 8 cm. Calculate:

a the length of side BC (2)

b angle C. (2)

3.12 What is the difference in height between a point 220 metres above sea level and another point 425 metres below sea level? (1)

3.13

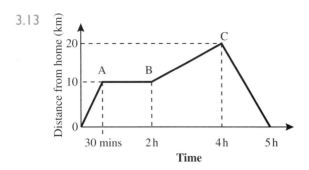

The travel graph shows a cyclist riding from home to point A, resting for a short period

before travelling on to point C, then returning home again.

a For how many minutes does he rest? (1)

b At what speed does he travel on the return journey? (1)

c What is his overall average speed? (2)

3.14

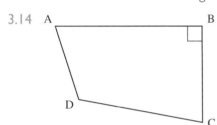

AB = 12 cm, AD = 6 cm, DC = 10 cm, BC = 8 cm and angle ABC is 90°.

a Copy the diagram to scale. (2)

b Draw the locus of points which are equidistant from points A and B. (2)

c Draw the locus of points which are equidistant from lines AB and BC. (2)

d Label the intersection of the two loci X. Measure the distance DX. (2)

3.15

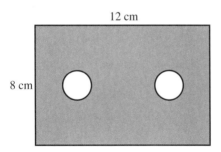

The diagram shows a steel sheet which has had two identical circular holes of radius r cm cut of it.

a Explain why the shaded area is $96 - 2\pi r^2$. (2)

b When the radius $r = 1$ cm, calculate:

  i the area of the shaded part (2)

  ii the shaded area as a percentage of the area of the whole rectangle. (2)

c Calculate the value of r when the shaded area is 90 cm². (2)

Core practice set 4

4.01 An irregular pentagon has 4 equal angles of 100°. Calculate the remaining angle. (2)

4.02 In Saudi Arabia, a soft drink costs 1 Saudi Riyal. If £1 = 5.8 SR, how many drinks can be bought for the equivalent of £3.20? (2)

4.03

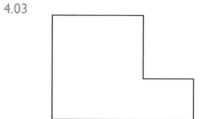

The shape in the diagram is an irregular hexagon and all the edges are either vertical or horizontal. What is the sum of the interior angles of the shape? (2)

4.04 a Write down the next two terms in each of the given sequences.

　　i　3, 6, 9, 12, ... (1)

　　ii　24, 12, 6, 3, ... (1)

　b The nth term of a sequence is given by $n^2 + 4$.

　　i　Find the 30th term. (1)

　　ii　Work out which term is equal to 125. (2)

　c Consider the sequence $\dfrac{2}{5}, \dfrac{3}{6}, \dfrac{4}{7}, \dfrac{5}{8}, \ldots$

　　i　Write down the next term. (1)

　　ii　Write down the 16th term. (1)

　　iii　Work out which term in the sequence is equal to $\dfrac{7}{8}$. (1)

　　iv　Write down the nth term. (1)

4.05

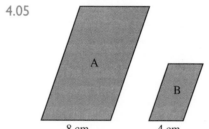

8 cm　　　4 cm

The two parallelograms are similar. Their base measurements are 8 cm and 4 cm, respectively. The area of parallelogram A is 40 cm². Calculate:

　a the perpendicular height of A (1)

　b the area of parallelogram B. (2)

4.06 a Simplify $3(x - 4) - 2(x + 3)$.   (2)

      b List the integer values of y for which $-2 < y \leq 4$.   (2)

      c Evaluate $4x^3 + 8x^2$

         i   when $x = 2$ (1)

         ii when $x = -3$.   (2)

      d Solve $5(x - 4) = 3(x + 2)$.   (2)

4.07

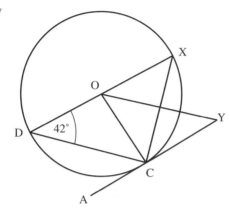

In the circle, O is the centre, line DOX is the diameter, line ACY is a tangent to the circle and angle CDX = 42°. Write down the values of:

a angle OCY   (1)

b angle CXD   (1)

c angle DCX.   (1)

4.08

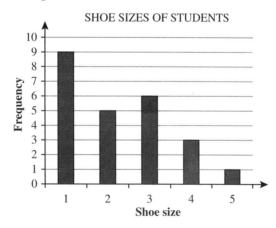

SHOE SIZES OF STUDENTS

The bar chart shows the shoe sizes of several children aged between 8 and 9 years old.

a How many children took part in the survey?   (2)

b Write down the mode.   (1)

c Write down the median.   (2)

d Write down the mean.   (2)

4.09 a Calculate the volume of a cube of side 4 cm. (1)

b A box, in the shape of a cuboid, is 28 cm long, 24 cm wide and 44 cm deep.
How many cubes of side 4 cm can fit into it? (2)

4.10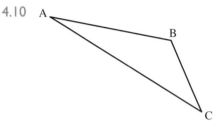

$\overrightarrow{AB} = \begin{pmatrix} 5 \\ -2 \end{pmatrix}$ and $\overrightarrow{BC} = \begin{pmatrix} 1 \\ -4 \end{pmatrix}$. Write down, as a column vector:

a $\overrightarrow{AC}$ (1)

b $3\overrightarrow{AC}$. (1)

4.11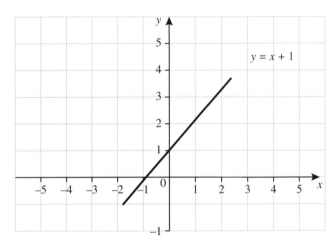

The graph of $y = x + 1$ is drawn on the grid.

a On the same grid, draw the graph of $y = 5 - x$. (2)

b Use your graphs to solve the simultaneous equations

$y - x = 1$

$y + x = 5$ (2)

4.12 A map has a scale of 1 : 30 000.

a A road on the map measures 3 cm long.

What is the real length of the road in kilometres? (2)

b Another road is actually 3.0 km. What would its length be on the map? (2)

4.13 Describe fully the symmetry of an isosceles trapezium. (2)

4.14

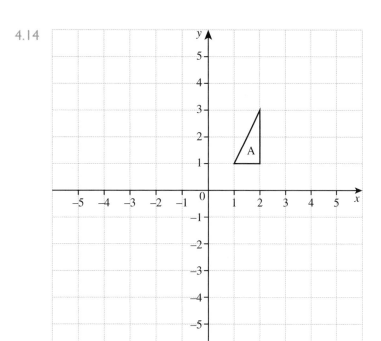

Copy the grid and perform the following transformations on A:

a   Reflection in the x-axis. Label the image B. (2)

b   Rotation by 180°, using the origin as centre of rotation. Label the image C. (2)

c   Enlargement of scale factor 0.5 from co-ordinate (4, 1). Label the image D. (2)

4.15   The population of a town increases by 5% each year. If in 2012 the population was 85 000, in which year is the population expected to exceed 100 000 for the first time? (3)

Core practice set 5

5.01 $x = \dfrac{3a - c^2}{de}$. Make a the subject of the formula. (2)

5.02   Calculate:

a 3^{-4} (1)

b y^0 (1)

c $4^2 \div 4^{-3}$ (1)

5.03   Factorise:

a $2x^2 - 8xy^2$ (1)

b $28a^3b^2c + 7a^4b^3c^2 - 14a^2b^2c^3$ (2)

4.04   Solve the equation $3y + 17 = 21 - 5y$ (2)

5.05   A school measures the dimensions of its rectangular playing field to the nearest metre. The length is recorded as 250 m and its width as 165 m. Express the range in which the length and width lie using inequalities. (2)

5.06   The owner of a shop bought 230 shirts for $2472.50.

   a   How much did she pay for each shirt?   (1)

   b   She put the shirts on sale at $12.90 each. Calculate the percentage
      profit on each.   (2)

5.07   a   Complete the table for the function $y = 4 - 2x - x^2$ for $-4 \leqslant x \leqslant 2$.   (3)

x	−4	−3.5	−3	−2	−1	0	1	1.5	2
y		−1.25	1	4		4	1		−4

   b   On a sheet of graph paper, draw the graph of $y = 4 - 2x - x^2$.   (5)

   c   Use your graph to estimate:

     i   the solutions of the equation $4 - 2x - x^2 = 0$ (2)

     ii   the maximum value of $4 - 2x - x^2$.   (1)

   d   On the same grid, draw the graph of $y = x$.   (2)

   e   Use the two graphs to solve the equation $4 - 2x - x^2 = x$.   (2)

5.08   a   The factors of 24 are 1, 2, 3, 4, 6, 8, 12 and 24. List all the factors of 36.   (1)

   b   The prime factors of 24 are $2 \times 2 \times 2 \times 3 = 2^3 \times 3$.

      Write, in a similar way, the prime factors of 36.   (1)

   c   Find the highest common factor of 24 and 36.   (2)

   d   Find the lowest common multiple of 24 and 36.   (2)

   e   Find the lowest common multiple of 24 000 and 36 000.   (1)

5.09   The ratio of the interior angles of a pentagon is $2 : 3 : 4 : 4 : 5$.

   Calculate the size of the largest angle.   (2)

5.10   Solve the following simultaneous equations:

$$2x - 3y = 7$$
$$-3x + 4y = -11$$ (3)

5.11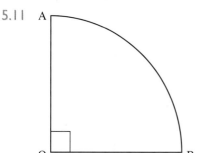

   The area of this quarter circle is 50.26 cm². Calculate the length of the radius.   (3)

5.12   Villages A, B and C lie on the edge of the Sahara desert. Village A is 29 km
   due north of village C, village B is 62 km due east of A.

   Calculate the shortest distance between villages C and B, giving your answer
   to the nearest 100 metres.   (3)

5.13   Find the total surface area of a cube of side 3 cm.   (2)

Extended exam-style practice questions

Practice papers contain short-answer questions and structured type questions. The marks for each part of the question are given on the right-hand side.

Extended practice set 1

1.01 Given that $4 \leqslant x \leqslant 7$ and $57 \leqslant y \leqslant 64$, find:

  a the greatest value of $\dfrac{y}{x}$ b the least value of $\dfrac{y}{x}$. (2)

1.02 The value of a house increases by 20% each year. It is valued at $20 000 today.

  a What will it be worth in two years' time? (1)

  b What was it worth one year ago? (2)

1.03 Solve the quadratic equation $x^2 + 2x = 1.35$, giving your answers to 2 decimal places. (5)

1.04 Find all of the angles in the following triangle. (4)

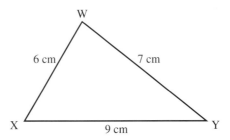

1.05 a Factorise $x^2 + 8x - 33$. (2)

  b Simplify $\dfrac{3x+4}{x^2+x-6} - \dfrac{1}{x+3}$ (3)

1.06 The co-ordinates of the points X and Y are $(-3, -1)$ and $(2, 1)$, respectively. Find:

  a the gradient of the line XY (2)

  b the length of the line segment XY. (2)

1.07 $f(x) = \dfrac{4x-2}{5}$.

  a Find $f(4)$. (1)

  b Solve $f(x) = 2$. (1)

  c Find $f^{-1}(x)$. (2)

1.08 y is inversely proportional to x^2. If $y = 1$ when $x = 0.4$, find:

  a the constant of proportionality (1)

  b the value of y when $x = 0.2$ (1)

  c the value of x when $y = 64$. (1)

1.09   Describe this speed–time graph in as much detail as possible.   (6)

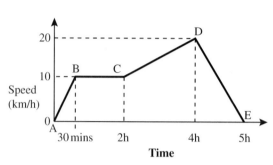

1.10

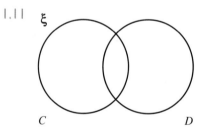

The diagram shows a rectangular-based pyramid where X is vertically above F.

a   Calculate the length BZ.   (2)

b   Calculate the length XF.   (2)

c   Calculate the angle XWF.   (2)

1.11   ξ

a   Shade the region in the Venn diagram which represents the subset $C \cap D'$.   (2)

b   Out of a group of 35 girls, 18 play netball, 16 play rounders and 4 play
    neither netball nor rounders. Find the number of girls who play rounders
    but not netball.   (3)

1.12   A student measures the diameter d of a wheel as 24 cm to the nearest
       centimetre.

a   Complete the statement

        $\_\_\_\_$ cm $\leqslant d <$ $\_\_\_\_$ cm   (1)

b   He knows that the value of π is such that $3.0 < \pi < 3.2$. Using this
    information, copy and complete his statement about the circumference, C:

        $\_\_\_\_$ cm $< C <$ $\_\_\_\_$ cm   (2)

1.13

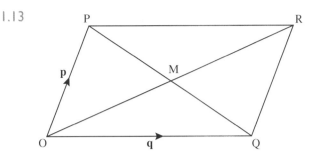

OPRQ is a parallelogram. **p** = $\overrightarrow{OP}$ and **q** = $\overrightarrow{OQ}$. Write in terms of **p** and/or **q**:

a $\overrightarrow{OR}$ (1)

b $\overrightarrow{RO}$ (1)

c $\overrightarrow{QP}$ (1)

d $\overrightarrow{QM}$ (1)

1.14

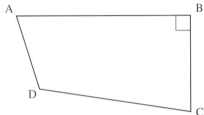

AB = 12 cm, AD = 6 cm,
DC = 10 cm and BC = 8 cm.
Angle B = 90°.

a   Copy the diagram to scale.   (2)

b   Draw the locus of points which are equidistant from points A and B.   (2)

c   Draw the locus of points which are equidistant from lines AB and BC.   (2)

d   Label the intersection of the two loci X. Measure the distance DX.   (2)

1.15 Three numbers are multiplied together.

The first number is called x, the second number is two greater than x and
the third number is two less than x. If the result is zero, form an equation and
find the value of x.   (3)

1.16 *Answer this question on graph paper.*

$$f(x) = \frac{12}{x} \qquad g(x) = (x - 8)(2 - x)$$

x	2	3	4	5	6	7	8	9
$f(x)$	6	4	3	a	b	1.7	c	1.3
$g(x)$	0	d	8	e	8	5	0	f

a   Complete the table of values.   (3)

b   Using a scale of 2 cm to 1 unit for the x-axis and 1 cm to 1 unit for
    the y-axis, draw the graphs of the above functions on the same grid.   (4)

c   Find the gradient of the $f(x)$ curve at the point where $x = 3.5$.   (3)

d   Find the solutions of x when $f(x) = 2$.   (2)

e   Show that the equation which is satisfied by the points of intersection
    of the graphs can be simplified to $x^3 - 10x^2 + 16x + 12 = 0$.   (3)

1.17 *Answer this question on graph paper.*

The vertices of a rectangle OPQR are $(0, 0)$, $(2, 0)$, $(2, 5)$ and $(0, 5)$, respectively.

a Taking 1 cm to represent 1 unit on each axis and marking each axis from -6 to $+6$, draw and label the rectangle OPQR. (3)

b The rectangle OPQR is mapped onto $O_1P_1Q_1R_1$ by the transformation matrix $\begin{pmatrix} 0 & 1 \\ 1 & 0 \end{pmatrix}$. Draw and label the rectangle $O_1P_1Q_1R_1$ on your diagram, describing the transformation. (2)

c Reflect the original rectangle OPQR in the y-axis. Label it $O_2P_2Q_2R_2$. (2)

d Write down the matrix which represents this transformation. (2)

Extended practice set 2

2.01 Calculate: a 2^{-4} b y^0 c $4^2 \div 2^{-2}$ (3)

2.02 Each interior angle of a regular polygon is $157.5°$.

Calculate the number of sides of the polygon. (2)

2.03 Solve for x and y: $5x + 2y = 13$ (4)
$$2x - y = 7$$

2.04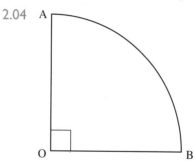

The area of the quarter circle is $28.28\ \text{cm}^2$. Calculate the length of the radius. (3)

2.05 a Factorise $3x^2 - 5x - 2$. (2)

b Simplify $\dfrac{2}{x} - \dfrac{1}{x+3}$. (2)

2.06 $x = \dfrac{2y - z^2}{ab}$. Make z the subject of the formula. (3)

2.07 $A = \begin{pmatrix} 4 & 3 \\ 2 & 1 \end{pmatrix}$, $B = \begin{pmatrix} -2 & -4 \\ 3 & 6 \end{pmatrix}$, $C = \begin{pmatrix} 2 & 4 & 6 \\ 1 & 3 & -3 \end{pmatrix}$. Calculate:

a A^2 (1) b AB (1) c BC (1) d $A^{-1}B^{-1}C$ (2)

2.08 A map has a scale of 1 : 40 000.

    a A road on the map is 10 cm long. What is the real length of the road in kilometres? (1)

    b The area of a farm on the map is 9 cm². What is the real area of the farm in hectares? (One hectare = 10 000 m².) (2)

2.09 Describe this distance–time graph *in as much detail as possible*. (5)

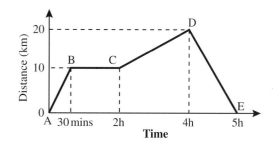

2.10 A water tank is in the shape of a cuboid, measuring 150 cm by 100 cm by 30 cm.

    a How many litres of water would the tank contain when full? (2)

    b The tank is initially empty and water flows into it from a pipe. The cross-sectional area of the pipe is 2.4 cm² and the water flows along the pipe at a rate of 35 cm/s. By calculating the volume of water flowing from the pipe in 1 second, find the time taken (to the nearest minute) to fill the tank. (4)

2.11 The table below shows the amount of money, $x, spent on books by a group of students.

Amount spent $x	$0 < x \leqslant 10$	$10 < x \leqslant 20$	$20 < x \leqslant 30$	$30 < x \leqslant 40$	$40 < x \leqslant 50$	$50 < x \leqslant 60$
Number of students	0	4	8	12	11	5

    a Calculate an estimate of the mean amount of money spent per student on books. (4)

    b Construct a cumulative frequency curve from the information in the table. (5)

    c Use the curve to find:

        i the median amount spent (2)

        ii the interquartile range. (2)

2.12 *Answer this question on graph paper.*

The vertices of a triangle ABC are (1, 2), (4, 2) and (4, 4), respectively.

    a Taking 1 cm to represent 1 unit on each axis and marking each axis from −6 to +6, draw and label the triangle ABC. (3)

    b The triangle ABC is rotated 90° anticlockwise about the origin onto $A_1B_1C_1$. Draw and label $A_1B_1C_1$. (2)

    c Find the matrix which represents this transformation. (2)

d Triangle $A_1B_1C_1$ is reflected in the *x*-axis onto $A_2B_2C_2$. Draw and label $A_2B_2C_2$. (2)

e Find the matrix which represents this transformation. (2)

Extended practice set 3

3.01 Calculate: **a** $8 + 7 \times 3$ **b** $\frac{1}{3}(9 \times 4 - 6 \div 2)$ (3)

3.02 A regular hexagon has sides of 4.5 cm. Calculate its area. (4)

3.03 Solve for *c* and *d*: $3c + 4d = -17$ (4)
$$2c - 2d = -2$$

3.04

A and B are both spheres.

Sphere A has a radius of 8 cm and sphere B has a radius of 2 cm. Find by calculation:

a the volume of sphere A (2)

b the surface area of sphere B (2)

c hence prove that the shapes are similar. (2)

[Volume of sphere $= \frac{4}{3}\pi r^3$, surface area of sphere $= 4\pi r^2$.]

3.05 Factorise completely:

a $16x^2 - 121y^2$ (2)

b $ax + ay + bx + by$ (2)

3.06 A lorry has a capacity of 50 000 litres. A model of the lorry is made using a scale of 1 : 40. Calculate the capacity of the model in millilitres. (3)

3.07 $a = \left(\dfrac{4y + b^2}{gh}\right)^2$. Make *b* the subject of the formula. (3)

3.08 The vector $\mathbf{a} = \begin{pmatrix} 7 \\ 2 \end{pmatrix}$ and $\mathbf{b} = \begin{pmatrix} -3 \\ -1 \end{pmatrix}$. Find:

a $\mathbf{a} + \mathbf{b}$ (1) **b** $2\mathbf{a} - \mathbf{b}$ (2) **c** $|\mathbf{a}|$, the magnitude of **a**. (2)

3.09 A map has a scale of 1 : 250.

a A house on the map is 4 cm long. What is the real length of the house in metres? (1)

b The area of a lake on the map is 10 cm². What is the real area of the lake in m²? (2)

3.10 Describe the speed–time graph *in as much detail as possible.* (6)

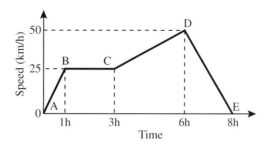

3.11 A train usually completes a journey of 180 km at an average speed of x km/h. One day engine trouble causes the average speed to be 20 km/h less than usual.

  a Write down an expression for the time taken, h_1, for the usual journey. (2)

  b Write down an expression for the time taken, h_2, for the slower journey. (2)

  c The time for the slower journey was 15 minutes more than the time for the usual journey. Write down an equation for x using your answers to parts (a) and (b), and hence show that:

  $$x^2 - 20x - 14400 = 0$$ (4)

  d Solve the equation $x^2 - 20x - 14400 = 0$ and hence calculate the usual average speed of the train. (4)

3.12 *Answer this question on graph paper.*

The table below shows the height of flowers as measured during an experiment.

Height (cm)	$0 < h \leq 5$	$5 < h \leq 10$	$10 < h \leq 15$	$15 < h \leq 25$	$25 < h \leq 50$
Frequency	20	40	60	80	50

  a Calculate an estimate of the mean height of the flowers. (4)

  b Construct a histogram from the information in the table. (Choose your own scale.) (5)

  c If two flowers are picked at random, state the probability that both flowers have a height greater than 10 cm. (2)

3.13 *Answer this question on graph paper.*

The vertices of a rectangle ABCD are (1, 2), (4, 2), (4, 4) and (1, 4), respectively.

  a Taking 1 cm to represent 1 unit on each axis and marking each axis from -10 to $+10$, draw and label the rectangle ABCD. (3)

  b The rectangle ABCD is rotated 90° clockwise about the origin onto $A_1B_1C_1D_1$. Draw and label $A_1B_1C_1D_1$. (2)

  c Find the matrix which represented this transformation. (2)

  d Rectangle $A_1B_1C_1D_1$ is reflected in the y-axis onto $A_2B_2C_2D_2$.

  Draw and label $A_2B_2C_2D_2$. (2)

  e Rectangle $A_2B_2C_2D_2$ is enlarged by scale factor 2, using the origin as centre of enlargement, onto $A_3B_3C_3D_3$. Draw and label $A_3B_3C_3D_3$. (2)

Extended practice set 4

4.01   a   If 25% of the 350 million sheep in the world were bred in Wales, and 2% remained there; calculate the number of sheep in wales.   (1)

      b   If 40% out of a class of 35 children have a mobile phone, what is probability that Sasha and Lewis have a mobile?   (2)

      c   Chandni eats one pizza, containing 500 calories, every day for one year. Calculate how many calories she consumes from pizzas over that period.   (2)

4.02   An irregular heptagon has 4 equal angles of 105°. If the remaining three angles are in the ratio 1 : 2 : 3, calculate the largest angle.   (3)

4.03   Arrange the following in order of size, smallest first:

        $0.5\,m^2$, $450\,cm^2$, $45\,500\,mm^2$ (2)

4.04   Describe *fully* the symmetry of this shape: (2)

4.05   Given the functions $f(x) = x^2 + 6$ and $g(x) = 2x + 1$, calculate:

      a $f(2)$ (1)   b $g(-3)$ (1)   c $g^{-1}(x)$ (2)   d fg^{-1} (2)

4.06   Given that Kinesh can save 15% of his salary every month and that his annual saving amount is £3525, what is his yearly salary?   (2)

4.07

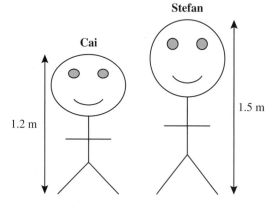

     Cai and Stefan are mathematically similar in shape; however Cai is 30cm shorter.

      a   If Cai weighs 100kg, what is the mass of Stefan?   (2)

      b   If they were both rolled flat by a passing steamroller and Cai covered a surface area of $10\,m^2$, what surface area would Stefan cover?   (2)

4.08

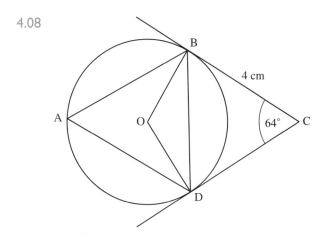

BC and CD are tangents to the circle, centre O. Angle BCD = 64°,
BC = 4 cm. Find:

a   angle BAD   (1)

b   angle CBD   (1)

c   angle BOD   (1)

d   chord length BD.   (3)

4.09

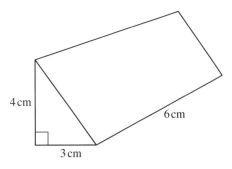

a   Draw the *accurate* net of the solid shown.   (3)

b   Calculate its volume and surface area.   (2)(2)

4.10   Ben plays football for his school's team. The probability that he scores is 0.2.
Each time he misses, he tries again.

a   Copy and complete the tree diagram below: (2)

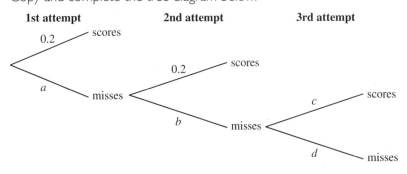

b Find the probability that, to succeed, it takes:

    i   exactly two tries (2)

    ii one, two or three tries (3)

    iii n tries. (2)

4.11 *Answer this question on graph paper.*

$f(x) = 4 - x - x^2$ $g(x) = x^3 + 1$

The tables below show some values for both functions:

x	−4	−3	−2	−1	0	1	2	3
$f(x)$	a	b	c	4	4	2	d	e

x	−2	−1.5	−1	−0.5	0	0.5	1	1.5
$g(x)$	−7	f	g	h	1	i	2	j

a Complete the tables for both functions. (3)

b Draw both graphs on the same grid. (4)

c Use your graph(s) to solve the equation $4 - x - x^2 = 0$. (2)

d Estimate the gradient of the $f(x)$ function where $x = -2$. (3)

e At which x value(s) does $f(x) = g(x)$? (2)

Extended practice set 5

5.01

Jennie uses a large 'jumbo pack' of black hair dye every week. Calculate:

a the cost per litre (2)

b the number of millilitres of hair dye obtained for one dollar (2)

c the cost price of the container if the shopkeeper made a 20% profit on its sale. (2)

5.02 By splitting into triangles (no overlapping), prove that an irregular dodecagon obeys the formula for calculating the total degrees inside any polygon. (4)

5.03 Factorise: a $6x^2 - 9x - 27$ b $144a^2 - 16b^2$ c $3 - 75y^2$ (6)

5.04   a   In a class, two students are chosen at random from 14 boys and 11 girls. Find the probability that :

        i   two boys are chosen   (2)   ii   a boy or a girl is chosen   (2)

     b   Express 340 as the product of its prime factors.   (2)

5.05   a   Phoebe and Sarah share a sum of money in the ratio 5 : 3. If Phoebe's share was $21.25, find the total amount of money they had to share.   (2)

     b   Mr Young enjoys blowing his own trumpet. If the mass of his trumpet is 4.8 kg and represents 4% of his mass, find the combined mass of both Mr Young and his trumpet.   (2)

5.06   Simplify $(a^{-1}b^0c^2d^{-3}) \times (2abc^{-2}d)$, giving your answer in its lowest terms.   (2)

5.07

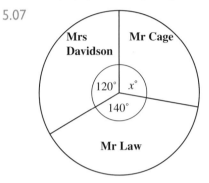

In a recent teacher popularity survey involving 720 pupils, the results were recorded and displayed as a pie chart.

     a   What fraction of voters voted for Mr Cage (in its lowest terms)?   (1)

     b   How many pupils voted for Mr Law?   (1)

     c   What percentage of pupils voted for Mrs Davidson?   (1)

5.08   On a recent fishing trip, Martin caught two sharks, Sam caught two tiny sardines and Loire foul-hooked an elderly catfish half the size of a shark. Given that the mass ratio of shark : sardine was 1500 : 1 and the mass of a sardine was 3 g, calculate the total mass of fish caught in kilograms.   (3)

5.09

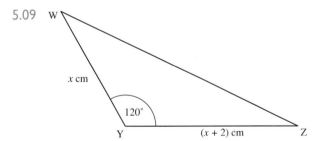

     a   Use the cosine rule to find an expression for WZ² in terms of x.   (4)

     b   When WZ is 7 cm, show that $2x^2 + 4x - 30 = 0$.   (3)

     c   Factorise $2x^2 + 4x - 30$.   (2)

     d   Solve the equation $2x^2 + 4x - 30 = 0$ and hence write down the lengths of WY and YZ.   (4)

5.10 Kayna and Zara are tailors. They make x jackets and y suits each week. Kayna does all the cutting and Zara does all the sewing. To make a jacket takes 5 hours of cutting and 4 hours of sewing. To make a suit takes 6 hours of cutting and 10 hours of sewing. Neither tailor works for more than 60 hours a week.

   a   For the sewing, show that $2x + 5y \leqslant 30$.   (2)

   b   Write down another inequality in x and y for the cutting.   (1)

   c   They make at least 8 jackets each week. Write down another inequality.   (1)

   d   Draw axes from 0 to 16 using 1 cm to 1 unit on each axis, and on your grid show the information in parts (a), (b) and (c), shading the unwanted regions.   (6)

   e   The profit on a jacket is $40 and on a suit is $110. Calculate the maximum profit they can make in a week.   (3)

Extended practice set 6

6.01   Give an example of:

   a   a negative number which is not an integer   (1)

   b   a prime number between 60 and 70   (1)

   c   any irrational number.   (1)

6.02 ξ

   a   Shade $A' \cup B'$ in the diagram.   (2)

   b   In a class of 44 students, 20 study physics, 28 study chemistry and 3 study neither. How many study both physics and chemistry?   (3)

6.03   To the nearest metre, a room measures 8 metres long by 6 metres wide.

   a   The actual length of the room is l metres. Write down the upper and lower limits of l.   (1)

   b   The actual area of the room is A metres^2. Calculate the upper and lower limits of A.   (2)

6.04

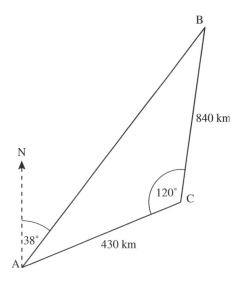

a   Calculate AB, the distance from town A to town B. (2)

b   Calculate angle BAC to the nearest degree. (2)

c   Find the bearing of town A from town B. (2)

d   A plane flew from town A to town B at an average speed of 400 km/h. If it left town A at 0840 hours, what time did it arrive at town B? (2)

6.05   Factorise: a $2x^2 - 8xy^2$ b $2y^2 + 7y + 6 =$ (4)

6.06   Solve the equation $3y + 17 = 21 - 5y$. (2)

6.07   Make x the subject of the formula: $y = \dfrac{c + 3x}{2}$ (3)

6.08   The values a and b satisfy the equation $a^2 b = k$, where k is a constant number.

a   If $a = 3$ when $b = 10$, find the value of b when $a = 2$. (2)

b   What happens to the value of b when the value of a is decreased by 50%? (2)

6.09   *Answer the whole of this question on graph paper.*

Adella, Alex and Joshua sell houses.

Adella charges $500, whatever the selling price. Alex charges 1% of the selling price.

Joshua charges $250 for selling prices up to $30 000. For selling prices more than $30 000, he charges $250 plus 2% of the value over $30 000.

a   Use a scale of 2 cm to represent a selling price of $10 000 on the horizontal axis and 2 cm to represent a charge of $100 on the vertical axis. On the same grid, draw the three graphs to show the charges made by Adella, Alex and Joshua for selling prices up to $80 000. Label your graphs clearly. (5)

b   i   For which selling price is Adella's charge the same as Alex? (2)

ii   For what range of selling prices does Joshua charge the least? (2)

iii   For which selling price, less than $50 000, does Alex charge $50 less than Joshua? (2)

6.10

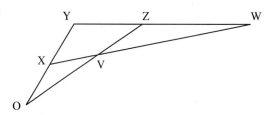

In the diagram, O is the origin, YZW is a straight line and X is the mid-point of OY.

$\overrightarrow{OY} = \mathbf{a}$, $\overrightarrow{OZ} = \mathbf{b}$, $\overrightarrow{YW} = 3\overrightarrow{YZ}$.

Find in terms of **a** and/or **b**, in their simplest form:

a $\overrightarrow{XY}$ (2)   b $\overrightarrow{YZ}$ (2)   c $\overrightarrow{XW}$ (2)   d the position vector of W (2)

e Given also that $\overrightarrow{XV} = \dfrac{1}{5}\overrightarrow{XW}$, find:

   i $\overrightarrow{OV}$ in terms of **a** and/or **b** (2)

   ii the ratio $\overrightarrow{OV} : \overrightarrow{VZ}$. (2)

Extended practice set 7

7.01 Solve the equation $5 - \dfrac{x}{0.5} = -11$. (2)

7.02 Solve for a and b: $4a - b = 11$ (3)

                $3a - 3b = 15$

7.03

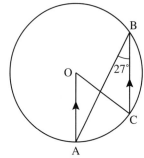

O is the centre of the circle and lines BC and OA are parallel.

Given that angle ABC is 27°, calculate:

a angle OAB (2)

b angle AOC. (2)

7.04 a Factorise $4 - 100a^2$. (2)

   b Simplify $\dfrac{2}{x^2 + 5x + 6} - \dfrac{1}{x + 3}$. (3)

7.05 Laura and Annabelle share a sum of money in the ratio 5 : 4. If Laura's share is $22.50, find the total amount of money shared altogether. (2)

7.06

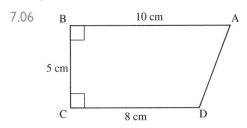

a   Draw this shape to scale. (2)

b   Construct the locus of points which are 6 cm from D. (2)

c   Construct the locus of points which are equidistant from A and B. (2)

d   Shade the region which is less than 6 cm from D and nearer to B than A. (2)

7.07   A train completes a journey of 400 km at an average speed of x km/h.

However, on one snowy day, ice on the track causes its average speed to be 20 km/h less than usual.

a   Write down and expression in terms of x for the usual time taken in hours. (1)

b   Write down a similar expression for the time taken for its slower journey. (1)

c   If the difference in time between the journeys was 45 minutes, write an equation in x and hence show that $3x^2 - 60x - 32\,000 = 0$. (4)

d   Solve the equation $3x^2 - 60x - 32\,000 = 0$, and hence write down the usual average speed of the train. (5)

7.08   Ten counters are placed into a bag, of which three are red, five are blue and two are green.

Random selections are made **without replacement**.

a   Complete the probability tree below for values a to d. (2)

b   Calculate the probability of obtaining:

i   a red and then a blue (2)

ii   two of the same colour (3)

iii   three blues in a row. (2)

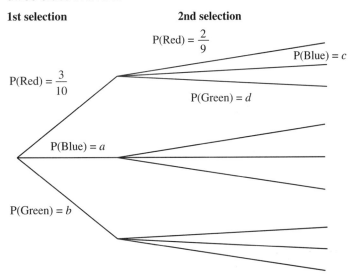

7.09

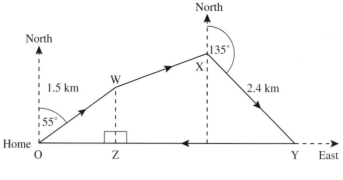

The diagram shows the path taken by a walker one sunny afternoon. Starting from home, he walks to W then X, then Y and back to his house. All distances are in kilometres.

a   Calculate the distances OZ and ZW, answers to one decimal place.   (2) (2)

b   Write down the vector $\overrightarrow{OW}$ in the form $\begin{pmatrix} x \\ y \end{pmatrix}$, where x and y are the components of the column vector.   (1)

c $\overrightarrow{WX} = \begin{pmatrix} 2 \\ 0.75 \end{pmatrix}$. Calculate: i   the length of WX, to 1 decimal place.   (2)

ii   the bearing of X from W, to the nearest degree.   (2)

d   Calculate the total distance walked.   (3)

Extended practice set 8

8.01   Prove with the use of two examples that Pythagoras' theorem will only work on a right-angled triangle.   (3)

8.02   The pressure, P, of a gas is inversely proportional to its volume, V, at a constant temperature.

If $P = 4$ when $V = 6$, calculate:

a P when $V = 8$ (2)

b V when $P = 12$.   (2)

8.03

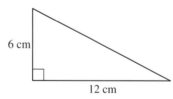

The triangle shown is to be reduced by a ratio of 1 : 3.

a   Calculate the area of the original triangle.   (1)

b   Calculate the area of the reduced triangle.   (2)

c   Calculate the ratio by which the area of the triangle has been reduced.   (2)

8.04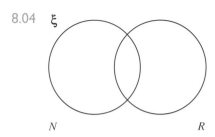

N   *R*

   a Shade the region in the Venn diagram which represents the subset $N' \cap R$. (2)

   b Out of a group of 25 girls, 15 play netball, 10 play rounders and 4 play neither netball nor rounders. Find the number of girls who play rounders but not netball. (3)

8.05 $\xi = \{x : 3 \leqslant x \leqslant 12 \text{ and } x \text{ is an integer}\}$, $C = \{\text{prime numbers}\}$, $D = \{\text{factors of 12}\}$.

   a List the sets: i $C \cap D$ (2)   ii $C \cup D$ (2)

   b State the value of $n(D')$. (2)

8.06 Calculate: a length of side BC (3)

                        b area of triangle ABC. (2)

8.07 If $f(x) = 4x - 6$, calculate:

   a $f(3)$ (1)   b $f(x) = 6$ (2)   c $f^{-1}(x)$ (2)   d $f^{-1}(-2)$ (1)

8.08 The spherical ball below is floating in a liquid with its centre O at a depth h below the surface. XZ is a diameter of the circular cross-section formed at the surface. When $r = 26$ cm and $h = 10$ cm,

   a Calculate:

      i Length of XZ (2)   ii Angle XOZ (2)

      iii Length of the arc XYZ. (2)

   b The area of surface above the water level is given by the formula $2\pi r(r - h)$. Find the area of surface above the liquid level. (2)

   c If the total surface area of a sphere is given by the formula $4\pi r^2$, find the area above the liquid level as a percentage of the total surface area of the sphere. (3)

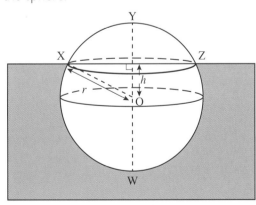

8.09 *Answer this question on graph paper.*

The vertices of a triangle ABC are $(1, 1), (3, 1), (3, 4)$, respectively.

a Taking 1 cm to represent 1 unit on each axis and marking each axis from −8 to +8, draw and label the triangle ABC. (3)

b The triangle ABC is reflected in the y-axis onto $A_1B_1C_1$.

    i Draw and label $A_1B_1C_1$. (2)

    ii Find the matrix which represents this transformation. (2)

c Triangle $A_1B_1C_1$ is enlarged from point X $(1, -1)$ by a scale factor of 2 onto triangle $A_2B_2C_2$. Draw and label $A_2B_2C_2$. (2)

d Triangle $A_2B_2C_2$ is then translated by the vector $\begin{pmatrix} 0 \\ -7 \end{pmatrix}$ to its new position $A_3B_3C_3$. Draw and label $A_3B_3C_3$. (2)

Answers to exam-style practice questions

Cambridge International Examinations bears no responsibility for the example answers to questions taken from its past question papers which are contained in this publication.

Unit 1

1.01 The next two prime numbers after 53 are 59 and 61.   (1 mark for each correct answer)

1.02   a Integers $= 2, 5$

      b Rational numbers $= 2, 5, -2.3, 0.3333\ldots$

      c Primes $= 2, 5$ (must have all numbers)

1.03 Sum $= 4 + 6 = 10$ (1 mark for identifying square/ triangular numbers, 1 for correct sum)

1.04   a

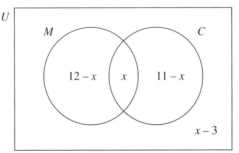

Of the 12 students that passed mathematics, some of these also passed chemistry, hence we have $12 - x$ in the mathematics-only region. We use the same logic for chemistry only.

To find the outside region: $20 - (12 - x) - x - (11 - x) = x - 3$

      b $x - 3 = 2$, so $x = 5$. So five students passed both tests.

Unit 2

2.01 9 marks as a percentage of $12 = \dfrac{9}{12} \times 100 = 75\%$

2.02   a 4 grams as a percentage of 200 grams $= \dfrac{4}{200} \times 100 = 2\%$

      b $\dfrac{8.7}{200} \times 100 = 4.35\%$

2.03   a Range $=$ highest value $-$ smallest value

           $= 350 - (-240)$

           $= 350 + 240 = 590\,^{\circ}\text{C}$

      b If Uranus is $-200\,^{\circ}\text{C}$, then $20\,^{\circ}\text{C}$ lower would be $-220\,^{\circ}\text{C}$, therefore the planet is Neptune.

2.04 We can convert all the values to decimals (using our calculator) and then compare:

$\dfrac{\pi}{4}$ (0.785) $\dfrac{1}{\sqrt{2}}$ (0.707) $\dfrac{3}{4}$ (0.75)   sin 47° (0.731)

We can see that the order should be:

$\dfrac{1}{\sqrt{2}}$ sin 47° $\dfrac{3}{4}$ $\dfrac{\pi}{4}$

Try to put the original form of the numbers in the answer spaces, and remember that the question states 'smallest first'.

2.05 a $\dfrac{4}{9}$ b $\dfrac{31}{99}$ c $1\dfrac{272}{999}$

Unit 3

3.01 a $8 \div 500 = 0.016\,\text{kg}$

b $0.016 = 1.6 \times 10^{-2}\,\text{kg}$ (numbers less than one have a negative power)

3.02 $4\,496\,000\,000\,\text{km} = 4.496 \times 10^{9}\,\text{km}$ in standard form.

(the digits moved 9 times relative to the decimal point)

3.03 a 783.265 square kilometres = 800 square kilometres (1 s.f.)

(we had to round the first digit)

b $800 = 8 \times 10^{2}$ square kilometres

3.04 $0.049 < 5\%\ (0.05) < \dfrac{5}{98}\ (0.051)$

(change the values to decimal equivalents and arrange accordingly)

3.05 Using a calculator (do brackets first, then power):

1745.953607 = 1746.0 (to 1 d.p.)

3.06 a 3460 (to 3 s.f.)

b 3463.59 (to 2 d.p.)

c 3500 (nearest 100)

Unit 4

4.01 $11.5 \leqslant h < 12.5$

4.02 Least possible area = 7.5 cm × 5.5 cm = 41.25 cm²

4.03 $12.15 \leqslant t < 12.25$

4.04 $58.925 \leqslant \text{mass} < 58.935$

4.05 $365.245 \leqslant \text{days} < 365.255$

4.06 Distance limits: $6250 \leqslant d < 6350$. Total distance $D = 6 \times 2 \times$ upper/lower limits.

So $6 \times 2 \times 6250 \leqslant D < 6 \times 2 \times 6350$

$75\,000 \leqslant D < 76\,200$

4.07 Upper and lower bounds of height: $1.635 \leqslant h < 1.645$

4.08 Maximum and minimum volume: $5.5^3 \leqslant V < 6.5^3$

So $166.38 \leqslant V < 274.63$

4.09 The upper bound for the distance travelled by one bicycle is 6.55 km.

So upper bound for total distance = $6.55 \times 9\,000\,000 = 58\,950\,000$ km.

4.10 Lower bound for radius is 3.05 cm, so lower bound for surface area = $4 \times \pi \times (3.05)^2 = 116.9$ cm (1 d.p.).

Unit 5

5.01 Euros = $\$600 \div 1.34 = €447.76$. Dollars = $447.76 \times 1.38 = \$617.91$

5.02 a Height of larger jug = $15 \times (4 \div 3) = 20$ cm

b Surface area = $1000 \times (4 \div 3)^2 = 1777.78$ cm²

5.03 a $210 : 240$ simplifies to $7 : 8$ (divide both values by 7)

b Teachers = $450 \div 9 = 5$

5.04 Real-life size = $25\,000 \times 10 = 250\,000$ cm (2.5 km)

5.05 100 km/h = 27.78 m/s (multiply by 1000, then divide by 60 and by 60 again)

5.06 Inversely proportional, so $t = \dfrac{k}{d^2}$, $k = td^2$

Using the values provided, $k = 0.2 \times 8^2 = 12.8$

Using $k = 12.8$, $t = \dfrac{12.8}{10^2} = 0.128$

5.07 a larger screen measurements = $\dfrac{5}{4} \times 44 = 55$ cm and $\dfrac{5}{4} \times 32 = 40$ cm

b fraction of screen areas = $\dfrac{44 \times 32}{55 \times 40} = \dfrac{1408}{2200} = \dfrac{7}{11}$

Unit 6

6.01 Percentage score = $\dfrac{22}{34} \times 100 = 64.7\%$

6.02 New price = $\dfrac{108}{100} \times \$300 = \$324$ (original price has been increased by 8%)

6.03 Sale price = $\dfrac{88}{100} \times £2000 = £1760$

6.04 a $\dfrac{25}{120} \times 100 = 20.8\%$ b $\dfrac{500}{3000} \times 100 = 16.7\%$

c $\dfrac{15}{240} \times 100 = 6.25\%$ d $\dfrac{50}{200} \times 100 = 25\%$

6.05 Using trial and improvement: let the original amount be x, when will the new amount = $2x$?

$x \times \dfrac{110}{100} \times \dfrac{110}{100} \times \dfrac{110}{100} \times$ etc. = 8 days

6.06 Lin's mark as a percentage of Jon's mark $= \dfrac{18}{12} \times 100 = 150\%$

6.07 a 2002 salary $= \dfrac{7200}{120/100} = \$6000$

b Percentage increase $= \dfrac{8100 - 7200}{7200} \times 100 = 12.5\%$

6.08 Sets made last year $= \dfrac{38\,500}{110/100} = 35\,000$

6.09 Let x represent number of questions attempted. 90% of $x = 135$,

so $x = \dfrac{135}{90/100} = 150$

Therefore number of questions incorrect $= 10\%$ of $150 = 15$

6.10 Yield last year $= \dfrac{10\,000}{125/100} = 8000$ litres

Unit 7

7.01 84 hours $= 72$ hours $+ 12$ hours $= 3$ days and 12 hours

Arrival date $=$ Thursday 26 May 2145 hours (9.45 p.m.)

7.02 Perimeter $= 4.5 + 4.5 + 2.8 + 2.8 = 14.6$ metres $= 1460$ centimetres

7.03 Using **STO** / **RCL** or bracket keys on calculator: answer $= 0.58$

7.04 Number of glasses $= 2500$ millilitres $\div 250 = 10$ glasses

7.05 Average speed $=$ distance $\div$ time $= (250 \times 1000) \div (4 \times 60 \times 60)$
$= 17.4\,\text{m/s}$

Unit 8

8.01 Alfredo receives $500 \times 9.95 = 4975$ Chinese yuan

8.02 Rihanna earns $\$276 \div \dfrac{4}{11} = \$759$

8.03 a Offer A, simple interest $= PTR/100 = 6000 \times 3 \times 7.4/100 = \$1332$

b Offer B, compound interest:

first year $= \$6000 \times 7/100 = \$420$, second year $= \$6420 \times 7/100 = \$449.40$, third year $= \$6689.40 \times 7/100 = \$480.86$

Total interest $= \$420 + \$449.40 + \$480.86 = \$1350.26$

8.04 Cost of holiday $= 245 \times 1.06 = \$259.70$

8.05 a Total after 20 years $= \$100 +$ simple interest $= \$100 + (100 \times 20 \times 7/100) = \$240$

b After 40 years $= \$100 +$ simple interest $= \$100 + (100 \times 40 \times 7/100) = \$380$

8.06 Using the formula, value $= \$440.90$

Unit 9

9.01 a The train stopped at 1000 hours, which is 60 minutes after it started.

b Average speed $= \dfrac{\text{distance}}{\text{time}} = \dfrac{100}{1} = 100\,\text{km/h}$

c The slope or gradient of the graph is less steep.

d Average speed $= \dfrac{\text{distance}}{\text{time}} = \dfrac{125}{1.5} = 83.3\,\text{km/h}$

9.02 Using a scale of 1 square = 1 foot (vertical axis), 1 square = 5 inches (horizontal axis), we have a constant (linear) graph, as shown below.

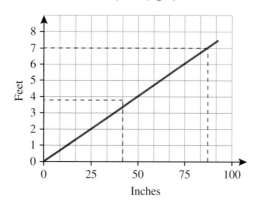

From the graph we can see that:

a 7 feet = approx. 85 inches

b 40 inches = approx. 3.6 feet

9.03 a Distance is the area under the triangle, $\dfrac{5 \times 30}{2} = 75\,\text{m}$

b Acceleration $= \dfrac{\text{change in speed}}{\text{time taken}} = \dfrac{5}{30} = 0.17\,\text{m/min}$

c Total distance travelled is the total area under the graph:

$$75 + (10 \times 30) + \dfrac{15 \times 30}{2} = 600\,\text{m}$$

9.04 Using a diagram to aid understanding:

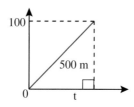

$500\,\text{m} = \dfrac{\text{time} \times 100}{2}$, so $t = 10$ seconds

9.05 Area = $\dfrac{60 \times 1000 \times \dfrac{30}{60 \times 60}}{2} = \dfrac{\dfrac{30\,000}{60}}{2} = 250\,\text{m}$ (change km to metres, seconds to hours)

9.06 a Acceleration = $\dfrac{\text{change in speed}}{\text{time taken}} = \dfrac{18}{30} = 0.6\,\text{m/s}^2$

b The area under the graph has been split into four parts (A, B, C and D).

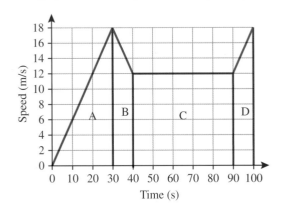

Calculating the area of each:

Area A = $\dfrac{30 \times 18}{2} = 270\,\text{m}$ (area of triangle)

Area B = $\dfrac{18 + 12}{2} \times 10 = 150\,\text{m}$ (area of trapezium)

Area C = $50 \times 12 = 600\,\text{m}$ (area of rectangle)

Area D = $\dfrac{18 + 12}{2} \times 10 = 150\,\text{m}$ (area of trapezium)

So total area = 270 + 150 + 600 + 150 = 1170 m

Unit 10

10.01 a i

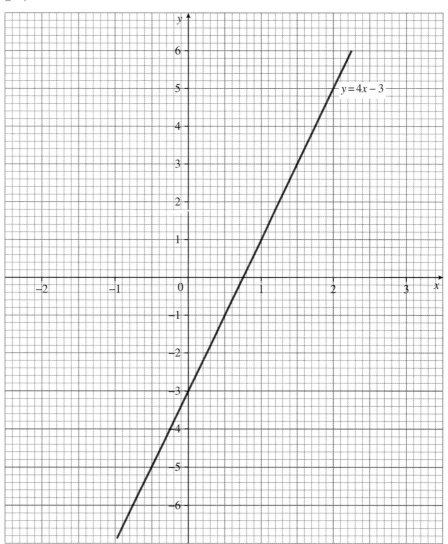

ii

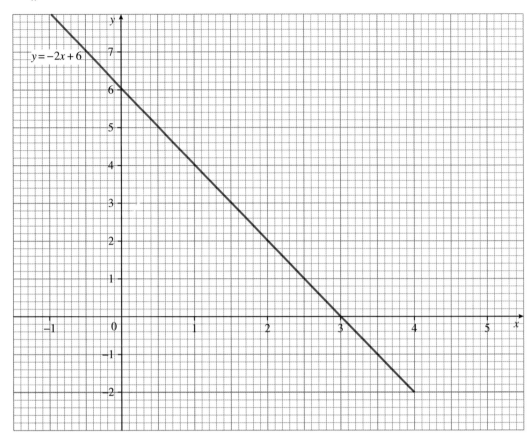

b i   Gradient $= \dfrac{4}{1} = 4$

   ii   Gradient $= \dfrac{-2}{1} = -2$

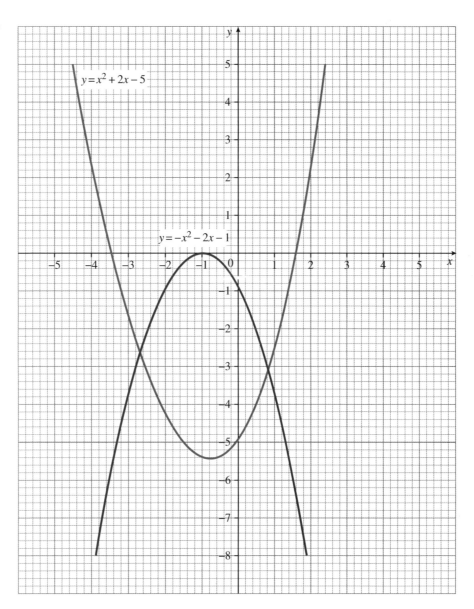

10.02 a, b

$y = x^2 + 2x - 5$

$y = -x^2 - 2x - 1$

10.03 a The letter m represents the gradient.

b Equation of line: $y = 2x + 5$ (y intercept $= 5$, gradient $= 2$)

c The table values are shown below:

x	-4	-3	-2	-1	0	1	2	3	4
$y = 12 - x^2$	-4	3	8	11	12	11	8	3	-4

d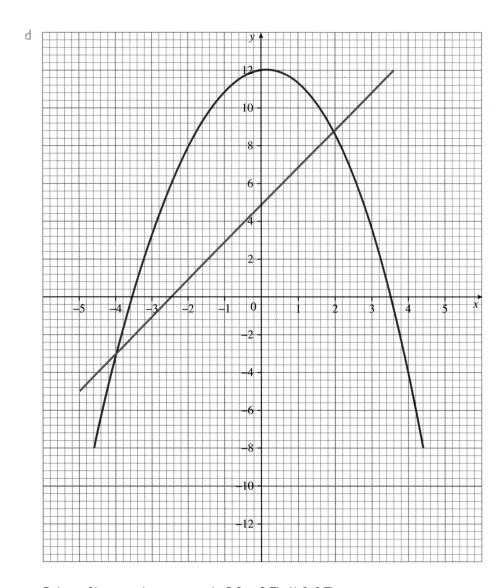

e Points of intersection, approx. $(-3.8, -2.7)$, $(1.8, 8.7)$

10.04 i a

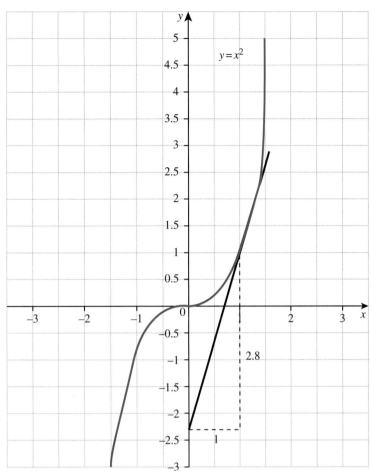

b Gradient = 2.8 (approx. 3)

ii a

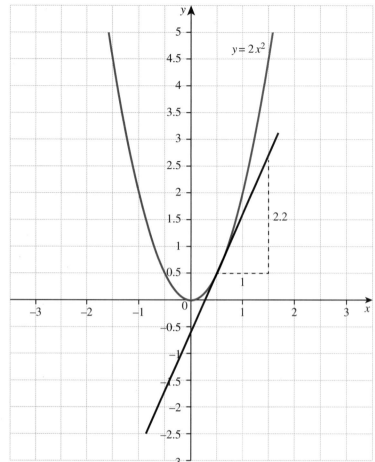

b Gradient = 2.2 (approx. 2)

iii a

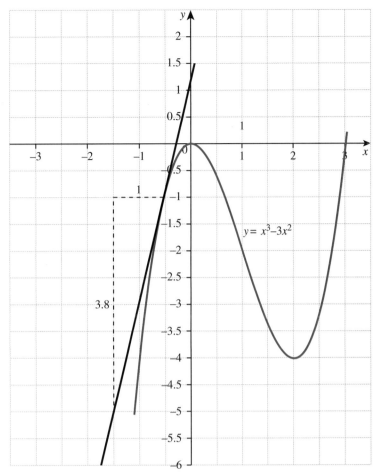

$y = x^3 - 3x^2$

b Gradient = 3.8 (approx. 4)

10.05 Calculated table values in red.

x	-2	-1.5	-1	-0.5	0	0.5	1	1.5	2
$y = x^3 + x - 2$	-12	-6.9	-4	-2.6	-2	-1.4	0	2.88	8

Then draw the graphs:

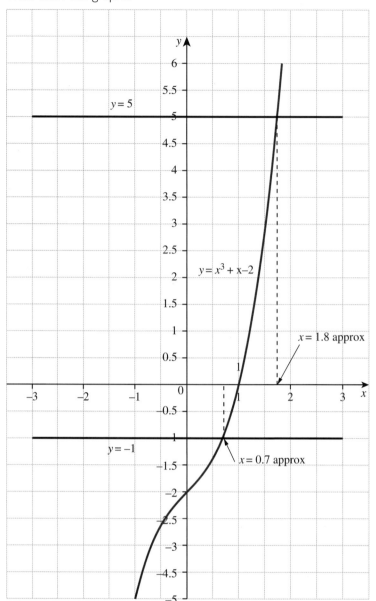

a $x^3 + x - 2 = -1$

Plot $y = -1$ and read off intersection: $x =$ approx. 0.7

b $x^3 = 7 - x$ (Note: $x^3 + x - 2 = 5$ is equivalent to $x^3 = 7 - x$)

Plot $y = 5$ and read off intersection: $x =$ approx. 1.8

Unit 11

11.01 a $m = 2, c = -5$ b $m = -5, c = 6$ c $m = 0.75, c = 3$

11.02 Line XY has equation $y = -2x + c$.

Using substitution, $(-7) = 2(6) + c$, so $c = -19$.

So the equation of line XY is $y = -2x - 19$.

11.03 Using the same method as above:

     a $y = 2x - 9$ b $y = -x + 7$

11.04 a Gradient of line A $= \dfrac{(0)-(5)}{(5)-(0)} = -1$

     b $m = 2, c = 5$ (same method as Q11.02)

     c i See red line on diagram.

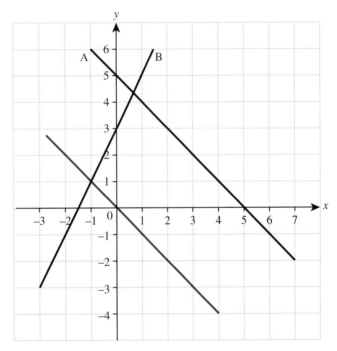

     ii $y = -x$

11.05 a Using Pythagoras, length of line $= \sqrt{(y\,\text{change})^2 + (x\,\text{change})^2}$

        $= \sqrt{(3)^2 + (3)^2} = \sqrt{18}$

     b By the same method, length $= \sqrt{(6)^2 + (9)^2} = \sqrt{117}$ c $\sqrt{72}$

11.06 a Midpoint $= (5, -1)$, gradient $= \dfrac{4}{6}$

     b Midpoint $= (5, 0)$, gradient $= \dfrac{-4}{8} = \dfrac{-1}{2}$

     c Midpoint $= (0, 0)$, gradient $= \dfrac{-4}{-8} = \dfrac{1}{2}$

11.07 Midpoint $= (4, 2)$, using the formula $\left[\dfrac{x_1 + x_2}{2}, \dfrac{y_1 + y_2}{2}\right]$

11.08 a Rearranging $3x + 2y - 8 = 0$, $2y = 8 - 3x$, $y = \dfrac{8 - 3x}{2}$

  b Gradient is the coefficient of x, so gradient $= \dfrac{-3}{2}$

  c Line crosses y-axis at $x = 0$. At this point, $y = \dfrac{8 - 3(0)}{2} = 2.5$, so co-ordinates are $(0, 2.5)$

11.09 Equation of line: $y = -\dfrac{1}{3}x + 7$

Unit 12

12.01 $y = 5(-4)(2) - 2(2) = -44$

12.02 $2x + 5y = w$, $2x = w - 5y$, $x = \dfrac{w - 5y}{2}$

12.03 a $\dfrac{8(3)}{(-8)} = -3$ b $4(2)^2 + 2(3)^3 = 34$ c $\dfrac{(2)^5}{2(-8)} = -2$

12.04 $\dfrac{2x + 3y^2}{5} = w$, $2x + 3y^2 = 5w$, $2x = 5w - 3y^2$, $x = \dfrac{5w - 3y^2}{2}$

12.05 $c = \dfrac{5d + 4w}{2w}$, $2wc = 5d + 4w$, $2wc - 4w = 5d$, $d = \dfrac{2wc - 4w}{5}$

12.06 $9x + 5x + 10 + 6x + 5 + 8x - 25 + 10x - 20 = 540°$, so $38x - 30 = 540°$, $x = 15°$

  Angles are $135°, 85°, 95°, 95°$ and $130°$

12.07 $54\,\text{cm} = y + y + (y - 3) + (y - 3)$, $54 = 4y - 6$, $y = 10\,\text{cm}$, so width $= 7\,\text{cm}$

12.08 $66 = \dfrac{x - 6}{2} + (x - 6) + x$, $132 = (x - 6) + 2(x - 6) + 2x$, $132 = 5x - 18$, $x = 30$

12.09 Present: son $= x$, Himesh $= x + 32$; 10 years ago: son $= 3(x - 10)$, Himesh $= (x + 32) - 10$

  $3(x - 10) = (x + 32) - 10$, $3x - 30 = x + 22$, $x = 26$. So: son is 26 and Himesh is 58.

Unit 13

13.01 a $ab + ac$ b $3ac - 3bc - 3c^2$

  c $k^2m^3 - k^2m^3n$ d $6x^2 + 12x^3$

13.02 a $6a + 12b - 9c - 12a - 6b + 15c = -6a + 6b + 6c$

  b $5x + 2$ c $5x^2 + 13x$

13.03 a $3y^2(2 + y)$ b $ab(3a + 2b)$ c $2a(3a + 2b - c)$

13.04 a $xy(x + y)$ b $2ab(x + b - a)$ c $3ab(b^2 - a^2 + a^2b^2)$

13.05 a $x^2 + 6x - 12$ b $2x^2 - 7x - 4$

    c $6x^4 - 3x^3 - 4x^3 + 2x^2 = 6x^4 - 7x^3 + 2x^2$

13.06 $4x^2 - 6xy - 6xy + 9y^2 - (9x^2 - 12xy - 12xy + 16y^2) = -5x^2 - 36xy - 7y^2$
    $= -(5x^2 + 36xy + 7y^2)$

13.07 a $m(s + t^2) - n(s + t^2) = (m - n)(s + t^2)$

    b $m(a - b) - n(a - b) = (m - n)(a - b)$

    c $2a(x + y) + b(x + y) = (2a + b)(x + y)$

13.08 a $(x - 7)(x + 5)$ b $(5x + 6b)(5x - 6b)$

    c $(4x + 1)(2x - 3)$ d $(2x + 5)(x + 1)$

Unit 14

14.01 a $f(-1) = (-1)^3 - 3(-1)^2 + 6(-1) - 4 = -14$

    b $gf(x) = 2(x^3 - 3x^2 + 6x - 4) - 1 = 2x^3 - 6x^2 + 12x - 9$

    c $g^{-1}(x) = \dfrac{x+1}{2}$

14.02 a $f^{-1}(x) = \dfrac{x+2}{3}, f^{-1}f(x) = \dfrac{(3x-2)+2}{3} = x$

    b $ff(x) = 3(3x - 2) - 2 = 9x - 8$

14.03 a $f\left(\dfrac{-1}{2}\right) = 2\left(\dfrac{-1}{2}\right) + 1 = 0$

    b $g(-3) = (-3)^2 - 1 = 8$

    c $h(-3) = 3^{-3} = \dfrac{1}{27}$

    d $f^{-1}(x) = \dfrac{x-1}{2}$

    e $gf(x) = (2x + 1)^2 - 1 = 4x^2 + 4x$

    f $fg(2) = 2((2)^2 - 1) + 1 = 7$

14.04 a $fg(-1) = ((-1) - 1)^2 - 1)^3 = 9$

    b $gh(x) = ((3x + 1) - 1)^2 = 9x^2$

    c $f^{-1}(x) = \sqrt[3]{x} + 1$

Unit 15

15.01 a $4x^2 = 4(5)^2 = 100$ b $(4x)^2 = (4(5))^2 = 400$

15.02 $\left(1\dfrac{1}{2}\right)^{-2} = \left(\dfrac{3}{2}\right)^{-2} = \left(\dfrac{2}{3}\right)^2 = \dfrac{4}{9}$

15.03 a $8^{-3x} = \dfrac{1}{4}, 2^{2(-3x)} = 2^{-2}, 2^{(-6x)} = 2^{-2}, x = \dfrac{1}{3}$

    b $2^{(x+1)} = 32, 2^{(x+1)} = 2^5, x = 4$

    c $5^{(x-4)} = 125, 5^{(x-4)} = 5^3, x = 7$

15.04 $10^{(y+1)} = 1, 10^{(y+1)} = 10^0, y = -1$

15.05 $3^{(x+2)} = 81, 3^{(x+2)} = 3^4, x = 2$

15.06 a $\left(\dfrac{p^4}{16}\right)^{0.75} = \left(\dfrac{p^4}{16}\right)^{\frac{3}{4}} = \dfrac{p^{4 \times \frac{3}{4}}}{16^{\frac{3}{4}}} = \dfrac{p^3}{2^{4 \times \frac{3}{4}}} = \dfrac{p^3}{8}$

     b $\sqrt[3]{\dfrac{1}{8}} = 2^q = \dfrac{1}{2} = 2^q = 2^{-1} = 2^q = -1 = q$

15.07 $(27x^3)^{\frac{2}{3}} = 3^{3 \times \frac{2}{3}} x^{3 \times \frac{2}{3}} = 3^2 \times x^2 = 9x^2$

15.08 a $\sqrt{32} = 32^{\frac{1}{2}} = 2^{5 \times \frac{1}{2}} = 2^{\frac{5}{2}} = 2^p$, so $p = \dfrac{5}{2}$

     b $\sqrt[3]{\dfrac{1}{8}} = \dfrac{1}{2} = 2^q$, so $q = -1$

15.09 a $x = 1$ b $y = -1$ c $z = \dfrac{3}{2}$

Unit 16

16.01 Rearrange second equation for y, $y = 4 - 3x$, then substitute into first equation:

     $8x + 2(4 - 3x) = 13, 8x + 8 - 6x = 13, 2x = 5, x = 2.5$, therefore $y = -3.5$

16.02 $3x + 1 = 4x - 4, x = 5$

16.03 a $p = 6$ b $m = 4$ c $4x - 28 = 2x - 10, 2x = 18, x = 9$

16.04 $4x + 4(2x) = 360°, 12x = 360°, x = 30°$, therefore exterior angles are $4 \times 30°$ and $4 \times 60°$.

     Interior angle + exterior angle = $180°$, so interior angles = $150°$ and $120°$.

16.05 Area = base $\times$ height $\times$ 0.5. $15 = x(x - 1) \times 0.5, 30 = x^2 - x$, so $x = 6$ or -5.

     So base is 6 cm and height is 5 cm.

16.06 Using the elimination method: $2y + 3(3y + 10) = 8, 2y + 9y + 30 = 8$, $y = -2, x = 4$

16.07 $3(2x - 5) > 8(x + 4), 6x - 15 > 8x + 32, -47 < 2x, -23.5 < x$

16.08 Using the quadratic formula: $x = \dfrac{-(5) \pm \sqrt{(5)^2 - 4 \times (1) \times (-8)}}{2 \times 1}$, so $x = -12.55$ or 2.55

16.09 $x^2 + 11x = -24, x^2 + 11x + 24 = 0, (x + 3)(x + 8) = 0, x = -3$ or -8

16.10 a mean mass of chocolate = $\dfrac{105}{x}$

     b mean mass of toffee = $\dfrac{105}{x + 4}$

     c $0.8 = \dfrac{105}{x} - \dfrac{105}{x + 4}, 0.8 = \dfrac{105(x + 4) - 105(x)}{x(x + 4)}$,

      $0.8x^2 + 3.2x = 420, x^2 + 4x - 525 = 0$

     d i $x^2 + 4x - 525 = (x + 25)(x - 21)$

       ii $x = -25$ or 21

     e total number of sweets = $21 + 25 = 46$

17.01

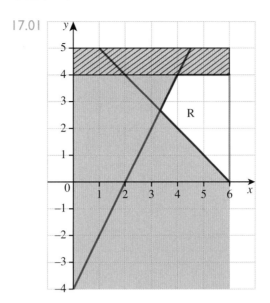

Lines drawn on grid are all shown as bold lines as they are inclusive.

The region required is left unshaded and labelled R.

17.02

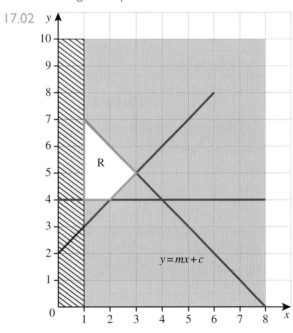

a   From the lines we can see the gradient m is -1 and the y-intercept c is 8.

So equation is $y = -x + 8$.

b   Unwanted region R is shown.

Unit 18

18.01 a   Acute   b Obtuse   c Reflex

18.02

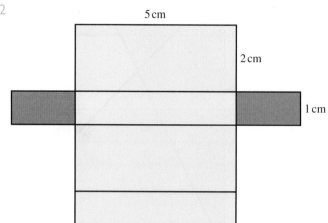

18.03 The cuboid has 6 faces, 8 vertices and 12 edges.

18.04 Point B is on a bearing of 070° and 8 km from point A.

18.05

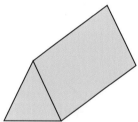

18.06 Volume of B $= \left(\dfrac{3}{12}\right)^3 \times 180 = 2.813\,\text{cm}^3$

18.07 Height of X $= \sqrt[3]{\dfrac{24}{3}} \times 10 = 20\,\text{cm}$

18.08 Area of reduced triangle $= 24 \times \left(\dfrac{85}{100}\right)^2 = 17.34\,\text{cm}^2$

(note that a reduction of 15% equates to 85% of the original length)

18.09 Area of island on map $= 100 \times \left(\dfrac{1}{20\,000}\right)^2 = 0.000\,000\,25\,\text{km}^2 = 2500\,\text{cm}^2$

18.10 a   Volume of smaller vase $= 1080 \times \left(\dfrac{2}{3}\right)^3 = 320\,\text{cm}^3$

b   Surface area of larger vase $= 252 \times \left(\dfrac{3}{2}\right)^2 = 567\,\text{cm}^2$

Unit 19

19.01

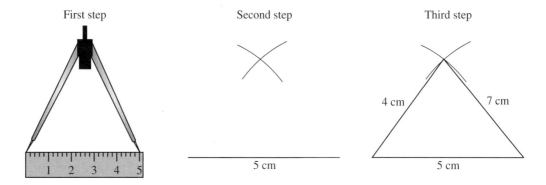

First step   Second step   Third step

19.02   Ensure that one arm of the angle is lined up with zero, then turn anticlockwise until you reach 120°.

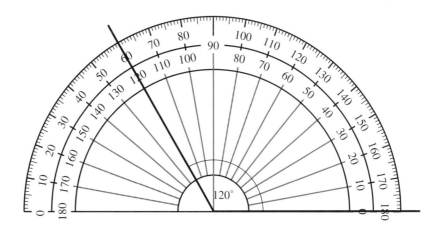

19.03   Draw the line XY, 7 cm. Set the compasses to approximately three quarters of the length of XY. Place the point of the compasses on one end of the line, e.g. point X. Draw an arc above and below. Without changing the compasses' setting, place the point of the compasses on the other end (point Y). Draw an arc above and below XY to cut the previous arcs. Check the distance is 4 cm to each end of the line.

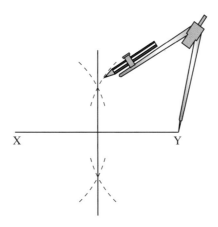

19.04 Draw lines of 13 cm and 7 cm at right angles to each other. Set compasses to 14 cm and draw an arc from the end of the 7 cm line, and then to 5 cm and draw an arc from the end of the 13 cm line.

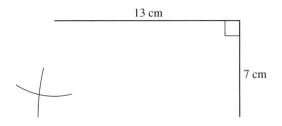

Join lines to where the arcs cut each other. Check the lengths using a ruler.

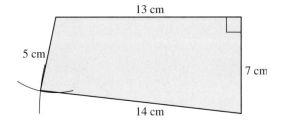

Unit 20

20.01 a   Parallelogram has no line symmetry but rotational symmetry of order 2.

b   A regular octagon has 8 lines of symmetry and rotational symmetry of order 8.

c   A rhombus has 2 lines of symmetry and rotational symmetry of order 2.

20.02 For example:

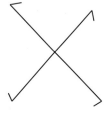

20.03 a   One line of symmetry, rotational symmetry of order 1.

b   Four lines of symmetry, rotational symmetry order 4.

c   Two lines of symmetry, rotational symmetry order 2.

20.04 Rotational symmetry of order 2.

20.05 a

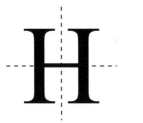

b Order 1 rotational symmetry; rotational symmetry of order 2.

20.06 a A cone:

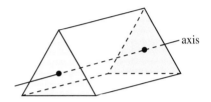

b A cube:

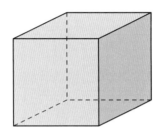

20.07 a A cuboid has 3 planes of symmetry.

b A tetrahedron has 6 planes of symmetry.

20.08 a Order 2 rotational symmetry.

b Order 1 rotational symmetry.

20.09 a

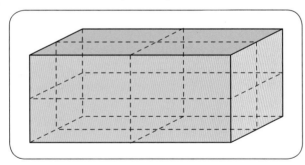

b Order of rotational symmetry = 3

Unit 21

21.01 a Sum of the interior angles: $x + x + 10 + x + 20 + x + 30 + x + 40 = 540°$

    b $5x + 100 = 540°, x = 88°$.

    c Largest exterior angle is supplementary to smallest interior angle, so $= 180 - 88 = 92°$

    d Exterior angles are $92° + 82° + 72° + 62° + 52° = 360°$

21.02 $x : 3x : 5x$, total $= 180°$, so $9x = 180°, x = 20°, 3x = 60°, 5x = 100°$

21.03 $4x + 30 + 3x + 10 + 3x + 2x + 20 = 360°, 12x + 60 = 360, x = 25°$.

    So angles $= 130°, 85°, 75°$ and $70°$.

21.04 a Angle B $= 60°$, BC $= 5$ cm (using Pythagoras)

    b $x = 120°, z = 240°, y = 90°$

21.05 $x = 22°$ (angles in same segment, same as angle BAC), $w = 30°$ (part of right-angled triangle CED). $z = 52°$ (alternate to $w° + 22°$), $y = 30°$ (same as w, angles in same segment equal).

21.06 i Cyclic

    ii $y = 25°$ (using isosceles triangle AOB), $x = 45°$ (alternate to $45°$), $z = 110°$ (supplementary to $x + y$).

    iii OCT $= 90°$ (tangent to centre of circle is a right angle).

    iv AOC $= 220°$ (angle at centre is twice the angle at the circumference).

Unit 22

22.01

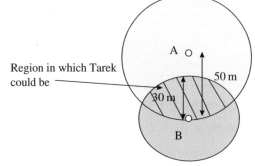

Region in which Tarek could be

22.02 a

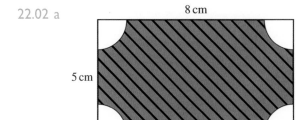

Note that the four excluded corners are constructed with a pair of compasses set to 1 cm.

b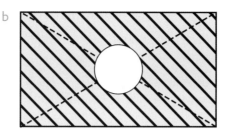

The shaded region shows the locus of points more than 3 cm from the centre of the garden.

Find the centre of the rectangle using a pair of compasses.

22.03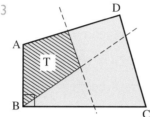

i   Actual length in metres of side BC = 11 metres

ii The size of angle ADC = 103°–105°

iii Construct angle bisector of ABC, then perpendicular bisector of line AD.

iv See region T on the top left corner of the diagram.

22.04

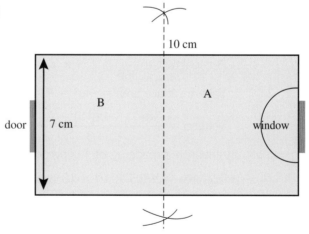

Construct a 2.5 cm boundary around the window using compasses and ruler.

The bisector of the length should be done with compasses and ruler. See possible arcs.

Possible positions of plants A and B are shown.

Unit 23

23.01 Area $= \pi r^2 = \pi(5)^2 = 78.6\,\text{cm}^2$. Circumference $= 2\pi r = 2\pi(5) = 31.4\,\text{cm}$

23.02 a Surface area $= 2\pi r(h + r) = 2\pi(3.5)(15 + 3.5) = 406.9\,\text{cm}^2$.
Volume $= \pi r^2 h = 577.3\,\text{cm}^3$

    b Surface area $= 2(6 \times 10) + 2(4 \times 6) + 2(4 \times 10) = 248\,\text{cm}^2$.
Volume $= 4 \times 6 \times 10 = 240\,\text{cm}^3$

    c Surface area $= 2(0.5 \times 6 \times 8) + (15 \times 8) + (6 \times 15) + (10 \times 15)$
$= 408\,\text{cm}^2$.

Volume $= 0.5 \times 6 \times 8 \times 15 = 360\,\text{cm}^3$

23.03 Side of square $= \sqrt{52.25} = 7.23\,\text{cm}$

23.04 a Volume $= \pi r^2 h = \pi(50)^2 \times 138 = 1\,083\,990\,\text{cm}^3$

    b $1\,083\,990\,\text{cm}^3 = 1\,083\,990 \div 100^3 = 1.08\,\text{m}^3$

23.05 a Using Pythagoras, AD $= \sqrt{3^2 - 1.5^2} = 2.6\,\text{cm}$

    b Area $= 0.5 \times \text{base} \times \text{height} = 0.5 \times 3 \times 2.6 = 3.9\,\text{cm}^2$

    c Volume $= \text{area of cross section} \times \text{length} = 3.9\,\text{cm}^2 \times 8\,\text{cm} = 31.2\,\text{cm}^3$

    d i Big box volume $= 0.5 \times 9 \times \sqrt{9^2 - 4.5^2} \times 16 = 561.2\,\text{cm}^3 = 18$

      ii Surface area $= 2(9 \times \sqrt{9^2 - 4.5^2}) + 3(16 \times 9) = 140.3 + 3(144)$
$= 572.3\,\text{cm}^2$

Note that we could also have used similar shapes methods to calculate the volume and surface area of the larger prism.

23.06 a Arc length $l = \dfrac{\theta}{360} \times 2\pi r = \dfrac{70}{360} \times 2 \times \pi \times 10 = 12.2\,\text{cm}$

    b Arc length $l = \dfrac{225}{360} \times 2 \times \pi \times 12 = 47.1\,\text{cm}$

23.07 a Sphere surface area $= 4\pi r^2 = 4 \times \pi \times 15^2 = 2827.8\,\text{cm}^2$

    b Volume $= \dfrac{4\pi r^3}{3} = \dfrac{4\pi(15)^3}{3} = 14\,139\,\text{cm}^3$

23.08 Tetrahedron is made up of 4 congruent equilateral triangles, so

surface area $= 4(0.5 \times 10 \times 10 \times \sin 60°) = 173.2\,\text{cm}^2$

23.09 Shape is made up of 2 sectors with angle 40° and radius 18 cm, and 2 smaller sectors with angle 140° and radius 6 cm.

Large sector area $= \dfrac{40}{360}\pi(18)^2 = 113.1\,\text{cm}^2$.

Small sector area $= \dfrac{140}{360}\pi(6)^2 = 44.0\,\text{cm}^2$.

Total area $= 2(113.1) + 2(44.0) = 314.2\,\text{cm}^2$.

Unit 24

24.01 Using Pythagoras: $AC^2 = 3.6^2 + 2.3^2$, $AC = 4.27\,cm$

24.02 a Angle $APB = 90°$ (angle in a semicircle, Unit 21)

b $\sin 40° = \dfrac{PB}{12}$, $PB = 7.7\,cm$

c Area of circle $= \pi r^2 = \pi \times 6^2 = 113.1\,cm^2$

24.03 a Using Pythagoras, $PQ^2 = 8.3^2 + 4.8^2$, $PQ = 9.59\,cm$

b Bearing of Q from P $= 180° + $ angle QPR, $\tan QPR = \dfrac{4.8}{8.3} = 30.0°$, bearing $= 180° + 30° = 210°$

24.04 a $AD = 2\,cm + 6\,cm = 8\,cm$

b Using Pythagoras, $DE^2 = AE^2 - AD^2$, $DE = 6\,cm$

c $\sin AED = \dfrac{8}{10} = 53.1°$

d $\dfrac{6}{CD} = \tan 40°$, $CD = 7.15\,cm$

e $CE = CD + DE = 7.15 + 6 = 13.2\,cm$

24.05 Using the cosine rule: $21^2 = (2x)^2 + x^2 - 2(2x)(x)(\cos 120°)$, $441 = 7x^2$, $x = 7.94$

24.06 Using the sine rule: a $\dfrac{\sin y}{35} = \dfrac{\sin 30°}{27}$, $y = 40.4°$

b $\dfrac{w}{\sin 40°} = \dfrac{14}{\sin 60°}$, $w = 10.4\,cm$

c $\dfrac{\sin x}{9} = \dfrac{\sin 60°}{10}$, $x = 51.2°$

24.07 a Area $= 0.5 \times 12 \times 13 \times \sin 80° = 76.8\,cm^2$

b $50 = 0.5 \times 14 \times 9 \times \sin x$, $x = 52.5°$

24.08 a Using Pythagoras, $AC = 10\,cm$, so $EC = 5\,cm$. $PE^2 = 13^2 - 5^2$, $PE = 12\,cm$

b Volume $= \dfrac{1}{3} \times (8 \times 6) \times 12 = 192\,cm^3$

c Angle PCA: $\cos C = \dfrac{5}{13}$, $C = 67.4°$

d Angle $MPN = 2 \times$ angle $MPE = 2 \times \tan^{-1}\dfrac{4}{12} = 36.9°$

e Using the cosine rule: $\cos B = \dfrac{6^2 + 13^2 - 13^2}{2 \times 13 \times 6} = 76.7°$

Unit 25

25.01 a Mean = $\frac{53}{8}$ = 6.63, median = 7, mode = 7

b Mean = $\frac{13}{9}$ = 1.44, median = −1.5, mode = −5, −4

25.02 Their ages are 10, 20 and 36 (20 has to be in the middle because it is in the middle, the sum must be 66 and the difference between the first and last numbers is 26).

25.03 Mode = 4 (highest frequency), median is 3.5 (50.5th position)

mean = (0 + 10 + 24 + 54 + 88 + 70 + 60 + 21 + 8) ÷ 100 = 3.35 books

25.04 a i

Number of people in a car	Tally	Number of cars
1	卌 l	6
2	卌 卌 卌 ll	17
3	卌 lll	8
4	卌 卌	9
5	卌 卌 l	11
6	卌 卌	9

ii

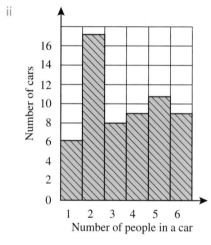

iii Mode = 2 (highest frequency)

iv Median = 30.5th position = 3

v Mean = [(1 × 6) + (2 × 17) + (3 × 8) + (4 × 9) + (5 × 11) + (6 × 9)] ÷ 60

= 209 ÷ 60 = 3.48

b Sector angle = $\frac{11}{60}$ × 360 = 66°

25.05 a Total height (men) = 15 × 1.70 = 25.5 m

b Total height (women) = 9 × 1.60 = 14.4 m

c Mean height = (25.5 + 14.4) ÷ 24 = 1.663 m

25.06 a Estimate of the mean = [(10 × 27) + (30 × 36) + (45 × 19)
+ (60 × 30) + (85 × 18)] ÷ 130

= (270 + 1080 + 855 + 1800 + 1530) ÷ 130 = 5535 ÷ 130
= 42.6 years

b Modal class = 20 ≤ x < 40 (class interval with largest frequency)

c i For the histogram, construct a table including an extra column showing
the frequency density:

Age	Frequency	Frequency density
0 ≤ x < 20	27	27 ÷ 20 = 1.35
20 ≤ x < 40	36	36 ÷ 20 = 1.80
40 ≤ x < 50	19	19 ÷ 10 = 1.90
50 ≤ x < 70	30	30 ÷ 20 = 1.50
70 ≤ x < 100	18	18 ÷ 30 = 0.60

Plot the histogram with frequency density on the vertical axis and age on
the horizontal axis:

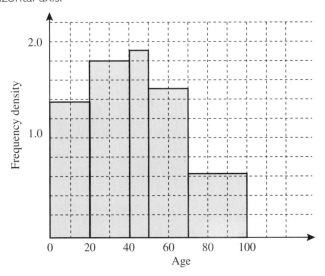

ii For the cumulative frequency diagram, construct a table including an extra
column for cumulative frequency:

Age	Frequency	Cumulative frequency
0 ≤ x < 20	27	27
20 ≤ x < 40	36	63
40 ≤ x < 50	19	82
50 ≤ x < 70	30	112
70 ≤ x < 100	18	130

Construct the curve with cumulative frequency on the vertical axis and age
on the horizontal axis. Read off the median and upper/lower quartiles.

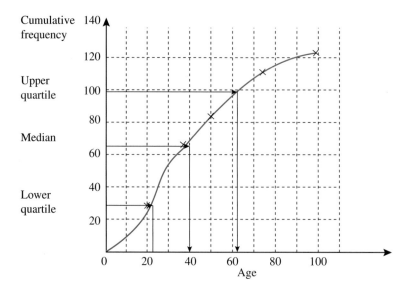

From the diagram:

Median = 40 years (approx.)

Upper quartile = 63 years (approx.)

Lower quartile = 24 years (approx.)

So the interquartile range = 63 − 24 = 39 years

Unit 26

26.01 a red ball = 6/10   b white ball = 0/10 = 0

c green ball = 4/9

26.02 a P(B) = 2/11   b P(vowel) = 4/11

c P(not Y) = 1 − P(Y) = 1 − 1/11 = 10/11

26.03 a P(even) = 51/101   b P(less than 15) = 13/101

c P(square) = 9/101 (4, 9, 16, 25, 36, 49, 64, 81, 100)

26.04 Expected number = 0.2 × 240 = 48

26.05 a Relative frequency = 22/50 = 0.44

b Best estimate = 110/200 = 0.55

26.06 a $P(\text{C and C}) = \dfrac{1}{11} \times \dfrac{1}{11} = \dfrac{1}{121}$

b $P(\text{E or A}) = \dfrac{1}{11} + \dfrac{2}{11} = \dfrac{3}{11}$

c $P(\text{M and then S}) = \dfrac{2}{11} \times \dfrac{1}{11} = \dfrac{2}{121}$

26.07 Santy must have not won on the first selection.

$P(\text{not WON then WON}) = \dfrac{995}{1000} \times \dfrac{5}{1000} = \dfrac{4975}{1000\,000}$

26.08 a P(tails and tails) = 0.3 × 0.3 = 0.09

 b P(head and tail and head) = 0.7 × 0.3 × 0.7 = 0.147

26.09 a P(B and B) $= \dfrac{4}{12} \times \dfrac{4}{12} = \dfrac{16}{144} = \dfrac{1}{9}$

 b P(R and G) + P(G and R) $= \left(\dfrac{3}{12} \times \dfrac{5}{12}\right) + \left(\dfrac{5}{12} \times \dfrac{3}{12}\right) = \dfrac{30}{144} = \dfrac{5}{24}$

26.10

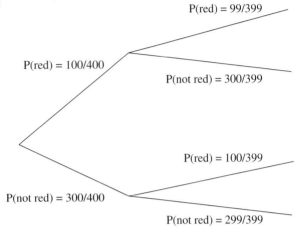

P(red) = 100/400

P(red) = 99/399

P(not red) = 300/399

P(not red) = 300/400

P(red) = 100/399

P(not red) = 299/399

 a P(red and red) $= \dfrac{100}{400} \times \dfrac{99}{399} = \dfrac{9990}{159600}$

 b P(no red and no red) $= \dfrac{300}{400} \times \dfrac{299}{399} = \dfrac{89700}{159600}$

 c P(red and then no red) $= \dfrac{100}{400} \times \dfrac{300}{399} = \dfrac{30000}{159600}$

Unit 27

27.01 a i $\mathbf{a} + 4\mathbf{b} = \begin{pmatrix} -1 \\ -10 \end{pmatrix}$ ii $\mathbf{b} - \mathbf{a} = \begin{pmatrix} -4 \\ 0 \end{pmatrix}$

 b D is at co-ordinate (−1, −2)

27.02 a −2**a** b −**b** c **a** + **b** d 2**c**

27.03 a i $\mathbf{p} + \mathbf{r}$ ii $\mathbf{r} - \mathbf{p}$ iii $\dfrac{2}{3}\mathbf{r} - \mathbf{p}$ iv $\mathbf{p} + \dfrac{1}{2}\mathbf{r}$

 b i $\dfrac{-3}{2}\mathbf{p} + \mathbf{r}$ ii $\dfrac{-3}{2}\mathbf{p}$

27.04 a i 2**c** ii −**d** + 2**c** iii $\dfrac{3}{4}\mathbf{d} + \dfrac{1}{2}\mathbf{c}$

 b $\overrightarrow{CE} = \dfrac{3}{4}\overrightarrow{BD} + (-\mathbf{c}) = \dfrac{-3}{4}(-\mathbf{d} + 2\mathbf{c}) - \mathbf{c} = \dfrac{1}{4}(2\mathbf{c} - 3\mathbf{d})$

Unit 28

28.01 a   Only **BA** and **CB** are possible (ensure that the column number of the first matrix is equal to the row number of the second).

b   Using the inverse formula:

$$\begin{pmatrix} \frac{1}{2} & \frac{3}{4} \\ \frac{1}{8} & \frac{1}{4} \end{pmatrix}^{-1} = \frac{1}{\left(\frac{1}{2}\times\frac{1}{4}\right)-\left(\frac{1}{8}\times\frac{3}{4}\right)}\begin{pmatrix} \frac{1}{4} & -\frac{3}{4} \\ -\frac{1}{8} & \frac{1}{2} \end{pmatrix} = 32 \times \begin{pmatrix} \frac{1}{4} & -\frac{3}{4} \\ -\frac{1}{8} & \frac{1}{2} \end{pmatrix} = \begin{pmatrix} 8 & -24 \\ -4 & 16 \end{pmatrix}$$

c   No inverse because determinant = 0

28.02 a $\mathbf{AB} = \begin{pmatrix} 2x+12 & 3x+6 \\ 8+6 & 12+3 \end{pmatrix}$

b   When **AB** = **BA**, $\begin{pmatrix} 2x+12 & 3x+6 \\ 8+6 & 12+3 \end{pmatrix} = \begin{pmatrix} 2x+12 & 12+9 \\ 2x+4 & 12+3 \end{pmatrix}$.

Equating matrices, $3x + 6 = 12 + 9$, so $x = 5$

28.03   Using matrix multiplication rules: $\begin{pmatrix} -58 \\ -23 \\ -1 \end{pmatrix}$

Unit 29

29.01

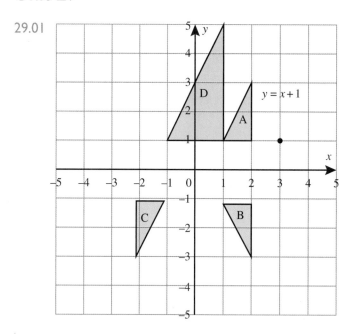

a   The triangle has flipped over the x-axis, resulting in the y co-ordinates changing sign.

b   A change of direction has occurred but each rotated point remains the same distance from the centre of rotation.

c After enlargement of scale factor 2, the image is now twice the size of the object.

Remember to check your results with compasses or tracing paper.

29.02 a Using matrix multiplication: $\begin{pmatrix} -2 & 0 \\ 0 & -2 \end{pmatrix}\begin{pmatrix} 3 & 4 & 3 & 0 \\ 4 & 0 & 1 & 0 \end{pmatrix} = \begin{pmatrix} -6 & -8 & -6 & 0 \\ -8 & 0 & -2 & 0 \end{pmatrix}$.

So the new co-ordinates of PQRS are: $(-6, 8), (-8, 0), (-6, -2), (0, 0)$. It has undergone an enlargement of scale factor -2 (an enlargement of scale factor 2 followed by a reflection in the line $y = x$).

29.03 a New co-ordinates of ABC: $(-2, 1), (-4, 1), (-4, 2)$; reflection in y-axis.

b New co-ordinates of ABC: $(2, -1), (4, -1), (4, -2)$; reflection in x-axis.

c New co-ordinates of ABC: $(-1, -2), (-1, -4), (-2, -4)$; reflection in line $y = -x$.

29.04 a The matrix which maps DEF to D′E′F′ is $\begin{pmatrix} 1 & 0 \\ 1 & -1 \end{pmatrix}$.

b The matrix which maps D′E′F′ to DEF is $\begin{pmatrix} 1 & 0 \\ 1 & -1 \end{pmatrix}$, the inverse matrix.

29.05

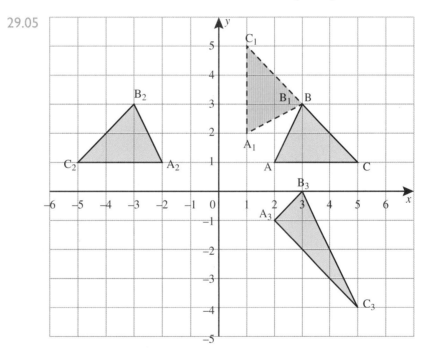

a–d See diagram.

e Transformation which maps ABC onto $A_2B_2C_2$ is reflection in the y-axis.

f i See diagram.

ii Shear transformation, y-axis invariant (if invariant line not mentioned must state shear factor 1, -1).

iii Matrix = $\begin{pmatrix} 1 & 0 \\ 1 & 1 \end{pmatrix}$

Core practice set 1

1.01 $y = 1, 2, 3, 5, 6$

1.02 a $200   b $96

1.03 12%

1.04 2 hr 18 min

1.05 CD = 10.8 cm, DE = 7.2 cm

1.06 $950 \leqslant w < 1050$

1.07 $14.20

1.08 a $24.8 \times 10^3 < 2.5 \times 10^5$ b 2.5×10^5 c 2.48×10^4

1.09 a Order 5   b 8 lines

1.10 4.68 cm²

1.11 a i Reflection in y-axis   ii Translation $\begin{pmatrix} 5 \\ -4 \end{pmatrix}$

      iii Rotation 90° anticlockwise about origin

    b Co-ordinates are (0, 1), (2, 1), (2, 5)

1.12 a 106°   b 200

1.13 a i $4x + 3y$ ii $4x + 3y = 80$

    b $6x + 9y = 174$

    c i Football shirts cost $11   ii Rugby shirts cost $12

[Total marks = 46]

Core practice set 2

2.01 a 0.75   b $\dfrac{3}{4}$

2.02 2.5

2.03 $y = 5$

2.04 13

2.05 a 3.9 cm   b 61°

2.06 a £60.80   b £72.96

2.07 Lucas receives $150, Amelie receives $200.

2.08 a 17   b 0.25

2.09 $\dfrac{y - c}{a} = x$

2.10 a $5x(y + 2)$ b $x(x - 4)$

2.11 Cork moves from left to right, etc., forming an arc.

2.12 a Values are 7 and 2   b Semicircle expected

  c i $x = 3.5$ and 0.6 ii -2

  d Values are 7 and 0   e Straight line graph cuts previous graph

  f $A = (-1, 5.9), B = (3.7, 1)$

2.13 a Frequencies: 1, 4, 4, 3, 11, 10, 7, 5, 3, 2   b 5.7   c 5

  d Mode $= 5$, range $= 9$

  e Height of bars equal frequencies, chart should be labelled and titled, with equal intervals for both axes.

[Total marks $= 54$]

Core practice set 3

3.01 a 38   b 13

3.02 15%

3.03 $\dfrac{9}{20} < 0.455 < 46\% < \sqrt{0.25}$

3.04 a RBR, RRB   b $\dfrac{2}{3}$

3.05 a 50 °C   b 49.7 °C

3.06 a 83 or 89   b $\sqrt{2}$ or π c E.g. -4.5

3.07 a $\begin{pmatrix} 1 \\ -2 \end{pmatrix}$ b $\begin{pmatrix} 11 \\ 6 \end{pmatrix}$

3.08 $a = 3, b = -2$

3.09 a Triangular prism   b 84 cm^2 c 36 000 mm^3

3.10 a £6535.95   b €3880

3.11 a 5.29 cm   b 48.6°

3.12 645 m

3.13 a 90 min   b 20 km/h   c 8 km/h

3.14 d DX $= 3.7$ cm

3.15 a Area of rectangle minus two circle areas $= (12 \times 8) - 2\pi r^2$

  b i 89.7 cm^2 ii 93.4%

  c $r = 0.98$ cm

[Total marks $= 56$]

Core practice set 4

4.01 140°

4.02 18 drinks

4.03 720°

4.04   a   i   15, 18   ii   1.5, 0.75

      b   i   904   ii   11th term

      c   i $\dfrac{6}{9}$ ii $\dfrac{17}{20}$ iii   20th term   iv $\dfrac{n+1}{n+4}$

4.05   a   5 cm   b   10 cm^2

4.06   a $x - 18$ b $-1, 0, 1, 2, 3, 4$

      c   i   64   ii -36

      d $x = 13$

4.07   a   90°   b   48°   c   90°

4.08   a   24   b   1   c   2   d   2.25

4.09   a   64 cm^3 b   462

4.10   a $\begin{pmatrix} 6 \\ -6 \end{pmatrix}$ b $\begin{pmatrix} 18 \\ -18 \end{pmatrix}$

4.11   b $x = 2, y = 3$

4.12   a   0.9 km   b   10 cm

4.13   1 line, rotation of order 1

4.14   a   Co-ordinates $(1, -1), (2, -1), (2, -3)$

      b $(-1, -1), (-2, -1), (-2, -3)$

      c $(2.5, 1), (3, 1), (3, 2)$

4.15   2016 (after 4 years)

[Total marks = 61]

Core practice set 5

5.01 $\dfrac{dex + c^2}{3} = a$

5.02   a $\dfrac{1}{81}$ or equivalent   b   1   c   1024

5.03   a $2x(x - 4y^2)$

      b $7a^2b^2c(4a + a^2bc - 2c^2)$

5.04 $y = \dfrac{1}{2}$

5.05 $249.5 \leqslant l < 250.5,\ 164.5 \leqslant w < 165.5$

5.06   a   \$10.75   b   20%

5.07   a   Values: $-4, 5, -1.25$ b   Inverted U-shape expected

      c   i $x = -3.2$ and 1.3   ii   5

      e $x = -4$ and 1

5.08   a   1, 2, 3, 4, 6, 9, 12, 18, 36

      b $2^2 \times 3^2$ c   12   d   72   e   72 000

5.09   150°

5.10 $x = 5, y = 1$

5.11   8 cm

5.12   68.4 km

5.13   54 cm²

[Total marks = 50]

Extended practice set 1

1.01   a   16   b   8.14

1.02   a $28 800   b $16 666.67

1.03 $x = 0.53$ or -2.53

1.04 $\angle W = 87.3°, \angle X = 51°, \angle Y = 41.7°$

1.05   a $(x + 11)(x - 3)$ b $\dfrac{2}{x-2}$

1.06   a $\dfrac{2}{5}$ b   5.4

1.07   a   2.8   b $x = 3$ c $\dfrac{5x+2}{4}$

1.08   a $k = 0.16$ b $y = 4$ c $x = 0.05$

1.09   A to B = constant acceleration of 20 km/h², B to C = constant speed of 10 km/h, C to D = constant acceleration of 5 km/h², D to E = constant deceleration of 20 km/h², total distance travelled = 57.5 km

1.10   a   7.8 cm   b   11.3 cm   c   71°

1.11   a   Shade all of C except the intersection   b   13 girls

1.12   a $23.5 < d \leqslant 24.5$ b $70.5 < C < 78.4$

1.13   a $\mathbf{p} + \mathbf{q}$ b $-\mathbf{p} - \mathbf{q}$ c $\mathbf{p} - \mathbf{q}$ d $\dfrac{1}{2}(\mathbf{p} - \mathbf{q})$

1.14   All construction arcs should be shown. DX = 4.8 cm

1.15 $x(x + 2)(x - 2) = 0, x = 0, 2$ or -2

1.16   a $a = 2.4, b = 2, c = 1.5, d = 5, e = 9, f = -7$ c -1

     d $x = 2.3$ or 7.8

     e   Rearrange algebraically $f(x) = g(x)$

1.17   b   Co-ordinates of rectangle are: $O_1 (0,0), P_1 (0,2), Q_1 (5,2), R_1 (5,0)$, reflection in $y = x$

     c $O_2 (0,0), P_2 (-2,0), Q_2 (-2,5), R_2 (0,5)$ d   Matrix $= \begin{pmatrix} -1 & 0 \\ 0 & 1 \end{pmatrix}$

[Total marks = 89]

Extended practice set 2

2.01   a $\dfrac{1}{16}$ b   1   c   64

2.02   16 sides

2.03 $x = 3, y = -1$

2.04   6 cm

2.05   a $(3x + 1)(x - 2)$ b $\dfrac{x + 6}{x(x + 3)}$

2.06 $z = \sqrt{2y - abx}$

2.07   a $\begin{pmatrix} 22 & 15 \\ 10 & 7 \end{pmatrix}$ b $\begin{pmatrix} 1 & 2 \\ -1 & -2 \end{pmatrix}$ c $\begin{pmatrix} -8 & -20 & 0 \\ 12 & 30 & 0 \end{pmatrix}$

       d   Impossible, determinant = 0, so no inverse

2.08   a   4 km   b   144 hectares

2.09   AB = constant speed of 20 km/h (1 mark), BC = stationary for 1.5 hours (1 mark), CD = constant speed of 5 km/h (1 mark), DE = returning to start point at constant speed of 20 km/h (2 marks)

2.10   a   450 litres

       b   Volume = 84 cm^3, time = 5357 seconds = 89 minutes (to nearest minute).

2.11   a   \$36.25

       b   Ensure cumulative frequency plotted against upper class limit

       c   i   median = \$38   ii   Interquartile range = 45 − 28 = \$17

2.12   b   Co-ordinates of triangle are $A_1 (-2, 1), B_1 (-2, 4), C_1 (-4, 4)$

       c $\begin{pmatrix} 0 & -1 \\ 1 & 0 \end{pmatrix}$

       d $A_2 (-2, -1), B_2 (-2, -4), C_2 (-4, -4)$ e $\begin{pmatrix} 1 & 0 \\ 0 & -1 \end{pmatrix}$

[Total marks = 62]

Extended practice set 3

3.01   a   29   b   11

3.02 $6(\dfrac{1}{2} \times 4.5^2 \times \sin 60°) = 52.6$ cm^2

3.03 $c = -3, d = -2$

3.04   a   2145 cm^3 b   50.3 cm^2

       c   Use ratios of $(8:2)^2$ and $(8:2)^3$ to show the connection between surface areas and volumes.

3.05   a $(4x - 11y)(4x + 11y)$ b $(a + b)(x + y)$

3.06 $\dfrac{50\,000}{40^3} = 781$ ml

3.07 $\sqrt{(\sqrt{agh} - 4y)}$

3.08 a $\begin{pmatrix} 4 \\ 1 \end{pmatrix}$ b $\begin{pmatrix} 17 \\ 5 \end{pmatrix}$ c 7.3 units

3.09 a 10m   b 62.5m²

3.10 AB = constant acceleration of 25 km/h² (1 mark), BC = constant speed of 25 km/h (1 mark), CD = constant acceleration of 8.33 km/h² (1 mark), DE = constant deceleration of 25 km/h² (1 mark), total distance travelled = 225 km (2 marks)

3.11 a $\dfrac{180}{x}$ b $\dfrac{180}{x-20}$

c $\dfrac{180}{x-20} - \dfrac{180}{x} = 0.25$, then simplify to $x^2 - 20x - 14400 = 0$

d 130.4 km/h

3.12 a 18.3

b $0 < h \leqslant 5 = 4\,cm^2, 5 < h \leqslant 10 = 8\,cm^2, 10 < h \leqslant 15 = 12\,cm^2,$
$15 < h \leqslant 25 = 16\,cm^2,$

$25 < h \leqslant 50 = 8\,cm^2$

c $\dfrac{190}{250} \times \dfrac{189}{249} = \dfrac{1197}{2075}$

3.13 b Co-ordinates of rectangle are: $A_1\,(2, -1), B_1\,(2, -4), C_1\,(4, -4), D_1\,(4, -1)$

c $\begin{pmatrix} 0 & 1 \\ -1 & 0 \end{pmatrix}$

d $A_2\,(-2, -1), B_2\,(-2, -4), C_2\,(-4, -4), D_2\,(-4, -1)$

e $A_3\,(-4, -2), B_3\,(-4, -8), C_3\,(-8, -8), D_3\,(-8, -2)$

[Total marks = 72]

Extended practice set 4

4.01 a 1750000   b $\dfrac{13}{85}$ c 730000 calories

4.02 240° (1 mark for calculating total degrees of 900, extra mark for finding one share of total degrees)

4.03 450 cm² < 45 500 mm² < 0.5 m²

4.04 1 line of symmetry, order 1 rotational symmetry (1 mark each)

4.05 a 10   b −5   c $\dfrac{x-1}{2}$ d 6.25

4.06 $25 000

4.07 a 195.3 kg   b 15.6 m² (allow a mark for stating the cube/squared ratio)

4.08 a 58°   b 58°   c 116°   d 4.24

4.09 b Volume = 36 cm³, surface area = 84 cm²

4.10 a $a = 0.8, b = 0.8, c = 0.2, d = 0.8$ (1/2 mark each)

b i 0.16   ii 0.488   iii $(0.2)0.8^{n-1}$

4.11   a $a = -8, b = -2, c = 2, d = -2, e = -8, f = -2.38, g = 0, h = 0.88,$
            $i = 1.13, j = 4.38$

            (1 mistake, lose 1 mark, otherwise no marks)

      c $x = -2.6$ or 1.6

      d   Gradient $= 2.8 \pm 0.5$ (allow 1 mark for tangent)   e $x = 1$

[Total marks = 60]

Extended practice set 5

5.01   a $2.90   b   345 ml   c $12.08

5.02   10 triangles should be present, which equals $1800°$, same as $(n - 2) \times 180°$ formula gives.

5.03   a $(3x - 9)(2x + 3)$ b $(12a - 4b)(12a + 4b)$

      c $3(1 - 5y)(1 + 5y)$

5.04   a   i $\dfrac{91}{300}$ ii   1   b $2^2 \times 5 \times 17$

5.05   a $34 (1 mark for finding Sarah's share was $12.75)

      b   124.8 kg (1 mark for finding Mr Young's mass was 120 kg)

5.06 $2bd^{-2}$ or equivalent

5.07   a $\dfrac{5}{18}$ b   280 pupils   c   33.3 %

5.08   11.256 kg

5.09   a $WZ^2 = 3x^2 + 6x + 4$

      b $49 = 3x^2 + 6x + 4, 3x^2 + 6x - 45 = 0 \ (\div 1.5)$ to get $2x^2 + 4x - 30 = 0$

      c $(2x - 6)(x + 5)$ d $WY = 3$ cm, $YZ = 5$ cm

5.10   a $4x + 10y \leqslant 60 \ (\div 2)$ to give $2x + 5y \leqslant 30$

      b $5x + 6y \leqslant 60$ c $x \geqslant 8$

      d   Plot graphs, region left unshaded will have boundaries $(8, 0), (8, 2.8), (9.2, 2.3)$ and $(12, 0)$

      e   9 jackets and 2 suits $= $580 profit

[Total marks = 60]

Extended practice set 6

6.01   a   Any negative decimal or fraction, e.g. -2.5

      b   61 or 67   c   E.g. $\pi, \sqrt{2}$

6.02   a   All regions shaded except $A \cap B$ b   7

6.03   a $7.5 < l \leqslant 8.5$ b $41.25 < A \leqslant 55.25$

6.04   a   1118.8 km   b   40.6°   c   218°   d   1127 hours

6.05   a $2x(x - 4y^2)$ b $(2y + 3)(y + 2)$

6.06 $y = 0.5$

6.07 $x = \dfrac{2y - c}{3}$

6.08   a $k = 90, b = 22.5$ b a quadruples or increases by 300%

6.09   b   i $50 000   ii $25 000 to $30 000   iii $40 000 and $20 000

6.10   a $\dfrac{1}{2}\mathbf{a}$ b $\mathbf{b} - \mathbf{a}$ c $3\mathbf{b} - 2.5\mathbf{a}$ d $3\mathbf{b} - 2\mathbf{a}$

      e   i $\dfrac{3}{5}\mathbf{b}$ ii $3 : 2$

[Total marks = 55]

Extended practice set 7

7.01 $x = 8$

7.02 $a = 2, b = -3$

7.03   a $27°$ b $54°$

7.04   a $(2 - 10a)(2 + 10a)$ b $\dfrac{-x}{(x + 2)(x + 3)}$

7.05 $40.50

7.06   Section shaded should be below the perpendicular bisector of AB but also within the circle. This will be a small area in the bottom right of the quadrilateral.

7.07   a $\dfrac{400}{x}$ b $\dfrac{400}{x - 20}$

      c $\dfrac{400}{x - 20} - \dfrac{400}{x} = 0.75$ then simplify to $3x^2 - 60x - 32 000 = 0$

      d   Usual speed = 113.8 km/h

7.08   a $a = \dfrac{5}{10}, b = \dfrac{2}{10}, c = \dfrac{5}{9}, d = \dfrac{2}{9}$

      b   i $\dfrac{1}{6}$ ii $\dfrac{14}{45}$ iii $\dfrac{1}{12}$

7.09   a   OZ = 1.2 km, WZ = 0.9 km   b $\begin{pmatrix} 1.2 \\ 0.9 \end{pmatrix}$

      c   i   2.1 km   ii $90 - 20.6 = 069°$

      d $1.5 + 2.1 + 2.3 + 1.65 + 2 + 1.23 = 10.78$ km

[Total marks = 56]

Extended practice set 8

8.01 E.g., choose a right-angled triangle showing that $c^2 = a^2 + b^2$, then pick a non-right-angled triangle showing that it does not obey Pythagoras' theorem.

8.02 a $k = 24, P = 3$ b $V = 2$

8.03 a $36\,cm^2$ b $4\,cm^2$ c $1:9$

8.04 a All of R shaded except the intersection   b 6 players

8.05 a i $\{3\}$ ii $\{3, 4, 5, 6, 7, 11, 12\}$ b 6

8.06 a $12.2\,cm$ b $44.2\,cm^2$

8.07 a 6   b 3   c $\dfrac{x+6}{4}$ d 1

8.08 a i $48\,cm$ ii $134.8°$ iii $61.2\,cm$

     b $2614\,cm^2$ c 30.8%

8.09 b i Co-ordinates are $A_1\,(-1, 1), B_1\,(-3, 1), C_1\,(-3, 4)$ ii $\begin{pmatrix} -1 & 0 \\ 0 & 1 \end{pmatrix}$

     c $A_2\,(-3, 3), B_2\,(-7, 3), C_2\,(-7, 9)$ d $A_3\,(-3, -4), B_3\,(-7, -4), C_3\,(-7, 2)$

[Total marks = 56]

Index